THE SCIENCE OF WEB SURVEYS

THE SCIENCE OF WEB SURVEYS

Roger Tourangeau
Frederick G. Conrad
Mick P. Couper

OXFORD
UNIVERSITY PRESS

Library of Congress Cataloging-in-Publication Data
Tourangeau, Roger.
The science of web surveys / Roger Tourangeau, Frederick G. Conrad, Mick P. Couper.
    p. cm.
Includes bibliographical references and index.
ISBN 978–0–19–974704–7
1. Social surveys—Methodology.   2. Social surveys—Data processing.   3. Internet surveys.
4. Questionnaires.   I. Conrad, Frederick G. (Frederick George), 1955–   II. Couper, Mick.   III. Title.
HM538.T68 2013
300.72'3—dc23
2012034133

9 8 7 6 5 4 3 2
Printed in the United States of America
on acid-free paper

CONTENTS

PREFACE

This book examines the virtues and limitations of Web surveys. It attempts to provide a comprehensive review of the literature on Web data collection. Although we have contributed many papers to this literature, this book is not just a summary of our work. For example, in Chapter 7, we report a meta-analysis of all the studies we could find that compare reports on sensitive topics in Web surveys with reports collected in other modes of data collection. Other chapters summarize work on issues, like coverage error in Web surveys, where we have not contributed much. Besides summarizing what is known, we have attempted to provide theoretical frameworks for understanding the properties of Web surveys. In addition, Chapter 8 provides our take on the issue of multimode surveys and lays out a mathematical model for understanding the errors in estimates that combine data collected in more than one mode.

The book adopts the total survey error framework and examines sampling and coverage (Chapter 2), nonresponse (Chapter 3), measurement (Chapters 4–7), and the issues involved in combining modes (Chapter 8). Chapters 2 and 8 are the most mathematical of the chapters. Chapter 2 examines statistical procedures that attempt to remove the biases from estimates derived from Web surveys, especially those based on samples of self-selected volunteers. Chapter 8 looks at the statistical properties of estimates based on data collected in multiple modes. Chapters 4 and 8 are the most practical and may be of most interest to those who are reading the book for guidance on conducting a Web survey. Chapter 4 covers basic design decisions for Web surveys, from input widgets to background colors. Chapter 8 summarizes all the recommendations presented throughout the earlier chapters. Chapters 4, 5, and 6 are the chapters that focus most on our own work on Web surveys, work that has concentrated on the special features of Web data collection, such as its visual character (Chapter 5), the ability to interact with respondents (Chapter 6), and its use of self-administration (Chapter 7).

Our work on Web surveys was made possible by a series of grants to the three of us and to our sometime partner in crime, Reg Baker at Market Strategies International. We are extremely grateful for the support we received from the National Science Foundation (NSF) and the Eunice Kennedy Shriver National Institute of Child Health and Human Development (NICHD). NSF provided initial funding for our work in the form of grants to Tourangeau and Couper (SES-9910882) and subsequently to

Tourangeau, Couper, Conrad, and Baker (SES-0106222). Later, NICHHD provided additional support to the project (5 R01-HD041386–01A1 and 2 RO1 HD041386–06A1). Needless to say, neither the National Science Foundation nor the National Institutes of Health is responsible for the conclusions we present here. Cheryl Eavey, who directs NSF's Methodology, Measurement, and Statistics (MMS) Program, has been an especially consistent supporter of our work and we are very grateful to her, but she can't be blamed for anything we say here.

Apart from his numerous intellectual contributions to the work (and his thoughtful comments on an earlier draft of this book), Reg Baker oversaw the administration of the series of Web surveys on which many of our conclusions are based. He was a full collaborator in this endeavor, in many ways our most valuable player. He did his best to keep us honest on the applied side of Web survey design and to keep us informed about what was happening in the real world. On our side, we did our very best to exceed the limits of mrInterview, the software environment in which our Web survey experiments were programmed, but never quite succeeded in bringing the program to its knees. We thank Reg and his very competent staff (including at various points Scott Crawford, Gina Hamm, Jim Iatrow, Joanne Mechling, and Duston Pope), who designed, implemented, and programmed most of our studies. Two other very helpful colleagues—Stanley Presser and Andy Peytchev—made it through an earlier draft of this book and provided excellent editorial suggestions to us. We are grateful for their help and encouragement. Rick Valliant vetted the statistical material in Chapter 2 and we greatly appreciate his able assistance. Catherine Tourangeau provided valuable help with Chapter 7 (slogging through lots of mode comparison studies) and also did the indexes for the book. We are grateful for her willingness to take on such tedious tasks and appreciate the skill with which she carried them out. And, of course, we had terrific help from a large number of excellent graduate students including Mirta Galešic, Courtney Kennedy, Becca Medway, Andy Peytchev, Cleo Redline, Hanyu Sun, Ting Yan, Cong Ye, and Chan Zhang. We never could have done this without them.

THE SCIENCE OF WEB SURVEYS

/// 1 /// INTRODUCTION

Since the inception of scientific surveys, researchers have often modernized and refined their methods of collecting data. The pace of this innovation in survey methods has, if anything, accelerated over the past three decades. This period has seen the almost universal adoption of computer-assisted methods for collecting survey data. Before the computer revolution, surveys had mainly relied on three methods of data collection—face-to-face interviews (in which interviewers contacted respondents in person, typically at the respondents' homes, read them the questions, and recorded their answers on paper questionnaires), telephone interviews (in which interviewers contacted respondents by telephone, but also read them questions and recorded their answers on paper questionnaires), and mail surveys (in which the researchers mailed a paper questionnaire to the respondents, who were supposed to fill it out it and mail it back). Each of these methods has gradually been supplanted by methods that incorporate computer technologies (see Chapter 5 in Groves, Fowler, Couper, Lepkowski, Singer, and Tourangeau, 2009, for a more detailed discussion of these developments).

Apart from the diffusion of desktop and laptop computers throughout the developed world, a second set of technological developments has transformed the way survey data are collected. This second set of developments involves how people communicate with each other. Telephone surveys gradually came to be accepted among survey researchers in the United States in the 1960s and 1970s as telephone service became virtually universal in the United States (Thornberry and Massey, 1988). Mobile telephone surveys have emerged as growing proportions of people use the devices in place of landline telephones (e.g., Brick, Brick, Dipko, Presser, Tucker, and Yuan, 2007). It's not hard to imagine the next steps in this process as new interview modes, such as SMS text questionnaires and desktop video interviews, are built to accommodate people's changing media preferences.

Web surveys represent an important advance in the evolution of self-administered questionnaires. Prior to the computer revolution, the only effective way to self-administer a questionnaire was for respondents to complete a printed paper form. Several automated methods of self-administration preceded the development of the World Wide Web—for example, "disk by mail" and email surveys—but these were short-lived and not widely adopted (Groves et al., 2009, Chapter 5). Other automated methods of self-administration are used in the context of face-to-face and telephone surveys, typically in conjunction with interviewer-administered questions. For example, face-to-face surveys sometimes use a combination of modes in which an interviewer asks some of the questions and the respondent directly interacts with a computer (with or without sound) for others. Similarly, many telephone surveys involve a hybrid methodology, in which respondents are contacted by live telephone interviewers and then switched to an automated Interactive Voice Response (IVR) system (Cooley, Miller, Gribble, Turner, 2000). But the widespread use of stand-alone, self-administered, automated questionnaires has become much more common since the Web became part of everyday life.

In many parts of the developed world, people spend much of their lives online, engaged in a variety of activities, including many that share features with survey responding—filing income taxes, applying for jobs, making travel reservations, and purchasing products and services (see, for example, Purcell, 2011). So, it is a natural extension to deploy questionnaires via the Internet. This is where people are—at least many of them—and they can rely on familiar routines and conventions when completing questionnaires this way. Moreover, the marginal cost for each additional case in a Web survey is extremely small compared to surveys done in other modes, where each completed case may require contact with an interviewer and thus entails interviewer payments and possibly travel costs. The marginal cost per case in Web surveys is even smaller than with paper questionnaires, where there are printing and postage costs for each additional case. The primary investment in conducting a Web survey is programming the questionnaire. This cost is fixed, irrespective of the number of cases, and is similar to the costs of programming instruments for computer-assisted interviews. If the survey uses email invitations and incentives with a fixed overall cost (such as a sweepstakes for participants), the total cost of a Web survey is essentially independent of the sample size.

Web surveys thus make large samples affordable to a much wider range of researchers than more traditional modes of data collection do. The attractive cost structure of Web surveys seems likely to assure the continued popularity and evolution of the mode. Questionnaires displayed in Web browsers, as is currently the norm, may gradually give way to app-based surveys on mobile devices and polls conducted within social media. Yet, despite their budgetary appeal, Web surveys come with inherent drawbacks that give rise to various forms of error.

1.1 THE TOTAL SURVEY ERROR APPROACH

To classify the errors affecting estimates from Web surveys, it is useful to adopt the *total survey error* framework (e.g., Groves, 1989). This perspective has a long history in survey research (see Groves and Lyberg, 2010, for a review). In the total survey error framework, errors are often divided into two main categories—those affecting how well the respondents represent the population of interest and those affecting the accuracy or validity of individual answers. The former errors arise from what is not observed.

For example, potential sample members may not have Internet access and so cannot take part in a Web survey; they are not in the "frame," that is, the set of members of the population who could potentially take part in the survey. Or sample members may not participate when they are invited to complete a survey, perhaps because the email invitation is intercepted by a spam filter before they see it. These errors of imperfect coverage (see Chapter 2) and nonresponse (see Chapter 3) are examples of non-observation errors. Of course, reliance on volunteer Web panels is another potentially important source of non-observation errors, since the panel members may not constitute a representative sample of the population of interest. All three types of problem—coverage, sampling, and nonresponse—will lead to biased survey estimates when people in the frame, those in the sample, and those who become respondents differ from their unobserved counterparts on the attributes being measured in the survey.

Errors that affect the accuracy or validity of the answers involve measurement and therefore what *is* observed in the survey. Measurement error is typically defined as the difference between what respondents report when they answer a survey question and the true value of the attribute being measured. This discrepancy is most often attributed to the social and cognitive processes that a respondent engages in while answering (see Chapters 4–7). For example, Web respondents might be particularly prone to take cognitive shortcuts (leading to more measurement error) or they might be more willing to disclose personal information (leading to less measurement error) than respondents in other modes. Measurement errors lie in the responses—the observations—and so are considered errors of observation.

Errors of non-observation. Imagine a Web survey question about health care utilization administered to members of an "opt-in" or volunteer panel. These panels are not constructed to resemble the population; members simply join, often to receive some form of incentive. If the proportion of panel members with health insurance is smaller than in the general public—perhaps one reason that people join the panel is to make ends meet while they are out of work and therefore without health insurance—then panel members may differ on a range of health-related characteristics. For example, they may use health care services less often than other members of the general public. The estimates derived from these respondents about their health care may well be biased because of this coverage error; the panel doesn't include the right proportion of people who have health insurance. It will not help if the particular sample of respondents recruited is randomly selected from the panel; the sample will reflect the coverage biases present in the overall panel. Alternatively, if having health insurance is unrelated to panel membership, there will be little coverage error—at least with respect to health insurance and any variables closely related to having health insurance. Coverage error might, of course, affect other survey variables, depending on the degree to which differences in the makeup of the panel and the population are related to those variables.

The logic is similar for nonresponse error. If certain characteristics are distributed differently among the nonrespondents than among the respondents, and if these characteristics are related to the survey variables, this discrepancy will produce nonresponse bias, but if an attribute is distributed similarly among respondents and nonrespondents there will be little or no bias, even with low response rates (see Groves, 2006). Imagine that a sample of Web survey panelists is invited to participate in a study about political participation. If the sample members with the least interest in politics decline the invitation to take part more often than those with more interest in the topic, this might erroneously inflate estimates of, say, voting rates; presumably the less-interested nonrespondents vote less often than the respondents. (In fact, Tourangeau, Groves, and Redline, 2010, found just such a bias in a mail and telephone survey on political topics; in their study, non-voters were less likely to respond to the survey than voters, leading to overestimates of the proportion of people who voted.) In contrast, there might be relatively little or no nonresponse error for survey measures that are not related to political interest.

There is nothing unique about the way nonresponse error functions in Web surveys, compared to other modes, as long as the sample is selected from a probability panel. Members of such panels are recruited on the telephone or face-to-face from conventional telephone or area probability frames. Recruits are asked to provide an email address at which they can receive Web survey invitations, and they are given Web access and a computer if they don't have them. These probability Web panels—for example, the Knowledge Networks panel in the United States or the Longitudinal Internet Studies for the Social Sciences (LISS) panel in the Netherlands—are designed to mirror key attributes of the population and, unlike opt-in panels, can be used to produce population estimates in a straightforward way (see Chapters 2 and 3).

In contrast, opt-in panels cannot support population estimates, at least using the traditional design-based approaches. Because the relationship between the panelists' characteristics and those of the general population is not known, nonresponse cannot really be tied to nonresponse error. As a result, the very low participation rates that are common in opt-in panels—sometimes in the single digits—may not threaten the results as they would with a probability panel. This is because, even if all those who were invited took part in the survey, there is still no real basis for generalizing beyond the participants when the participants are drawn from an opt-in panel. With opt-in panels, self-selection problems are likely to distort the estimates more than nonresponse, even when the participation rates are low.

Errors of observation. Measurement in Web surveys has much in common with measurement in other predominantly visual and self-administered modes, such as mail surveys. However, the problems may be worse in Web surveys that rely on volunteer panels, because the members of such panels may not answer as carefully as respondents in other modes. One example of measurement error associated with the visual display of questions, and found in Web surveys, is *primacy effects*. With textual (as opposed to spoken) questions, respondents tend to choose answers that appear early in a list of answer categories rather than those that come later, even though the later ones might actually be more appropriate. Galešic, Tourangeau, Couper and Conrad (2007) tracked eye movements of Web respondents answering a question with a long list of answer options and found that, at least some of the time, primacy effects occurred because respondents simply didn't read the response options at the end of the list. The phenomenon of primacy effects, originally observed with paper administration (Krosnick and Alwin, 1987), is sometimes attributed to *satisficing*— that is, to performing satisfactorily and sufficiently but not optimally (cf. Simon, 1956). In contrast, when interviewers ask similar types of questions orally, respondents tend to exhibit a preference for the more recently presented options (those at the end of the list), producing *recency* effects. Thus, primacy effects seem to reflect visual presentation more than presentation online. In fact, it is entirely feasible to present spoken questions in Web surveys (see Chapter 6); in this case, we might expect to see recency rather than primacy effects.

In Web surveys, respondents almost always complete their task without an interviewer. The absence of an interviewer has long been known to improve respondents' reporting about sensitive topics (e.g., Tourangeau and Yan, 2007), whether the survey uses a mail questionnaire or an automated mode of data collection, such as computer-assisted self-interviewing (CASI) or IVR. Web surveys seem to offer similar advantages to these other forms of self-administration. Kreuter, Presser and Tourangeau (2008) reported that respondents reported more academic problems (such as failing grades) in a Web survey than in an interviewer-administered telephone survey or an IVR survey (see Chapter 8). And, by comparing respondents' answers to university records, Kreuter and her colleagues confirmed that the increased reporting was in fact more accurate reporting. This reduction in measurement error is almost surely the result of self-administration.

Some researchers are concerned that panel members participate in surveys mostly for the monetary rewards and don't worry too much about the quality of the information they provide. This can be seen in a behavior known as speeding—answering too quickly to have read the questions, let alone to have thought carefully about the answers. Surely, speeding cannot be good for data quality (see Chapter 6). However, it may occur whenever respondents self-administer a questionnaire. The reason speeding is associated with Web surveys is that it can be detected in Web surveys. It is almost impossible to measure response times under ordinary conditions with a paper questionnaire, but it is quite easy to measure response times automatically in online questionnaires. Again, the measurement error resulting from speeding in Web surveys may have little to do with the Web per se; speeding and similar problems may be inherent problems with self-administration, whether the questions are on paper or online.

1.2 ROADMAP OF THE BOOK

This book follows the main distinctions made in the total survey error framework. We give more attention to errors of observation than errors of non-observation in Web surveys, in part reflecting the focus of our own work and that of others who have investigated the strengths and weaknesses of Web data collection. Chapter 2 discusses sampling and coverage error. A key point in Chapter 2 is that, unlike other survey modes, with Web surveys there is no "native" frame construction technique. Telephone surveys often use random-digit dial (RDD) samples, face-to-face surveys often use area probability samples, and mail surveys are often based on address frames, but there is no analogue to these methods of frame construction for Web surveys. The most obvious counterpart would be a comprehensive list of email addresses. Such lists often exist for specific populations, such as students at a university, customers of certain businesses, or employees of large companies, but there is no such list for the general population, either in the United States or elsewhere. In addition, many people have multiple email addresses and some share addresses. Because of these problems, probability Web panels intended to represent the general population have been recruited from among the members of RDD or area probability samples. The members of opt-in panels and other non-probability samples are usually recruited on the Web, through online advertisements or other methods; but however the panelists are recruited, it is generally impossible to measure exposure to the invitation and therefore impossible to estimate the probability of recruitment into the panel.

Chapter 3 is concerned with nonresponse. Although nonresponse does not necessarily imply nonresponse error, it is far easier to measure *rates* of nonresponse than the associated nonresponse errors, and not surprisingly, more studies have examined the former than the latter. Still, Chapter 3 reviews the small body of studies that have investigated nonresponse error in Web surveys. In addition, the chapter reviews research on response rates in Web surveys and their determinants (prenotification, the mode and content of the invitation, the number of contacts, and incentives). It appears that response rates, where they can be meaningfully measured, are noticeably lower in Web surveys than in other modes. While this does not necessarily mean that there is more nonresponse error in Web surveys, it does suggest that Web surveys may be at higher risk of nonresponse error than surveys using more traditional methods of data collection. Finally, Chapter 3 discusses breakoffs and item nonresponse. These are easier to measure and study in Web surveys than in other modes, since Web surveys can capture the behaviors preceding missed questions or breakoffs when they occur.

We devote much of the remainder of the book to measurement and measurement error in Web surveys. Chapter 4 introduces the general topic, focusing on the vast array of options available to the Web survey designer. One such option is paging (presenting one or a few questions per page) versus scrolling (presenting the entire questionnaire as one scrollable form). The paging approach seems to offer some measurement advantages for long questionnaires (such as fewer missing observations), but scrolling is generally considered more appropriate for short questionnaires. In addition to such questionnaire-level options, there are many question-level options. One concerns whether to present a group of questions that share a common response scale as a grid (that is, a matrix). The evidence points to a number of problems arising from conventional grids, but new design approaches, some of them interactive, may help overcome these problems while preserving the main advantages of grids—conserving space on screen, reducing the number of page downloads, and reinforcing the relatedness of similar items. This is addressed in Chapter 4, along with other design considerations, such as whether to use radio buttons or check boxes for the response options.

Chapter 5 examines how the visual features of Web surveys can affect measurement. When the questions in a Web survey contain response scales, respondents may interpret the scales based on incidental visual features—that is, features that the designers never intended them to use. For example, designers may use different colors to reinforce the fact that the scale is bipolar, using one color for scale points indicating disagreement and another color for the scale points indicating agreement. This leads respondents to interpret the end points as more conceptually distinct (further apart) than when a single color is used and to concentrate their responses in a smaller and more positive region of the scale (Tourangeau, Couper, and Conrad, 2007). Images included with the questions can have the same kind of unintended impact on measurement. Respondents seem to incorporate the images into their interpretation of the question or to use images as standards of comparison for their judgments. For example, Couper, Conrad, and Tourangeau (2007) presented an image of either a sick woman in a hospital bed or a healthy woman out jogging and asked respondents to rate their own health. Those who had been exposed to the image of the sick woman rated their health as better than those exposed to the healthy woman—the visual analogue of a context effect produced by an earlier question. Chapter 5 also reviews evidence that not all content on a Web survey page is equally visible, in part due to respondents' strategies for processing information on Web pages. A good example of this is the primacy effect mentioned earlier, in which respondents seem not to consider all options in the list. The study by Galešic and her colleagues (Galešic et al., 2007) provides evidence that at least some respondents never really see the response options at the end of the list; in addition, the study shows that the successive options in the list receive progressively less attention from respondents.

Web surveys can be interactive in the sense that the questionnaire reacts to what the respondent does. Chapter 6 covers interactive features available to designers that can potentially reduce—but may sometimes introduce—measurement error. For example, a grid can be designed so that the rows dynamically change color when a response option is selected, simplifying navigation and reducing missing data (e.g., Couper, Tourangeau, and Conrad, 2009). On the other hand, progress indicators—feedback on how much of the questionnaire has been completed—are intended to promote completion but may actually increase breakoffs by communicating that many questions are left. Similarly, including a video recording of an interviewer or a computer-animated virtual interviewer can improve respondents' understanding of the questions (Conrad, Schober, Jans, Orlowski, Nielsen, and Levenstein, 2008; Fuchs and Funke, 2007), but can also introduce "interviewer effects" (Conrad, Schober, and Nielsen, 2011; Fuchs, 2009) and social desirability biases (Fuchs, 2009; Lind, Schober, Conrad, and Reichert, under review). Some interactive features are known to improve response accuracy when respondents use them, but they are often not used. Online definitions are a case in point. We know from laboratory studies (e.g., Conrad, Schober, and Coiner, 2007) that the more respondents are exposed to definitions—whether they request them or the system volunteers them—the more accurate answers become. But in a study by Conrad, Couper, Tourangeau, and Peytchev (2006), only 13 percent of the respondents ever used the definitions. So, while interactivity can sometimes improve the accuracy of responses, it is far from a panacea.

In the decision about whether to deploy a Web survey, a fundamental consideration is how the estimates will compare to those from other modes. Chapter 7 examines this issue with respect to two potential sources of differences across modes: self-administration of sensitive questions and cognitive burden. With respect to the first of these, there is strong evidence that Web administration preserves the well-known benefits of self-administration over interviewer administration and seems to improve reporting about as much as self-administration of paper questionnaires. For example, Chang and Krosnick (2009) report that white respondents provide more undesirable racial views on the Web than on the telephone; Denniston, Brener, Kann, Eaton, McManus, Kyle, Roberts, Flint, and Ross (2010) found that their respondents, who were high school students, reported more risky behaviors in Web questionnaires than on paper; and Kreuter, Presser, and Tourangeau (2008) report an advantage of Web over telephone interviews and show that this is accompanied by an improvement in accuracy. A meta-analysis reported in Chapter 7 confirms the advantage of Web over telephone administration for collecting sensitive information and also reveals a nonsignificant advantage for Web over paper reporting.

With respect to cognitive burden, Web responding seems to help several types of questions. Fricker, Galešic, Tourangeau, and Yan (2005) reported superior performance on scientific knowledge questions, a result echoed for political knowledge in a study by Strabac and Aalberg (2011). For scale items—batteries of items that tap into similar constructs and should on logical grounds be intercorrelated—Web administration produced higher predictive validity in the Chang and Krosnick (2009) study; vote intentions in a US presidential election were better predicted by related variables when voting intentions were measured online than on the telephone. These advantages for online responding are presumably due to respondents' ability to control the pace and timing of their task, attributes Web surveys share with other forms of self-administration. The literature reviewed in Chapter 7 also hints that Web survey data may be better in some cases than data from paper questionnaires.

In addition to reviewing the main findings and themes of the book, Chapter 8 —the final chapter—grapples with the issue of mode effects, especially the issue of combining data across modes in mixed-mode surveys. Should researchers try to minimize differences in the data collected in different modes by implementing questionnaires that avoid mode-dependent features? This is sometimes called the *unimode* approach. Or is it better to design questionnaires to produce the highest quality data possible in each mode, playing to their strengths, even if this results in mode differences? This is sometimes called the *best practices* approach. We present a mathematical model for mode effects in Chapter 8; one implication of the model is that when the purpose of the survey is to produce point estimates, particularly of factual phenomena, the best practices approach is generally most appropriate; however, when the purpose of the survey is to make comparisons across groups or treatments, especially for subjective phenomena, the unimode approach is generally the most appropriate. Finally, the chapter presents a list of recommendations for practice derived from the empirical findings discussed in the book.

1.3 THE PURPOSE AND SCOPE OF THE BOOK

Although we provide a set of design recommendations in Chapter 8, and there are other recommendations sprinkled throughout the book, our focus is more on scientific evidence about Web surveys than about practice. We draw on scientific studies from both the statistical and social sciences that concern the quality of the data and estimates from Web surveys. Much of this work is ongoing as the book goes to press, so we cite many conference papers which may eventually become peer-reviewed publications but are not yet published. To the extent possible, we have based the book on findings that will, we believe, stand up over time, even as the technology and methods used in Web surveys continue to evolve. We have attempted to provide a comprehensive review of what is known about Web surveys and their error properties.

Still, in many instances, our conclusions apply to other survey modes as well. Web surveys share many attributes or affordances (i.e., the actions made possible by a user interface; Norman, 1988) with other modes. They are generally visual; so are paper questionnaires. They are generally self-administered; so are paper questionnaires, as well as computer-assisted self-interviewing (CASI), audio-CASI (ACASI), and interactive voice response (IVR) questionnaires. They are automated; so are all the computer-assisted modes. They can be interactive; so are modes of data collection that are interviewer-administered. As a result, some—even many—of the phenomena we explore in the book may also characterize other modes that share relevant features or capabilities. In many instances, we discuss enduring issues for survey design that are brought to the fore by the peculiarities of Web surveys. For example, Chapter 5, on visual issues affecting measurement, discusses the impact of the spacing between the response options and shows that uneven spacing can alter respondents' interpretation of the underlying scale. Such visual distortion could be produced by settings on the browser or monitor that are out of the designer's control. Similar phenomena would almost certainly be observed if the spacing were similarly distorted in a paper questionnaire, but this unlikely to happen; there is virtually no variation in the display of information in a paper questionnaire, at least not when the survey designers follow best practices. So the issue is one of visual presentation in general, but it is far more likely to crop up in a Web than in a paper questionnaire. Similarly, our discussion of mixed-mode surveys and mode effects in Chapter 8 applies to any combination of modes. However, a "Web option" is often added to government or academic surveys whose primary mode of data collection is mail or telephone; these combinations are attractive because of the difficulties of contacting and inviting sample members to take part in a Web survey solely via email. Thus, our discussion of mixed-mode designs addresses general concerns in survey methodology that are of particular concern for Web surveys.

Web surveys have had an enormous impact on the survey profession. It is remarkable how much research attention Web surveys have received in such a short time. While many challenges remain, especially with regard to errors of non-observation, Web surveys offer a great deal of promise in terms of improved data quality or reduced measurement error. Indeed, the Web has facilitated the development of forms of measurement that would be difficult if not impossible to implement in other modes of data collection. The challenge—and opportunity—for researchers remains that of reducing the effects of the representational shortcomings of the Web while exploiting its measurement advantages.

/// 2 /// SAMPLING AND COVERAGE ISSUES FOR WEB SURVEYS

One of the major attractions of Web surveys for many researchers is their relatively low cost. Unfortunately, this low cost often reflects a nearly complete disregard of the sampling principles that are applied in most high-quality government or academic surveys designed to make inferences to broad populations. Although there are many populations for which probability samples can be drawn for Web surveys—such as members of professional associations, registered users of a website, or college students—the coverage and sampling challenges for inference to general populations (such as the population of adults in the United States) are considerable. Couper's (2000) widely-cited review paper on Web surveys distinguishes eight types of Web survey, and three of the eight types involve non-probability samples. Table 2.1 below (adapted from Couper's paper) shows the eight types. The reliance of many Web surveys of general populations on non-probability sampling raises several questions that we address in this chapter. First, why aren't probability samples used more often? Second, what biases are likely to be introduced by the use of non-probability samples? This question leads us to explore the characteristics of people who have access to the Internet and thus can take part in Web surveys as compared to those who don't have access. Third, given the differences between the population with Web access and the population without access, can statistical procedures be used to eliminate or at least reduce the resulting biases? We begin by differentiating the various types of Web surveys.

2.1 TYPES OF WEB SURVEYS AND THE USE OF PROBABILITY SAMPLING

Types of Web surveys. Couper (2000) groups Web surveys into two major categories, those that use probability sampling and those that don't.[1] We begin with

---

[1] A probability (or random) sample is one in which every element in the population of interest has a nonzero and calculable probability of selection. That is, no elements are omitted by design and the researchers can assign a selection probability to each element. The selection probabilities need not be the same for every element.

TABLE 2.1. Types of Web Survey and the Use of Probability Sampling

Type of Survey	Definition
NON-PROBABILITY SAMPLES	
1) Polls for Entertainment	Polls that make no claims regarding representativeness (e.g., CNN Quick Vote); respondents are typically volunteers to the Web site hosting the survey
2) Unrestricted self-selected surveys	Respondents are recruited via open invitations on portals or frequently visited Web sites; these are similar to the entertainment polls
3) Volunteer opt-in panels	Respondents take part in many surveys as members of a Web panel; panel members are usually recruited via invitations on popular Web sites (e.g., Harris Poll Online)
PROBABILITY SAMPLES	
4) Intercept surveys	Sample members are randomly or systematically selected visitors to a specific Web site, typically recruited via pop-up invitations
5) List-based samples	Sample members are selected from a list of some well-defined population (e.g., students or staff at a university), with recruitment via email or mail
6) Web option in mixed-mode surveys	A Web option is offered to the members of a sample selected through traditional methods; initial contact often through some other medium (e.g., advance letter)
7) Pre-recruited panels of Internet users	A probability sample, selected and screened to identify Internet users, is recruited to participate in a panel
8) Pre-recruited panels of the full Population	A probability sample is recruited to take part in a Web panel; those without Internet access are provided with access

Note: This typology is drawn from Couper (2000). Reprinted with permission from Couper, 2000.

the non-probability samples. The first two types of non-probability surveys (polls for entertainment purposes and unrestricted self-selected surveys) consist of ad hoc groups of volunteers—typically, visitors to a Web site (or multiple Web sites) who are asked to take part in a survey. In some cases, the findings from the resulting "surveys" are not intended to be taken seriously (these are the entertainment polls, in Couper's scheme), but in other cases the results are presented as though they were scientifically valid (these make up Couper's second category, the unrestricted self-selected surveys). Couper (2007) presents several examples of papers based on such surveys published in the medical and health literature. Volunteer opt-in or access panels, Couper's third type of Web survey, are very common, and several firms make members of their panels available to market and other researchers. These panels are often quite large, with hundreds of thousands or even millions of members, but the response rates to any specific survey request are often very low. It may be that relatively few of the panel members are still active and thus don't respond; it is also possible that active panel members are invited to complete so many surveys that they have gotten choosy about which ones they complete. Whether the problem is members dropping out of the panel entirely or their failure to respond to specific survey requests, nonresponse may worsen any initial self-selection biases.

Self-selected volunteer panels have their scientific uses, and much of the work summarized in this book makes use of such panels. Whether such panels can be used to represent any larger population is open to question. In some cases, the results are intended to project to the general population, and sophisticated weighting procedures are used to reduce the coverage and nonresponse biases associated with the use of self-selected panelists for this purpose (see, for example, Taylor, Bremer, Overmeyer, Siegel, and Terhanian, 2001). Section 2.3 below discusses the evidence regarding the effectiveness of these weighting methods for removing or reducing bias.

What about probability sampling on the Web? Couper distinguishes five types of Web surveys that use probability sampling, but even taken together, surveys using probability sampling are likely to constitute a small minority of all Web surveys. The first type of survey that does use probability sampling is the intercept survey, in which a random or systematic sample of visitors to a particular Web site is selected over a specified time frame and invited to complete a survey.[2] Although this form of sampling does produce a probability sample, it is drawn from a restricted population (visitors to a specified Web site or set of Web sites within a particular time frame). The conclusions are limited to such visitors rather than the broader population; if the former is the population of interest, then there is no coverage issue. This type of Web survey is often used to gather evaluations of the Web site or of the transactions that take place there (such as retail sales). Couper also points out that there are advantages to selecting visitors as they arrive at the Web site: this method permits the selection of all visitors, including those who leave without completing any transactions. The invitation to complete the survey can appear as respondents leave the Web site, but the selection occurs as they arrive. The key challenge for this type of Web survey is nonresponse, rather than coverage or sampling error.

Another instance in which Web surveys are based on probability sampling are surveys of circumscribed populations (such as the employees at an individual firm

---

[2] A systematic sample is one that includes every nth element on the frame, starting with a randomly selected element. A frame is a list of the members of some population or a set of materials, like a list of the blocks in a city or county, from which a list of the elements themselves can be constructed. With a Web survey, the frame consists of the visitors to the Web site during the specified period and it offers complete coverage of the population (so long as the population is defined as the visitors to the Web site during the particular time window in which sampling was carried out). Strictly speaking, this sort of sample design yields a probability sample of the population of *visits* to the site rather than the population of visitors, but as Couper (2000) notes, cookies can be used to prevent multiple selections of the same visitor (at least those that use the same computer and browser each time), producing an approximately equal probability sample of visitors.

or students at a university) with near-universal access to the Internet. The frame may or may not include email addresses. Invitations may be sent by email or by mail, depending on the availability and quality of the address information on the frame (we return to the issue of invitations in Chapter 3). Regardless of the method of invitation, all respondents complete the survey online. In general, when a list frame is available for a population, when it provides complete (or nearly complete) coverage of that population, and when the members of the population have access to the Internet, then this strategy can yield high-quality survey estimates—estimates with little or no coverage bias. (We discuss the mathematics of coverage bias in more detail later in this chapter.)

Some surveys start out using conventional methods of sampling (such as sampling from a list or from an area frame) but offer the Web as one method for responding to the survey among several possible methods. This strategy sidesteps the sampling and coverage issues that offer major difficulties for most Web surveys. For example, the National Center for Education Statistics has conducted the National Study of Postsecondary Faculty (NSOPF) since 1987. The most recent version of the study, carried out in 2003 and 2004, first selected a sample of degree-granting institutions and then, within each of the sample institutions, selected samples of the eligible instructional staff. Those selected for the study could complete a Web version of the questionnaire or participate in a telephone interview; ultimately, about 76 percent of the respondents completed the survey via the Web (see Heuer, Kuhr, Fahimi, Curtin, Hinsdale, Carley-Baxter, and Green, 2006, for details about the NSOPF: 04). As long as other modes of responding are available, lack of access to the Internet among some portion of the target population doesn't necessarily introduce any coverage bias.

The last two types of Web surveys that employ probability sampling share the same general approach. Both rely on some traditional method (such as random-digit dialing, or RDD) to select a general population sample; both then either screen the members of that sample to identify those with Internet access (this is Couper's seventh type, the pre-recruited panels of Internet users) or provide Internet access to those who don't already have it in order to represent the entire general population (this is Couper's final category, pre-recruited panels of the full population). Couper (2000) cites the Pew Research Center (Flemming and Sonner, 1999) and the Gallup Organization (Rookey, Hanway, and Dillman, 2008) as examples of the seventh type of Web survey. In principle, such samples represent the population with Internet access, not the entire population, and as we document below, there can be large differences between the two. This type of Web survey has become less popular, with researchers either gravitating toward the cheaper opt-in approach or including the non-Internet population by providing access to nonusers, as discussed below. The Gallup panel remains a notable exception, but uses mail surveys to cover the non-Internet population.

The Knowledge Networks panel in the United States (e.g., Krotki and Dennis, 2001; Smith, 2003) and the Longitudinal Internet Studies for the Social Sciences (LISS) panel in the Netherlands (www.lissdata.nl) would be examples of the eighth type, a probability sample that represents the general population. The Knowledge Networks panel members were selected via RDD[3] and recruited over the telephone; the LISS panel was selected from population registries. In both cases, members of the sample who otherwise couldn't participate were provided with Internet access. More recently, the Face-to-Face Recruited Internet Survey Panel (FFRISP) in the United States recruited members of an area probability sample to join a Web panel; they were offered a computer and Internet access as an inducement to take part (see Sakshaug, Tourangeau, Krosnick, Ackermann, Malka, DeBell, and Turakhia, 2009, for a description of the FFRISP sample).

Although the pre-recruited panels start as representative samples, nonresponse can jeopardize this representativeness. The recruitment process for such panels involves multiple steps, and potential panelists can drop out at each one. The researchers must first locate and contact members of the sample; the sample members must then agree to join the panel and in addition allow any necessary equipment to be installed; typically, potential recruits must complete some baseline questionnaire that allows the researchers to determine their eligibility for individual surveys later on; those who join the panel must remain active over time; and finally panelists must respond to the specific survey requests that are sent to them. Even if the success rates at each stage are very high, the cumulative response rate may be low, and cumulative response rates in the 10 to 20 percent range are typical (cf. the discussion in Berrens, Bohara, Jenkins-Smith, Silva, and Weimer, 2003, pp. 6–7; Callegaro and DiSogra, 2008). We take a closer look at nonresponse in Web surveys in Chapter 3.

Obstacles to the use of probability sampling. Most modes of data collection are, in fact, bundles of features that can on occasion be unbundled (see the discussion in Chapter 4 of Groves, Fowler, Couper, Lepkowski, Singer, and Tourangeau, 2009). For example, most (or at least many) telephone surveys involve generating a sample of telephone numbers using some form of RDD sampling, contacting sample households by telephone (sometimes after an advance letter has been sent), and completing telephone interviews that are done by live interviewers. Still, there is no fundamental reason that the sample *has* to be selected via RDD or that the interviews can't be carried out using recorded interviewers (as in interactive voice response). Similarly, many, if not most, surveys that use face-to-face interviews also use area probability sampling—this combination is employed by a large number of federal surveys in the United States—though face-to-face interviewing can also be used in conjunction with other methods of sampling. For the traditional modes of data collection, then, a method of data collection is often yoked with a specific sampling frame and method of sampling.

As Couper's typology makes clear, there is no such link between Web surveys and any particular method of sampling. Of the Web surveys that use probability sampling, some rely on intercept sampling, some on list samples, and some on methods

---

[3] Knowledge Networks now uses address-based sampling (ABS) for sample selection and panel recruitment (see DiSogra, 2009).

of sampling (such as RDD) that are usually associated with other modes of data collection. Why has no method of sampling become the typical method for Web surveys? The answer would seem to be the absence of a good sampling frame for Web surveys of the general population. The key requirements for a good sampling frame are:

1) Good coverage of the target population (that is, the frame should include a high proportion of the target population);
2) Relatively low rates of duplication, or "multiplicity" (that is, the frame should include most members of the population only once or should make it easy to determine the number of times each member is included); and
3) Up-to-date information that allows the researchers to contact members selected for the sample.

Since email is the method generally used for contacting and recruiting members of Web samples, the ideal sampling frame for Web surveys would be a list of the email addresses of all members of the population. In addition, a frame of email addresses would allow researchers to avoid the multiple sampling, contacting, and recruitment steps associated with pre-recruited probability samples that use more traditional methods of sampling, such as RDD. For some populations (such as students at a university), such list frames may be available, and surveys based on frames consisting of lists of the members of the population (with their email addresses) often achieve both acceptably high response rates and relatively low data collection costs.

Of course, there is no up-to-date and complete list of residential telephone numbers in the United States either, but the absence of a list frame hasn't prevented the emergence of standard methods for selecting telephone samples. (Lists of *listed* residential telephone numbers do exist, but unlisted numbers constitute a substantial fraction of all residential numbers, so most surveys do not rely on these lists.) Telephone numbers in the United States follow a standard format; each number consists of exactly ten digits, with the first three numbers representing the area code, the next three the prefix, and the final four the suffix. It is possible to get complete and up-to-date lists of all active area code-prefix combinations; moreover, it is possible to identify area code-prefix combinations that have one or more residential listings. List-assisted RDD sampling (Casady and Lepkowski, 1993; Lepkowski, 1988) exploits these facts, generating a sample of potential telephone numbers from active area code-prefix combinations that include at least one (or in some versions, at least three) listed residential numbers. A sample of area code-prefix combinations is selected and then four-digit suffixes are randomly generated and appended to produce a potential telephone number. A reasonably high proportion of the numbers generated in this way turn out to be working residential numbers (Brick, Waksberg, Kulp, and Starer, 1995)—although that fraction appears to be dropping—so that list-assisted sampling offers a cost-effective method for representing the population of households with a telephone.

To date, no equivalent method has been developed for sampling Internet users. The closest analogue to RDD sampling would be a method for randomly generating email addresses. Almost all Internet users have email, and we suspect that most of them are linked only to one or two email addresses (as they are linked only to one or two telephone numbers); email addresses have the further virtue of providing a means for researchers to contact the members of the sample. Unfortunately, email addresses (unlike telephone numbers) do not follow any standardized format, but can vary in length and in other ways. Thus, any attempt to generate a random set of email addresses is likely to include a very high fraction of nonworking email addresses; in addition, any scheme for generating email addresses is likely to exclude large numbers of real email addresses that follow formats that weren't anticipated when the algorithm for generating potential email addresses was developed. Because there is no standardized format for email addresses, and because there isn't any other frame for Internet users with acceptably high levels of coverage, most attempts to select probability samples for Web surveys rely on some traditional method of sampling that is typically used with another mode of data collection. It is, of course, possible that in the future some method for generating probability samples of email addresses or some other method for selecting probability samples of Internet users will be developed, but for the near term this appears unlikely. Further, given concerns over spam, the large-scale generation and transmission of messages to randomly generated email addresses is unlikely to prove feasible in practice.

Statistical consequences of non-probability sampling. What difference does it make if a sample consists of self-selected volunteers rather than a probability sample from the target population? The key statistical consequence is bias—unadjusted means or proportions from non-probability samples are likely to be biased estimates of the corresponding population means or proportions. Equation 2.1 (cf. Bethlehem, 2010, Equation 15) shows that the size and direction of the bias depend on two factors—one reflecting the proportion of the population with no chance of inclusion in the sample (for example, people without Web access or people who would never join a Web panel) and one reflecting differences in the inclusion probabilities among the different members of the sample who could in principle complete the survey:

$$(2.1) \quad Bias = E(\bar{y} - \bar{Y})$$
$$= P_0(\bar{Y}_1 - \bar{Y}_0) + \frac{Cov(P,Y)}{\bar{P}}.$$

In Equation 2.1, $\bar{y}$ represents a sample mean (or a sample proportion) based on those who complete the Web survey; $\bar{Y}$ represents the corresponding population mean or proportion; P_0 the proportion of the population of interest with no chance at all of participating in the survey (e.g., those without Web access); $\bar{Y}_1$, the mean among those with a non-zero probability of taking part; $\bar{Y}_0$, the mean among those with zero probability of taking part; $Cov(P,Y)$, the covariance between the probabilities of participation (P) and the survey variable of interest (Y) within the population with at least some chance of taking part; and $\bar{P}$, the mean probability of participation among those with a nonzero probability of taking part.

According to the equation, the bias due to the use of samples of volunteers rather than probability samples has two components. The first term in the second line of Equation 2.1 reflects the impact of the complete omission of some portion of the population of interest; it is the product of the proportion of the target population that is excluded from the sample entirely and the difference between the mean for this group and the mean for the remainder of the population. (In the next section of this chapter, we explore some of the differences between those with Web access and those without it.) The second term in the second line of the equation reflects the impact of differences in the inclusion probabilities (among those with nonzero probabilities); to the extent that these probabilities covary with the survey variable of interest (y), then the second bias component will be nonzero. Although Equation 2.1 applies to the unweighted sample mean, $\bar{y}$, it provides some useful distinctions for understanding how more complex estimators affect the bias. In non-probability samples, p and $\bar{P}$ are generally unknown or inestimable. Furthermore, in both probability and non-probability samples, $\bar{Y}$ is not known—if it were, there would be little or no need to do the survey. Thus, coverage bias cannot be estimated in practice for most survey variables of interest.

2.2   COVERAGE ISSUES FOR WEB SURVEYS

This section discusses trends in Internet access in the United States and explores the differences between those with Internet access and those without it. The proportion without Internet access corresponds to P_0 in Equation 2.1; the differences between those with Internet access and those without it correspond to the ($\bar{Y}_1 - \bar{Y}_0$) term in that equation.

As a preliminary matter, it is useful to discuss what we mean by Internet access. The various surveys that monitor Internet access in the U. S. use several different items that embody slightly different conceptions of access to measure the proportion of the population that is online. For example, the Current Population Survey (CPS), which is carried out by the US Bureau of the Census on behalf of the Bureau of Labor Statistics, has periodically included supplemental modules assessing Internet access. One item asks about Internet access from home ("Does anyone in this household connect to the Internet from home?"). Additional questions ask about access from work ("Does…use the computer at work to connect to the Internet or use email?") or school. Depending on the nature of the survey (and on whether it is work-related), access from either site may be more relevant to determining the likely level of coverage for a Web survey. The Health Information National Trends Survey (HINTS), sponsored by the National Institutes of Health, also includes items on Internet access; the key question in that survey asks, "Do you ever go online to access the Internet or World Wide Web, or to send and receive email?" Finally, the Pew Internet & American Life Project periodically conducts surveys that ask about Internet use ("Do you use the Internet at least occasionally?" and "Do you send and receive email at least occasionally?").[4]

It is not clear which of these approaches (if any of them) is the best way to assess the likely coverage of an Internet survey. Some of the items measure Internet access and some of them measure use. Some of the items measure access or use at the household level and some of them measure it at the person level. The household level is the appropriate measure for panels that recruit entire households (such as the Knowledge Networks and LISS panels). Regardless of the exact wording of the questions, these items may overestimate the size of the population likely to be covered in a Web survey. Clearly, those who access the Internet only rarely (say, from their local library) or those who have access only at work are unlikely to be represented in most Web surveys. A further problem is that methods of Internet access are rapidly changing, with smart phones and tablet computers replacing desktop computers as the main devices for going online (Purcell, 2011; Purcell, Rainey, Rosenstiel, and Mitchell, 2011). It is not clear that the existing questions adequately reflect these technological developments.

Trends in coverage. Regardless of these differences in item wording, the trends in Internet coverage both in the United States and Europe are clearly upward, but appear to be leveling off. Figure 2.1 summarizes the data from the CPS supplements, HINTS, and the Pew surveys and shows similar figures from Eurostat data on Internet access in Europe. According to the CPS, about 69 percent of all households in the United States had Internet access at home in 2009, up from 18 percent in 1997. According to HINTS, more than 68 percent of the adult population had access to the Internet in 2007, up from 61 percent in 2005. The Pew surveys indicate a rise from about 50 percent of adults with Web access in mid-2000 to about 78 percent in the spring of 2011. Despite many differences across the surveys (for example, the Pew data are from telephone surveys with households selected via RDD whereas the CPS data are based on an area probability sample interviewed face-to-face or by telephone), the trends are reasonably consistent across the three surveys; all three show continuing but slowing growth in the proportion of the general population with access to the Internet. Some of the apparent reversals in this overall trend probably reflect changes in the methods used by a given survey. For example, HINTS changed items after 2003 (when it asked "Do you go on-line at all?") and in 2007, HINTS switched from RDD to a combination of mail and telephone data collection. Similar trends are apparent throughout the developed world; according to the International Telecommunications Union (2007), about 62 percent of the population in developed countries had Internet access, and Eurostat estimates that about Internet access was about 71 percent among the adult population of the European Union in 2010.

The data plotted in Figure 2.1 raise the issue of whether everyone (or nearly everyone) will have Internet access at some point, in which case the coverage issue

---

[4] In the remainder of this chapter, we use the terms "Web access" and "Internet access" interchangeably. We use the term "Internet users" to refer to those having Internet access.

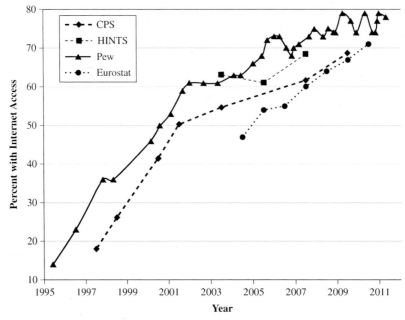

FIGURE 2.1. Trends in Internet access in the United States and the European Union. Although all three U. S. surveys (the CPS, HINTS, and Pew) show steady growth in the percentage of the adult population with Internet access, that growth appears to be leveling off. The trend in the European Union is similar to that in the United States, with perhaps a slight lag in Internet access in the EU.

for Web surveys (though not the sampling issue) would disappear. Ehlen and Ehlen (2007) have presented a model for predicting changes in the size and make-up of the population making the switch from landline telephones to cellular telephones only, what they refer to as "cell-only lifestyle adoption." A similar model presumably would apply to the adoption of the Internet lifestyle. According to Ehlen and Ehlen's model, the size of the population adopting the new lifestyle depends on two main factors—the rate of habit retention (a sort of behavioral inertia factor) and the incentives for adopting the new lifestyle:

$$(2.2) \quad \log Y_t = \log K_t + \lambda \log Y_{t-1} + \varepsilon_t$$

In Equation 2.2, Y_t represents the proportion of the population that has adopted the lifestyle at time t (in our case, accessing the Internet from home); Y_{t-1} represents the proportion in the previous period, time $t-1$; K_t represents the incentives for adoption at that time, and λ is the rate of habit retention from the previous period, time $t-1$. K_t reflects such variables as the costs associated with adopting the new lifestyle and the respondent's income. Clearly, the cost of Internet access is stabilizing; as a result, whether Internet access becomes universal (and how quickly that happens) will depend largely on the behavioral inertia factor. Unfortunately, when we fit the model summarized in Equation 2.2 to the Pew data using nonlinear regression methods, we find a relatively poor fit (the r^2 is about 0.20); apparently, the Pew observations

TABLE 2.2. Percentage of U.S. Population with Internet Access by Demographic Subgroup

Subgroup	HINTS 2007	HINTS 2005
Male	66.4%	61.3%
Female	70.6	60.9
18–34 years old	80.3	74.4
25–49 years old	76.0	67.4
50–64 years old	68.4	59.3
65–74 years old	45.1	32.7
75 and older	21.6	17.6
Less than high school	27.0	22.9
High school graduate	56.8	49.1
Some college	80.4	74.1
College graduate	91.0	87.2
Hispanic	49.3	36.2
Non-Hispanic Black	56.8	52.5
Non-Hispanic White	75.0	68.4
All Other	74.2	60.9

Note: Data from the Health Information National Trends Surveys (HINTS) 2005 and 2007.

are too close together in time to yield stable estimates of the habit retention factor. The other time series plotted in Figure 2.1 contain too few points to provide stable estimates of λ either.

The "digital divide." As Equation 2.1 makes clear, the omission from Web surveys of the more than 30 percent of the adult population without Internet access can lead to problems (more specifically, to substantial coverage biases) if those with access to the Internet differ from those without access on the survey variables. There is considerable evidence that the online population does differ in many ways from the population without access. Table 2.2 shows how the rates of coverage differ across demographic groups. There are large differences in the proportion of the population with access to the Internet by age, race, and education. Internet access declines monotonically with age and increases monotonically with education (and income); non-Hispanic Blacks and Hispanics are less likely to have access to the Internet than non-Hispanic Whites and others. These differences in rates of Internet access, sometimes labeled the "digital divide" (Lenhart, Horrigan, Rainie, Allen, Boyce, Madden, and O'Grady, 2003; Norris, 2001), imply serious risks of coverage bias in Web surveys that are intended to produce results that can be generalized to the full population. Relative to the general population, the U.S. Internet population is younger, better educated, wealthier, and more likely to be White. Bethlehem (2010) reports similar differences in the European Union between those with Web access and those without it.

It is relatively easy to correct for demographic differences between the Internet population and the general population as a whole, such as the differences apparent in Table 2.2, through standard weighting adjustments. (We discuss these weighting

TABLE 2.3. Percentage of Population or Population Subgroup with Selected Health and Attitudinal Characteristics

Survey/Characteristic	With Internet Access	Full Population	Target Population for Study
2003 MICHIGAN BRFSS			
Rates health "good" to "excellent"	89.8%	84.9%	Michigan residents
Has health care coverage	90.7	89.3	age 18 and older
Has personal doctor or health care provider	84.0	83.6	
Participated in exercise in past month	82.6	78.2	
Told that he/she has diabetes	5.5	7.9	
Told that he/she has high blood pressure	22.6	26.8	
Limited in usual activities because of arthritis or joint symptoms	23.1	27.2	
2002 HEALTH AND RETIREMENT STUDY			
Has high blood pressure	44.0	54.8	US population age
Has heart disease	16.0	25.3	50 and older
Has arthritis	48.9	61.9	
Depressed	10.6	18.6	
Lonely	11.7	21.2	
Enjoys life	93.3	95.7	
Has difficulty dressing	3.7	8.7	
Has difficulty walking several blocks	14.9	31.2	
2002 GENERAL SOCIAL SURVEY			
Feels warmly toward blacks	63.6	61.2	US population age
Voted in 2000 election	71.5	65.0	18 and older

Note: The figures in top panel are from Tables 3 and 5 in Dever et al. (2008); those in the middle panel are taken from Schonlau et al. (2009), Table 3; those in the bottom panel are from Lee (2006b). See the original sources for more detail (such as exact item wordings).

procedures in the next section of this chapter.) But the real issue is whether those with Internet access differ from those without it on characteristics that are likely to be of substantive interest in a survey—that is, on the y variables in Equation 2.1. The top two panels of Table 2.3 show how those with Internet access differ from those without access to the Internet on a number of health variables; the bottom panel of the table examines two attitudinal variables from the General Social Survey. The estimates displayed in Table 2.3 are representative of the larger sets of variables examined in the papers by Dever, Rafferty, and Valliant (2008) and Schonlau, van Soest, Kapteyn, and Couper (2009). Table 2.3 includes both of the variables that Lee (2006b) examined.

The figures in the top panel of Table 2.3 are drawn from the Michigan Behavioral Risk Factor Surveillance System (BRFSS) survey, a survey that uses RDD sampling and is done by telephone. The survey is intended to represent the adult household population in the state of Michigan and includes both respondents with access to the Internet and respondents without access. The Michigan BRFSS collects information on a range of health-related variables, including how the respondents assess their own health status, whether they are covered by health insurance, and whether a doctor has ever told them they have diabetes. As is apparent from the top panel of the table, those with Internet access report themselves to be in better health than those without access, resulting in overestimates of good health and underestimates of poor health compared to the general population. The figures in the middle panel of the survey are from the Health and Retirement Survey (HRS), which collects data via several modes from a sample originally selected as an area probability sample; as with the Michigan BRFSS, the HRS sample includes respondents with Internet access and respondents without it. Although the HRS represents a very different population (persons 50 years and older in the United States) from the Michigan BRFSS, the pattern of health differences is very similar to the one shown in the top panel of the table. Again, respondents with Internet access (the first column of percentages) appear to be healthier than the full population (the second column of percentages), with lower reported rates of high blood pressure, heart disease, loneliness, depression, and so on. The final panel looks at two "attitudinal" variables, using data from the General Social Survey, which conducts face-to-face interviews with a national sample of persons 18 or older. There are significant differences between those with Internet access and those without access on one variable (whether the respondent reported voting in the 2000 Presidential election) but not on the other (whether the respondent reports feeling warmly toward blacks). The remaining differences in the table are all statistically significant, with one exception (the difference in the percentages reporting that they have a personal physician or health care provider).

Overall, then, the figures in Table 2.3 suggest that the digital divide is *not* restricted to demographic characteristics, but extends to a wide range of health variables (see Dever et al., 2008, and Schonlau et al., 2009, for further evidence on this point); in addition, the final panel suggests that it may extend to attitudinal variables as well. Those with Internet access seem to differ on a variety of characteristics from those who have not yet gotten online (see also Couper, Kapteyn, Schonlau, and Winter, 2007). As we shall see in the next section, adjusting for demographic differences (e.g., the variables in Table 2.2) does not always reduce the bias in the substantive variables (e.g., those in Table 2.3).

2.3 STATISTICAL CORRECTIONS FOR COVERAGE AND SAMPLING BIAS

As Lee (2006a) points out, there are several potential sources of error that can bias the estimates from Web surveys based on volunteer Web panels (Couper's third type of Web survey). For our purposes, it is useful to distinguish between three of these potential error sources:

1) **Coverage error**, or differences between the population represented in the survey (such as the adult population with Internet access) and the target population for the survey (the full population of adults);
2) **Selection error**, or differences between the survey population (Internet users) and those who are recruited into the panel and selected to take part in the specific survey; and
3) **Nonresponse error**, or differences between those selected for the survey and those who actually complete it.

Regardless of what method of sampling is used, coverage errors occur in *any* Web survey that excludes those without Internet access but nonetheless attempts to characterize the entire population. The first component of the bias equation for an unweighted mean, Equation 2.1, reflects this source of error. As this equation shows, if the Internet population and the full population do not differ on the variable of interest, then the coverage bias will be zero; but if there are differences between the two populations, these differences will bias the survey estimates. The second source of error reflects problems in the recruitment or sampling process that introduce systematic discrepancies between the Internet population and the sample for a given survey. For example, with opt-in panels, there is no guarantee that the volunteer panel members resemble the larger population of Internet users on the survey variables. If the likelihood of recruitment (and selection) is related to values on the variables of interest, this will introduce error into the estimates (as indicated by the covariance term in Equation 2.1). For example, voters may be more likely than nonvoters to join a panel that features political surveys; this difference in response propensities will bias estimates of turnout. This error component is eliminated when probability sampling is used to select panel members. The final error source is nonresponse error, and we defer discussion of this error source until Chapter 3.

Post-stratification adjustments. Survey researchers have devised several statistical methods intended to reduce coverage and selection bias. All of the methods involve adjusting the weights assigned for the survey participants to make the sample line up more closely with population figures. These same methods are also sometimes used to compensate for nonresponse bias as well (see Kalton and Flores-Cervantes, 2003, for a useful review of weighting methods, including the four discussed here).

The first method that has been used to adjust for the sampling and coverage problems in Web surveys is known variously as ratio adjustment, post-stratification, or cell weighting ("cell weighting" is the term used by Kalton and Flores-Cervantes, 2003). This procedure adjusts "the sample weights so that the sample totals conform to the population totals on a cell-by-cell basis" (Kalton and Flores-Cervantes, page 84). The procedure is quite simple—the weight for each respondent (typically, the inverse of the case's selection probability) in a weighting cell (or post-stratum) is multiplied by an adjustment factor:

$$(2.3) \quad w_{2ij} = \frac{N_j}{\sum^{n_j} w_{1ij}} w_{1ij} \; ,$$

in which w_{2ij} is the adjusted or post-stratified weight, w_{1ij} is the unadjusted weight, and the adjustment factor is the ratio between the population total for cell j (N_j) and the sum of the unadjusted weights for the respondents in that cell. (Sometimes the "population" total is actually an estimate based on a good survey.) For many Web surveys, the initial weights are all one. After adjustment, the weighted sample totals for each cell exactly match the population totals. Population (π_j) and sample proportions ($\sum^{n_i} w_{1ij} / \sum^n w_{1j}$) can be used in place of the population (N_j) and sample totals ($\sum^{n_j} w_{1ij}$) in Equation 2.3 to produce the same adjusted weights.

Post-stratification will eliminate the bias due to selection or coverage problems provided that, within each adjustment cell, the probability that each case completes the survey is unrelated to that case's value on the survey variable of interest. This condition is sometimes referred to as the *missing at random* assumption (Little and Rubin, 2002). In terms of Equation 2.1, a post-stratification adjustment will eliminate the bias if the expected within-cell covariance between the participation probabilities (P) and the survey variables (Y) goes to zero:

$$Cov(P,Y \mid \underline{X}) = 0$$

where X is the vector of categorical variables that are cross-classified to form the adjustment cells. This condition of zero covariance can be met is several ways: The participation probabilities can be identical within each cell; the values of the survey variable can be identical within each cell; or values for the two can vary independently within the cells. As a practical matter, post-stratification will reduce the magnitude of the bias whenever the absolute value of the within-cell covariance term is less than the overall covariance term:

$$(2.4) \quad \left| Cov(P,Y \mid \underline{X}) \right| < \left| Cov(P,Y) \right|$$

Most survey statisticians use post-stratification in the belief that the inequality in 2.4 holds, not that the bias disappears entirely.

We note that sample matching attempts to *start* with a Web sample that matches some set of target population figures (Rivers and Bailey, 2009). With this method, a subsample of Web panel members is selected for a particular survey and the subsample is chosen to represent the population composition correctly. Any residual deviation between the sample make-up and the make-up of the population is corrected statistically via propensity weighting (discussed below). Sampling matching would presumably have an impact on bias similar to the impact of post-stratification.

Raking. Raking (or rim weighting) also adjusts the sample weights so that sample totals line up with external population figures, but the adjustment aligns the sample to the *marginal* totals for the auxiliary variables, not to the cell totals. For example, if population figures are available for males and females and for those with a college degree and those without one, the adjusted sample weights would bring the sample totals into line with the figures for males and females and for college graduates and those with less education, but not necessarily for males with college degrees or females without college degrees. There are several situations where raking might be preferred to post-stratification. Population figures may not be available for every adjustment cell formed by crossing the auxiliary variables. Or there may be very few participants in a given cell, so that the adjustment factors become extreme and highly variable across cells. Or the researchers may want to incorporate a large number of variables in the weighting scheme, too many for a cell-by-cell adjustment to be practical.

Raking is carried out using iterative proportional fitting (the same algorithm used to fit log-linear models). First, the sample weights are adjusted to agree with the marginal totals for one of the auxiliary variables, say, the sex of the respondents. The adjustment factor is computed in the same way as the one described in Equation 2.3, only the population target is based on the marginal total (say, the total number of males). Then, the weights are adjusted to agree with the marginal totals for the next auxiliary variable (education level) and so on until adjustments have been made for each of the auxiliary variables. The adjustment process for later variables (education) may have thrown off the totals for earlier variables (sex) so the process is repeated until the weights no longer change. (Convergence is usually rapid, but need not be; see the discussion in Kalton and Flores-Cervantes, 2003, page 86).

Raking reduces or eliminates bias under the same conditions as post-stratification (that is, when the covariance between the probability of participation and the survey variable is reduced after the auxiliary variables are taken into account), but assumes a more stringent model (in which the interactions between the auxiliary variables can be ignored or produce only small additional reductions in bias).

Generalized regression (GREG) modeling. GREG weighting is an alternative method of benchmarking sample estimates to the corresponding population figures. This approach assumes a "linear relationship between an analysis variable y and a set of covariates" (Dever, Rafferty, and Valliant, 2008, page 57). The GREG estimator for the total for y corrects the initial sample estimate using that linear relationship:

$$(2.5) \quad \hat{T}_{Gy} = \hat{T}_{1y} + \sum_{j}^{p} b_j (T_{xj} - \hat{T}_{1xj})$$

in which $\hat{T}_{Gy}$ is the estimated total for variable y based on the adjusted weights; $\hat{T}_{1y}$ is the corresponding estimate based on the unadjusted weights (that is, $\hat{T}_{1y} = \sum_{i}^{n_r} w_{1i} y_i$, with n_r representing the number of respondents); T_{xj} is the population total for covariate x_j; $\hat{T}_{1xj}$ is the sample estimate of the total for that covariate (based on the unadjusted weights); and the b's are the regression coefficients for the p covariates estimated through weighted least squares (the weights in the weighted regression are the unadjusted sample weights, w_{1i}). As Kalton and Flores-Cervantes (2003; see page 88) point out, in the simplest case (with a single covariate x), the adjusted weight becomes:

$$w_{2i} = w_{1i} + \left(T_x - \hat{T}_{1x}\right)(x_i - \bar{x}) / \sum_{i}^{n_r} (x_i - \bar{x})^2,$$

in which w_{1i} is the initial weight for respondent i; w_{2i} is the GREG weight; T_{xj} and $\hat{T}_{1x}$ are the population value and the sample estimate for the covariate total (as in Equation 2.5 above); x_i is respondent i's value on the covariate; and $\bar{x}$ is the sample mean on the covariate.

As with post-stratification and raking, GREG weighting eliminates the bias when, conditional on the covariates, there is no relationship between the likelihood of that a respondent will complete the survey and his or her values on the survey variables of interest.

Propensity scoring. Researchers have used one additional method for adjusting survey weights to remove or reduce bias—propensity score adjustment (PSA) or propensity weighting. At least seven published papers have examined the use of propensity score adjustment to improve Web survey estimates by reducing biases due to noncoverage or selection or both (Berrens et al., 2003; Dever et al., 2008; Lee, 2006b; Lee and Valliant, 2009; Schonlau, van Soest, and Kapteyn, 2007; Schonlau et al., 2009; and Schonlau, Zapert, Simon, Sanstad, Marcus, Adams, Spranca, Kan, Turner, and Berry, 2004). A propensity score is the predicted probability that a case will end up in one group rather than another—for example, the probability that someone will be among those that have Internet access (versus not having access). The technique was originally introduced as a way of coping with confounds in observational studies between cases who got a given treatment and similar cases who did not (Rosenbaum and Rubin, 1984). Such confounds are likely to arise whenever there is nonrandom assignment of cases to groups as in nonexperimental studies. Propensity score adjustment simultaneously corrects for the effects of multiple confounding variables on which the members of the two groups differ.

With Web surveys, the two groups are typically defined as the respondents to a Web survey (for example, the Web panel members who completed a specific Web questionnaire) and the respondents of a "calibration" or reference survey (for example, the respondents to an RDD survey conducted in parallel with the Web survey). The calibration survey is assumed to have little or no coverage or selection bias so that it provides a useful benchmark to which the Web survey results can be adjusted (see Lee and Valliant, 2008, for a useful discussion of propensity weighting; we lean heavily on their treatment here).

The first step in propensity weighting is to fit a model predicting the probability of membership in one of the groups. The usual procedure is to fit a logistic regression model:

$$\log(p(\underline{x})/(1-p(\underline{x})) = \alpha + \sum_{j}^{p} \beta_j x_j \,,$$

in which $p(\underline{x})$ is the probability that the case will be in the group of interest (e.g., will complete the Web survey); the x's are the covariates; α is an intercept term; and the β's are logistic regression coefficients. (It isn't absolutely necessary that the fitted propensity come from a logistic regression model, but in practice this is what has typically been done.) Next, cases are grouped (often into quintiles) based on their predicted propensities, that is, their value for $\hat{p}(\underline{x})$. Third, the existing weight for the case is adjusted by dividing by the predicted propensity of the case:

$$(2.6) \quad w_{2i} = \frac{w_{1i}}{\hat{p}_i(\underline{x})} \,.$$

If the cases have been grouped in propensity strata, then the mean (or harmonic mean) of the propensities in the stratum would be used in place of $\hat{p}_i(\underline{x})$ in the denominator of Equation 2.6.[5] As Lee and Valliant (2008) point out, propensity adjustments work best when the logistic regression model includes predictors that are related to both the propensities and the substantive variables (Little and Vartivarian, 2004, make the same point about post-stratification adjustments). Simulations by Lee and Valliant (2009) show that even when the calibration sample completely covers the target population, propensity adjustments alone do not completely remove the coverage bias in an Internet sample.

Comparison of the correction methods. Several of these methods are closely related to each other. Both GREG and raking are special cases of calibration weighting. Post-stratification is, in turn, a special case of GREG weighting. With calibration weighting, adjusted weights (w_{2i}) are found that are as close as possible to the unadjusted weights (w_{1i}) but are calibrated in the sense that the weighted sample totals now equal the population totals on one or more auxiliary variables (x_j):

$$T_{1xj} = \sum_{i}^{n_r} w_{2i} x_{ij} \,.$$

In the case of post-stratification variables, the auxiliary variables are simply a set of binary variables indicating whether each member of the population is in each post-

---

[5] If the purpose of the weight is to adjust to the calibration sample rather than to the full population, the adjustment takes the following form (see Schonlau et al, 2007) rather than that given in Equation 2.6:

$$w_{2i} = \frac{(1-\hat{p}(\underline{x}))w_{1i}}{\hat{p}(\underline{x})} \,.$$

stratum. Different measures of the distance between the unadjusted and adjusted weights lead to different forms of the calibration weights. All three forms of calibration estimation—GREG, raking, and post-stratification—are associated with linear models. For example, the model for post-stratification is that the expected value of a survey variable ($E(y_{ijk})$) from cell jk is the grand mean (u) plus a term representing the deviation between the grand mean and the cell mean (α_{ij}):

$$E(y_{ijk}) = u + \alpha_{jk}.$$

The raking model assumes that this cell deviation can be captured by main effect terms. If there are two adjustment variables, then the model would be:

$$E(y_{ijk}) = u + \alpha_j + \beta_k,$$

where α_j is the effect associated with level j of the first variable and β_k is the effect associated with level k of the second variable.

To understand the other assumptions on which the models rest, it will help to reproduce Equation 2.1 here:

$$Bias = P_0(\bar{Y}_1 - \bar{Y}_0) + \frac{Cov(P,Y)}{\bar{P}}$$

As we noted earlier, post-stratification eliminates coverage and selection bias (in means or proportions) when two conditions are met. First, every case in the population must have some nonzero chance of participation (that is, all the p's must be greater than 0 for every member of the target population). If so, then the first component of the bias in Equation 2.1 will be zero. Second, the data must be missing at random—that is, within the cells formed by cross-classifying the covariates, there can no longer be any relationship between the probability that a given case will become a respondent and that case's value on the survey variable y. When this second condition is met, the second term in Equation 2.1 becomes zero. Clearly, the same adjustment will have more or less effect on the biases for estimates derived from different survey variables.

Raking eliminates the bias under these same two conditions but imposes one further constraint on the model—that the interactions among the covariates can be ignored. GREG adjustments as we noted assume a more general model in which there is *some* linear relationship between one or more auxiliary variables and the survey variable of interest.

Propensity scoring goes even further in that it assumes that all the information in the covariates is captured by the propensity score. This condition is often referred to as strong ignorability. For the bias to be eliminated by a propensity weighting model, then, conditional on the fitted propensities, a) the distribution of values of the survey variable must be unrelated to what group the case came from (for example, the pool of Web respondents versus the pool of respondents to the calibration survey), and b) the survey outcomes must be unrelated to the covariates. These conditions imply that

$$Cov(P, Y \mid \hat{p}(\underline{x})) = 0 .$$

They are unlikely to be met in practice. As we shall see below (in Table 2.4), much of the bias remains after propensity adjustments are made. In part, this may reflect the fact that propensity scoring does not affect the other component of the bias, $P_0(\overline{Y}_1 - \overline{Y})$, that reflects the omission of those with no chance of participation. This point is confirmed in the simulations done by Lee and Valliant (2009).

There are two potential advantages to using methods like GREG weighting or propensity scoring rather than the seemingly simpler methods of post-stratification or raking. First, adjustments to the weights may reduce the bias of estimates but they can also increase their variance. For example, Lee (2006b) found that propensity score adjustments increased the standard errors of the estimates by 38 to more than 130 percent. Raking is thought to reduce this inflation factor relative to post-stratification adjustments; GREG weighting and propensity scoring are thought to reduce variance inflation even further (Kalton and Flores-Cervantes, 2003). Dever and her colleagues (2008, page 57) report the GREG model incorporating the largest number of covariates produces "slightly larger SEs [standard errors]" than similar models with fewer covariates. Still, as we note below, any adjustment based on a calibration survey is likely to increase the variance of the estimates from the Web survey.

Second, cell weighting and raking are both easiest to carry out with a small number of categorical covariates; with both GREG and propensity weighting adjustments, it is easy to incorporate numerical covariates as well. Further, GREG and propensity weighting are quite flexible. The models can include or exclude interaction terms and the methods can cope with cells that have no respondents; such zero cells pose problems for post-stratification and raking adjustments. Thus, GREG weighting and propensity adjustments may reduce the impact of the adjustments on the variance of survey estimates and give researchers greater flexibility in the covariates that the adjustment models can incorporate.

A final consideration differentiating the four approaches is that propensity models can only incorporate variables that are available for both the Web survey sample and the calibration sample; the other methods require only that external benchmarks can be found for variables that are available for the respondents to the Web survey.

Effectiveness of the adjustment procedures. So far, we've examined the four adjustment methods mainly from a mathematical point of view, but the key issue is how well the procedures work in practice. Several studies have examined this question and Table 2.4 summarizes the results of eight of them. We omit a ninth study (Yoshimura, 2004) that isn't described in enough detail to be included. All of these studies employ similar overall strategies to evaluate the impact of weighting adjustments. Three of the studies take estimates from a Web sample and compare them to estimates from a parallel RDD survey before and after adjusting the Web estimates. The adjustments use one or more of the methods described earlier. For example, Berrens and his colleagues compare 13 estimates from a Harris Interactive (HI) Web

TABLE 2.4. Studies Evaluating Statistical Adjustments for Web Surveys

Study	Calibration Survey/Web Survey(s)	Adjustment Method	Results		
			n of Estimates (Outliers)	Mean (Median) Reduction in Bias	Mean (Median) Absolute Relbias after Adjustment
Berrens, Bohara, Jenkins-Smith, Silva, & Weimer (2003)	RDD Survey/ Harris Interactive (January)	Raking	13 (0)	10.8 (19.4)	26.6 (8.3)
	Harris Interactive (July)	Propensity scoring	13 (2)	31.8 (36.7)	17.1 (4.7)
	Knowledge Networks	Raking	13 (0)	-3.0 (-2.3)	20.6 (15.9)
Dever, Rafferty, & Valliant (2008)	Full Michigan BRFSS/BRFSS Internet Users	GREG estimator (7 covariates)	25 (0)	23.9 (70.0)	4.3 (2.3)
Lee (2006b)	Full General Social Survey/ GSS Internet users	Propensity scoring	2 (0)	31.0 (31.0)	5.4 (5.4)
Lee & Valliant (2009)	Full Michigan BRFSS/BRFSS Internet Users	Propensity scoring (30 covariates)	5 (0)	62.8 (60.8)	5.8 (6.9)
		Propensity scoring plus GREG estimator		73.3 (80.8)	4.3 (3.9)
Schonlau, van Soest, & Kapteyn (2007)	RDD Survey/Rand Web panel	Propensity scoring (demographic variables)	24 (5)	24.2 (24.6)	21.1 (14.4)
		Propensity scoring (all variables)	24 (3)	62.7 (72.6)	10.3 (3.7)
Schonlau, van Soest, Kapteyn, & Couper (2009)	Full HRS sample/ HRS Internet users	Propensity scoring	33 (0)	43.7 (60.0)	25.8 (14.4)
Schonlau, Zapert, Simon, Sanstad, Marcus, Adams, Spranca, Kan, Turner, & Berry (2004)	RDD Survey/ Harris Interactive	Post-stratification	34	NA	NA
		Propensity scoring	34	NA	NA

(Continued)

TABLE 2.4. *(Continued)*

Study	Calibration Survey/Web Survey(s)	Adjustment Method	Results		
			n of Estimates (Outliers)	Mean (Median) Reduction in Bias	Mean (Median) Absolute Relbias after Adjustment
Yeager, Krosnick, Chang, Javitz, Levendusky, Simpser, & Wang (2011)	Various external benchmarks/ Seven non-probability Web samples	Raking			
	Survey 1		19 (2)	42.0 (40.3)	8.2 (5.1)
	Survey 2		19 (0)	38.7 (60.4)	8.4 (4.2)
	Survey 3		19 (1)	53.3 (42.3)	7.0 (4.6)
	Survey 4		19 (2)	30.6 (33.3)	7.0 (4.6)
	Survey 5		19 (3)	35.3 (22.2)	7.7 (5.9)
	Survey 6		19 (2)	37.4 (32.9)	7.3 (6.3)
	Survey 7		19 (1)	57.0 (62.1)	7.7 (6.6)

Note: Reduction in biases and relative biases (Relbias) are expressed as percentages. Means in the last two columns are computed after deletion of outliers; the medians include all observations.

survey of its Web panel members with estimates from an RDD survey; they rake the Web estimates and see how that affects the differences between the estimates from the Web and RDD surveys. Four of the studies didn't actually conduct Web surveys but instead compare estimates based on the subset of respondents to a face-to-face or telephone survey who do have Internet access to estimates based on *all* respondents in the survey. Lee (2006b) compares estimates derived from the subset of General Social Survey (GSS) respondents who have Internet access with estimates based on all the GSS respondents, including those without Web access. Both groups responded in a face-to-face interview, but only the group with Internet access would have been represented in a Web survey asking the same questions. Thus, the comparison provides an estimate of the coverage bias both prior to and after weighting adjustments to compensate for coverage bias. (Unlike the studies that involve actual Web surveys, the comparisons in the second group don't confound differences in the populations with measurement differences produced by the mode of data collection.) The final study (Yeager, Krosnick, Chang, Javitz, Levendusky, Simpser, and Wang, 2011) uses a somewhat different methodology; it compares estimates from seven volunteer Web samples with external benchmarks from the Current Population Survey (CPS), the American Community Survey (ACS), the National Health Interview Survey (NHIS), and other sources, before and after adjusting the Web survey estimates via raking. The CPS, ACS, and NHIS are all high-quality area probability samples that do not use Internet data collection.

We used a couple of measures to gauge the effectiveness of the weighting adjustments. First, we computed the average reduction in bias:

$$100 \times \left(1 - \frac{\sum \left| d_{adj,i} \right| / \left| d_{u,i} \right|}{n} \right)$$

where $d_{adj,i}$ is the difference between the estimate from the Web survey (or from the portion of the sample with Web access) and the same estimate for the calibration sample (or from the full sample or external benchmark) *after* adjustment to the Web sample weight and $d_{u,i}$ is the difference *prior* to the adjustment. The reductions in bias are expressed as percentages. Second, we computed the mean absolute value of the remaining relative biases after adjustment; the absolute relative bias is the absolute value of the difference between the adjusted estimate from the Web sample ($\hat{y}_{adj}$) and the corresponding benchmark ($\hat{y}_{cal}$) over the benchmark estimate:

$$100 \times \left(\frac{\left| \hat{y}_{adj} - \hat{y}_{cal} \right|}{\hat{y}_{cal}} \right)$$

The "Web" sample may in fact be the Internet users in a larger sample that includes both users and non-users and the "calibration" sample, the full sample including members of both groups or an estimate drawn from another survey (in the case of the Yeager et al., 2011, study).

Neither of these measures of the impact of the weighting adjustments is perfect. Both assume that the estimates from the calibration sample or external source are unbiased or at least closer to the population values than either the unadjusted or adjusted estimates from the Web sample. In addition, the weighting adjustments sometimes increase the bias, resulting in negative reductions in errors. If the original unadjusted estimates produce small biases, the adjustments can easily double the size of the bias (that is, the ratio $\left| d_{adj,i} \right| / \left| d_{u,i} \right|$ can exceed 2.0). We ignored adjusted estimates that yielded such large increases in bias in calculating the mean reduction on error (and note the number of such outliers that we discarded). Table 2.4 also includes median values for our two indicators of the impact of the weighting adjustments. The medians are less affected by extreme values.

The results are quite consistent across the eight studies (and with Yoshimura, 2004) and support four general conclusions. Regardless of which method of adjustment is used,

1) The adjustments remove only part of the bias, at most around three-fifths (Schonlau, van Soest, and Kapteyn, 2007);
2) The adjustments sometimes increase the biases relative to unadjusted estimates, sometimes by factors larger than 2 (these are the outliers in Table 2.4);
3) The relative biases that are left after adjustment are often substantial, often shifting the estimates by 20 percent or more.

4) There are large differences across variables, with the adjustments sometimes removing the biases and other times making them much worse.

Overall, then, the adjustments seem to be useful but fallible corrections for the coverage and selection biases inherent in Web samples, offering only a partial remedy for these problems.

All the estimates in Table 2.4 are estimates of simple means or proportions. Berrens and his colleagues also examine more complex estimates of relations between variables (Berrens et al., 2003). They conclude that "although many differences arose, across a variety of tests..., the Internet samples produced relational inferences quite similar to the telephone sample" (page 21). It remains to be seen whether that conclusion will prove to be a general one.

It is worth making one final point about these adjustment procedures. Any procedure that adjusts estimates from a large Web survey using data from a relatively small calibration survey (for example, a parallel RDD survey) is likely to sharply increase the variance of the estimates (Bethlehem, 2010, Equation 18; Lee, 2006b), although this may not be reflected in the variance estimates themselves. This variance inflation is not just the byproduct of the increased variability of the weights, but reflects the inherent instability of the estimates from the calibration survey. Because that survey uses a more expensive method of data collection, it will generally have a much smaller sample than the Web survey it is used to correct. As a result, the estimates from the calibration survey are likely to be highly variable and thus are likely to introduce considerable additional variation into the adjusted Web survey estimates. This variance inflation is exactly what Lee (2006b) reports in her simulation study.

2.4 SUMMARY

Many, perhaps most, Internet surveys do not use probability sampling and, among those that do, most rely on traditional methods of sampling (such as RDD) that are used more often in conjunction with other methods of data collection. Web surveys that attempt to characterize the full population are prone to coverage bias (unless they provide Web access to those without it), and those that use non-probability samples are prone to selection biases as well. Still, the few efforts to recruit probability samples of the general population and provide Web access to all members of these panels have run into practical difficulties, including high cumulative levels of nonresponse across the multiple stages of sampling and recruitment and high recruitment and data collection costs.

Whether and to what degree coverage problems bias the estimates from Web surveys depends in part on the size of the population that is not yet online and on the differences between those with access to the Internet and those without it. Although the Internet population has grown rapidly in the past 20 years, the rate of growth appears to be slowing (see Figure 2.1), and Internet penetration is far from complete in the United States and Europe. The digital divide remains a fact of life and is apparent both in the demographic characteristics of Internet users and nonusers (see, for example, Table 2.2) and in variables more likely to be of interest in surveys (Table 2.3). Since the adjustment procedures (and related methods such as sample matching) rely on demographic variables, they may fail to adjust for differences in substantive variables that are not strongly related to demographic characteristics.

Many Web surveys use statistical corrections in an effort to remove, or at least reduce, the effects of coverage and selection biases on the estimates. The studies summarized in Table 2.4 indicate that, regardless of the exact method used, the adjustment procedures typically remove less than half of the bias in the estimates and often substantial biases remain after adjustment. Sometimes the adjustments backfire and increase the bias. Even when they reduce bias, the adjustments often come with a penalty of increased variance (Bethlehem, 2010; Lee, 2006b). Clearly, considerable work is needed to find better methods for selecting Web samples and for reducing the problems that incomplete coverage can produce.

/// 3 /// NONRESPONSE IN WEB SURVEYS

In an era of falling response rates (Atrostic, Bates, Burt, and Silberstein, 2001; Curtin, Presser, and Singer, 2005; de Leeuw and de Heer, 2002), nonresponse is a challenge for all surveys, but it may be a special problem for Web surveys. There are at least three reasons for this. First, as we saw in Chapter 2, Web surveys often start out with unrepresentative samples. They often omit the portion of the intended target population that lacks Internet access. In addition, Web samples often consist of self-selected volunteers who are not a representative sample of the Internet population, let alone the general population. It is not clear how nonresponse errors and coverage errors relate, but it seems likely that these two sources of error often cumulate so that low response rates make the effects of coverage errors (and of any biases due to self-selection) even worse. That is, the same types of people who are less likely to have Internet access or to join a Web panel, such as minority group members or people in low-income households, are also less likely to respond to a Web survey if they are asked to take part in one. Second, as we shall see in this chapter, response rates to probability-based Web surveys tend to be lower than those for comparable surveys using more traditional methods of data collection (Lozar Manfreda, Bosnjak, Berzelak, Haas, and Vehovar, 2008; Shih and Fan, 2008). Although response rates are at best a weak indicator of nonresponse error (e.g., Groves, 2006; Groves and Peytcheva, 2008), they are related to the *risk* of nonresponse error. Thus, it is likely that Web surveys are prone to relatively high levels of nonresponse error. Third, Web surveys suffer from a form of nonresponse—breakoffs—that is relatively rare in interviewer-administered surveys. It is not clear how these high breakoff rates affect the overall levels of nonresponse error in Web surveys.

Because of the special wrinkles involved in Web surveys, including their use of non-probability samples and the high levels of breakoffs they experience, we begin this chapter by discussing the definitions of nonresponse and nonresponse error for Web surveys. Subsequent sections of the chapter examine studies that attempt to assess the level of nonresponse error in Web surveys, factors that affect unit nonresponse rates, design choices that affect breakoffs, and item nonresponse.

3.1 DEFINING NONRESPONSE AND NONRESPONSE ERROR IN WEB SURVEYS

Chapter 2 presented a discussion of the difference between probability-based and non-probability Web surveys. Here we briefly discuss the implications of this distinction for nonresponse error.

Probability samples. Probability samples have the explicit goal of characterizing the population from which the sample was drawn; nonresponse error is one potential source of inferential error, or bias. Nonresponse bias results from the differences between the initial sample and the pool of respondents for whom data are actually obtained. The effect of nonresponse on a sample mean largely reflects the covariance between the probability that a given sample member will respond (his or her response propensity, or p) and his or her value on the survey variable of interest (Y):

$$(3.1) \quad E(\bar{y}_r) - \bar{Y} = \frac{Cov(P,Y)}{\bar{P}},$$

in which $E(\bar{y}_r)$ is the expected value of the unadjusted sample mean (based on the respondents); $\bar{Y}$ is the population mean being estimated; $Cov(P,Y)$ is the covariance term; $\bar{P}$ is the mean response propensity in the population (or the expected response rate for the survey). This equation (due to Bethlehem, 2002) is parallel to the one presented for coverage bias in Equation 2.1. Like the earlier equation, it focuses attention on the association between the propensity to respond and the variable of interest rather than on the nonresponse rate (see Groves, 2006) as the key to nonresponse bias; it also underscores the fact that one estimate in a survey may be biased by nonresponse while another is not. If there are members of the sample with zero propensity to respond (that is, sample members who would *never* respond to this survey under any circumstances), then a second term must be added to the bias equation:

$$E(\bar{y}_r) - \bar{Y} = P_0(\bar{Y}_1 - \bar{Y}_0) + \frac{Cov(P,Y)}{\bar{P}}.$$

In this version of the equation, the first term on the right side represents the impact of the omission of the zero propensity sample members from the respondent pool; P_0 is the proportion of the population with no chance at all of taking part (those with propensities of zero), $\bar{Y}_0$ is the mean on the survey variable of interest among the zero propensity group, and $\bar{Y}_1$ is the mean among the rest of the population, those with a non-zero propensity to take part.

High nonresponse rates (or low response rates) can also affect the variance of key estimates, by reducing the sample size and thus inflating standard errors and confidence intervals. This can be countered by increasing the initial sample size. Given the low unit costs in Web surveys, this is a more attractive option than in other survey modes, where increasing initial sample sizes may greatly increase costs.

Non-probability Web surveys. With non-probability samples, the issue of nonresponse is part of the larger problem of whether the set of respondents resembles the target population on the key variables of interest that we discussed in

Chapter 2. Nonresponse error reflects the differences between the respondents to the survey and the larger pool of volunteers from which the respondents were drawn (e.g., the members of an online panel), but because the inference is not to the members of the opt-in panel but to some larger target population, calculating response rates as indicators of error makes little sense. For some types of non-probability sample, such as one-time samples recruited from Web sites (Type 2 in Table 2.1), the denominator for the response rate calculations may be unknown, rendering the notion of a response rate meaningless.

Many publications based on volunteer online panels report "response rates" (see Couper, 2007). Because of the longstanding association of response rate with probability samples, the AAPOR Task Force on Online Panels (AAPOR, 2010) recommended against using the term "response rate" for surveys based on such panels. Instead, Callegaro and DiSogra (2008) suggest using "completion rate" for the proportion of opt-in panel members responding to a specific survey request, while the ISO standard 26362 (ISO, 2009) recommends the use of the term "participation rate," defined as "the number of respondents who have provided a usable response divided by the total number of initial personal invitations requesting participation." The latest edition of the AAPOR Standard Definitions (AAPOR, 2011) recommends the term "participation rate" and we will use that term here for surveys based on opt-in panels.

Forms of nonresponse. Survey researchers have traditionally made a distinction between unit and item nonresponse, with partially-completed surveys as an intermediate category. Unit nonresponse is the failure to obtain answers to *any* of the survey questions. An example is a mail survey that is not returned, for whatever reason. Breakoffs are cases who begin the survey but do not complete it. The breakoff rate is the proportion of cases who start the survey without finishing it and the completion rate is the complement of the breakoff rate. Item nonresponse is the failure to obtain answers to selected questions in an otherwise complete questionnaire. An example would be a mail survey returned and completed, except for a few items with missing data. Web surveys allow for somewhat richer data on breakoffs and item nonrespondents. If a unique URL or login code is sent to sample members, one can track whether they clicked on (or typed in) that URL, thereby demonstrating that they received and acted upon the invitation, even if they didn't complete the survey. Similarly, for paging Web surveys (Peytchev, Couper, McCabe, and Crawford, 2006), the point of breakoff can be identified (facilitating analysis of reasons for such breakoffs; see Peytchev, 2009), and the responses up to that point are still available for analysis.

In the next section of this chapter, we review studies that attempt to measure the effects of nonresponse on estimates from Web surveys. Then, in the following sections, we examine unit nonresponse, breakoffs, and item nonresponse.

3.2 NONRESPONSE ERROR IN WEB SURVEYS

Who responds to Web survey requests and how do they differ from those who don't respond? Having started a Web survey, who completes the survey and who breaks off before the end? These questions, and the more interesting question of *why* some respond while others do not, involve nonresponse error. Much of the work on non-response in Web surveys has focused on response rates rather than on nonresponse errors. We review that work in Sections 3.3 and 3.4 of this chapter. The few excep-tions are studies based on Web samples for which there was prior information about the sample members, either from an earlier screening interview or from the sampling frame; in these studies, it is possible to determine how the respondents differ from the nonrespondents and from the larger population they are intended to represent, at least on the variables obtained prior to the survey.

In one such study, Fricker, Galešic, Tourangeau, and Yan (2005) began with an RDD telephone survey, with a 42.3 percent response rate (AAPOR RR3). Those who completed a short screening interview and who reported having Internet access were randomly assigned either to a follow-up Web survey or to a telephone survey. Cases assigned to the Web condition were sent an email invitation following the interview, while those assigned to the telephone group continued on to the main survey immediately following the screener. The Web survey obtained a 51.6 percent response rate, compared to a response rate of 97.5 percent for those continuing on by telephone. Despite this difference in the response rates, Fricker and his colleagues found no significant differences in the demographic makeup of the two samples. Both samples provided a reasonable representation of the Internet population (as derived from CPS data), but neither sample represented the US general population very well. The researchers also found no significant differences between the two samples on attitudes toward science and support for scientific research. However, they did find significantly higher knowledge scores for Web respondents than for tel-ephone respondents. They speculate that these differences may be due to the faster pace of the telephone survey rather than to differences in nonresponse error for the two modes. We discuss this study further in Section 7.3.

In another example of this approach to studying nonresponse error, Couper, Kapteyn, Schonlau, and Winter (2007) carried out a Web survey with respondents from the Health and Retirement Study (HRS). The HRS is a panel survey of people 50 years old and older in the United States. In the 2002 wave of the HRS, respondents who reported using the Internet (about 30 percent of the sample) and who expressed willingness to participate in a follow-up Web survey (about 75 percent of the Internet users) were subsequently mailed an invitation to participate in the Internet survey. Of those invited to complete the Internet survey, 80.6 percent did so. Among those who a) participated in the HRS, b) reported using the Internet, and c) agreed to partici-pate in a Web survey, Couper and his colleagues (2007) found significant differences between those who actually responded to the Web survey request and those who did not on several key variables (including race/ethnicity, employment status, and self-rated health). Furthermore, the sample members who had been harder to inter-view in the 2002 HRS were also significantly less likely to participate in the Web survey. Several other demographic and health-related variables were significantly related to reported willingness to participate. Despite these differences between respondents and nonrespondents, Couper and his coauthors (2007) found that the biggest source of error in the Web survey was coverage error—differences between those with Internet access and those without—in this population. Conditional on Internet access, the differences between those who did and did not respond to the Web survey were much smaller, and coverage bias was a larger contributor to overall bias in this sample than nonresponse bias.

Bandilla, Blohm, Kaczmirek, and Neubarth (2007) conducted a similar study, using the 2006 German General Social Survey (ALLBUS) as the base. Among all ALLBUS respondents, 46 percent reported having Internet access; of these, 37 percent expressed willingness to participate in a follow-up Web survey, and 24 percent actually did so. Bandilla and his colleagues found significant differences in education and frequency of Internet use between those who said they were willing to do the Web survey and those who said they were not willing, but these differences were smaller when they compared actual Web respondents to nonrespondents.

Another source of indirect information on nonresponse error comes from comparisons of members of different volunteer online panels that vary in participation rates in the same Web survey. In one such comparison, a single survey was fielded independently by 19 different panels in the Netherlands (Vonk, van Ossenbruggen, and Willems, 2006). The study-specific participation rates ranged from 18 percent to 77 percent across the 19 panels, with an overall participation rate of 50 percent. The investigators found no meaningful differences between estimates from the panels with low response rates and those with high response rates. Similar results for the U.S. are reported by Yeager, Krosnick, Chang, Javitz, Levendusky, Simpser, and Wang (2011), although there was considerable variation across panels in terms of which estimates were closer to the "true" value, as measured using external data. No one panel was consistently more accurate than the others, and participation rates were not a good indicator of likely error in the estimates from a given panel. This latter finding parallels one reported by Groves (2006; see also Groves and Peytcheva, 2008) for probability samples.

Other studies have examined differences between respondents and nonrespondents on the limited demographic variables available on the frame, often for student populations, and do not find substantial differences. But these are relatively homogeneous populations with demographic variables providing little help in understanding differences between respondents and nonrespondents. This brief review suggests there remains a lack of work on nonresponse error in Web surveys (as there is for work on nonresponse error in all modes).

3.3 RESPONSE AND PARTICIPATION RATES IN WEB SURVEYS

In this section, we discuss the response and participation rates achieved in Web surveys and compare those to the response obtained in other modes of data collection.

Response rates for probability samples. Two recent meta-analyses have compared response rates to Web surveys with those in other modes of data collection.

Lozar Manfreda and colleagues (Lozar Manfreda et al., 2008) conducted a meta-analysis of 45 experimental mode comparisons between Web and other survey modes (mostly mail), with random assignment of sample members to mode. They found that, on average, response rates to the Web surveys were 11 percentage points lower than those in the alternative mode. When the analysis was restricted to the 27 studies in which the other mode was mail, the average difference in response rates was 12 percentage points in favor of mail.

Shih and Fan (2008) restricted their meta-analysis to 39 studies directly comparing Web to mail. They found an average unweighted response rate of 34 percent for Web surveys and 45 percent for mail surveys, for an overall difference of 11 percentage points, very close to the difference found by Lozar Manfreda and her colleagues. Shih and Fan further examined five different study features in an attempt to account for these mode differences. The type of population surveyed had a significant effect, accounting for about a quarter of the effect size. The smallest difference between Web and mail response rates (about 5 percentage points) was for college populations, while the largest (about 23 percentage points) was for surveys of professionals.

Both meta-analyses found considerable variation in the response rate differences, with response rates for Web surveys occasionally exceeding those of the other mode. But the number of studies is not sufficiently large to tease out the source of these differences or to identify under what circumstances Web surveys may yield higher response rates than other modes.

Response rates for probability-based panels. A few panels have used offline methods to recruit participants to the panels, in some cases (Knowledge Networks, LISS, and FFRISP) providing Internet access to panel recruits lacking access. The problem is that the cumulative rate of recruitment across the various stages is often quite low.

Two panels have used face-to-face recruitment with members of area probability samples. The Dutch LISS (Longitudinal Internet Studies for the Social Sciences) panel used an address frame and telephone and face-to-face recruitment. Scherpenzeel and Das (2011) report that in 75 percent of eligible households, someone completed the short recruitment interview or answered a subset of the core questions. Among these, 84 percent expressed willingness to participate in the panel and 76 percent of those actually registered for panel membership, yielding a cumulative recruitment rate of 48 percent. In the United States, the FFRISP (or "Face-to-Face Recruited Internet Survey Platform") panel achieved a response rate of 49 percent for the household screener (among eligible households), 92 percent for the recruitment interview (among screened households), and 87 percent for enrollment in the panel (among those who completed the recruitment interview), yielding a cumulative recruitment rate of 39 percent (Krosnick, Ackermann, Malka, Yeager, Sakshaug, Tourangeau, DeBell, and Turakhia, 2009; Sakshaug, Tourangeau, Krosnick, Ackermann, Malka, DeBell, and Turakhia, 2009).

Two other panels use other methods of recruitment. The Knowledge Networks (KN) Panel, used RDD telephone contact with an RDD sample until 2009, when it switched to a mix of RDD and address-based sampling (DiSogra, Callegaro, and Hendarwan, 2009). For a specific example from 2006, Callegaro and DiSogra (2008) report a mean household recruitment rate of 33 percent (AAPOR RR3) and a household profile rate (the proportion of panelists who completed the profile questionnaire after joining) of 57 percent, for a cumulative recruitment rate of about 18 percent. The Gallup Panel (Rookey, Hanway, and Dillman, 2008) contacts members of an RDD sample by telephone. Screened households that agree to join the panel are assigned to the Internet mode if they report using the Internet at least twice a week and provide an email address; otherwise they are assigned to the mail mode. Rookey, Hanway, and Dillman (2008) report a 26 percent response rate (AAPOR RR3) to the telephone interview, with approximately 55 percent of those who completed the interview agreeing to join the panel. This yields an overall rate of about 14 percent.

In all these cases, the panels also suffer from attrition over the life of the panel, along with nonresponse to specific surveys sent to panelists. For example, Rookey, Hanway, and Dillman (2008) report monthly attrition rates of 2 to 3 percent for the Gallup Panel, and a response rate of 57 percent (completed surveys over the number of panel members invited) for one survey sent in 2006. Callegaro and DiSogra (2008) report an 84 percent response rate to one survey in the KN panel. Scherpenzeel and Das report response rates in the 60 to 70 percent range for individual surveys sent to LISS panel members.

These examples show the challenges of recruiting and retaining Web panel members selected using probability methods. The response rates and nonresponse bias at the recruitment stage may be similar to that for other modes of data collection. But, because of the additional losses following recruitment, the initial nonresponse problem is compounded. Still, once panelists have completed the screening interview or profile survey, additional information is available to assess (and potentially adjust for) nonresponse bias for individual surveys and attrition bias across the life of the panel.

Response rates for non-probability panels. Participation rates for Web surveys based on volunteer online panels are more difficult to determine. Few vendors provide details on the methods they use to recruit panel members. Typically, they use a variety of online and offline recruitment methods (see AAPOR, 2010; Miller, 2006), making it hard to estimate the rate of uptake among potential recruits. But we do know that "click-through" rates for banner ads are very low, typically less than 1 percent of page exposures (see, e.g., Alvarez, Sherman, and VanBeselaere, 2003; MacElroy, 2000; Page-Thomas, 2006; Tuten, Bosnjak, and Bandilla, 2000); the click-through rate is the proportion of persons exposed to an ad who click on it and are transferred to the survey. The online volunteer panels are in a constant state of churn, with inactive members dropped, new members recruited, and email addresses updated, making the estimation of recruitment rates even harder. Although the participation rates of individual surveys are often not reported, two bits of evidence suggest that the rates of participation may be falling precipitously.

First, we have been conducting our experiments using members of leading online panels in the United States over the past several years. We have seen participation rates decline from a high near 20 percent in 2002 to the low single digits since 2006, with a survey done in June-July 2010 yielding a participation rate of just 1 percent Similarly, in 2008, one of our surveys required invitations to almost 62,000 members to yield 1,200 completes, for a 1.9 percent participation rate. With one panel claiming about 1.2 million US members at the time, this meant that about one in twenty of all panel members were invited to that survey. A second piece of evidence comes from a study conducted by comScore Networks in 2004 (Miller, 2006). That study, based on the online activities of over a million volunteers, found that 30 percent of all online surveys are completed by just 0.25 percent of the US population. Furthermore, comScore reported that these highly active individuals belonged to seven online panels, on average, and completed nearly one survey every day. Similar evidence of multiple panel memberships comes from a study in the Netherlands (Vonk, van Ossenbruggen, and Willems, 2006). We suspect that the number of the number of survey solicitations sent to panel members has skyrocketed as the demand for online research has grown.

Although these numbers do not provide information on the nonresponse bias of surveys from volunteer online panels, they do point to the difficulty with which responses are obtained. The data suggest that the demand for survey respondents is exceeding the supply. As Tourangeau (2007) noted, survey data have become a commodity and the amount of data—rather than the quality—seems to be the only thing that counts for some consumers of survey data.

In summary, then, response rates across all types of Web surveys appear to be lower than for other modes and—as in other modes—appear to be declining. It is still not clear, however, whether this is an inherent feature of the mode. It is possible that because Web surveys are still relatively new, we simply have not yet developed the strategies to increase response rates in Web surveys as we have with more traditional modes of data collection. The next section discusses methods for increasing response and participation rates in Web surveys.

3.4 FACTORS AFFECTING PARTICIPATION IN WEB SURVEYS

Many of the methods used in an effort to increase response and participation rates in Web surveys have been borrowed from earlier modes of data collection. These include prenotification that a survey request is coming, multiple contact attempts, and incentives. Several studies have also examined the effects of various features of the invitation on response and participation rates in Web surveys.

Prenotification. Does prenotification increase response rates in Web surveys, as it does in other modes? Dillman, Smyth, and Christian (2009, p. 244) note that "research has consistently shown that a prenotice will improve response rates to mail surveys by three to six percentage points" (although see Singer, Van Hoewyk, and Maher, 2000). Can the same be expected for Web surveys? The limited research on the topic suggests that the mode in which prenotification is given may be more important than the sheer act of prenotification.

Crawford, McCabe, Saltz, Boyd, Freisthler, and Paschall (2004) found that a mail advance letter produced a significantly higher response rate than an advance email (52.5 percent versus 44.9 percent) in a Web survey of college students. Similarly, Kaplowitz, Hadlock, and Levine (2004) compared prenotification via postcard with no prenotification in a survey of college students and found that the postcard produced a significantly higher response rate than no prenotification (29.7 percent versus 20.7 percent). Harmon, Westin, and Levin (2005) tested three types of prenotification in a survey of applicants to a government grant program. One group was sent an email prenotice with an attached letter (in PDF) from the sponsoring agency; a second was sent an email with an attached letter from the data collection firm; and the third was sent a letter by mail from the sponsoring agency. The highest response rate was obtained for the group that got the advance letter by mail (69.9 percent) rather than by email (64.4 percent for the group who got the attached letter from the sponsor and 63.6 percent for the group who got the attached letter from the data collection firm). Bosnjak, Neubarth, Couper, Bandilla, and Kaczmirek (2008) compared an SMS prenotice with an email prenotice and no prenotice in a survey among college students. The SMS prenotice produced a significantly higher (84 percent) response rate than either the email prenotice (71 percent) or no prenotice (72 percent).

These findings suggest that advance notice sent by email may not offer any advantage over no prenotification, but advance notice sent in some other mode (letter, postcard, or SMS) may increase Web survey response rates. It is possible that much of the nonresponse to Web surveys comes from failure to receive (because of the widespread use of spam filters) or to read email messages, and prenotification in another mode may alert the recipient to the upcoming email invitation. Of course, an advance letter or postcard requires a mailing address, which may not be available for some samples. In addition, mailing an advance letter increases the cost of data collection. However, Kaplowitz, Hadlock, and Levine (2004) found that a postcard prenotice was not significantly more expensive than no prenotice, given the improvement in response rates. Another advantage of a mailed prenotice is that it makes it easier to use prepaid incentives.

The invitation. With respect to the invitation itself, some researchers have touted the advantages of email invitations (see, e.g., Couper, 2008a). Such invitations are cheap, timely, and give respondents quick and easy access to the survey through a clickable URL. However, because of the prevalence of spam and the sheer volume of email that many people receive, email may no longer be the preferred method for sending invitations to take part in Web surveys. Further, the effectiveness of email invitations depends on the quality of the information on the sampling frame; minor errors in an email address will result in delivery failure, unlike mailed invitations where minor errors in the address are better tolerated. To date, however, there has been little research on the mode of invitation to a Web survey. In one exception, Kaplowitz, Lupi, Couper, and Thorp (2012) tested a postcard versus an email invitation to a Web survey of college faculty, staff, and students. The email invitation significantly outperformed the postcard invitation for both faculty (33 percent versus 21 percent) and staff (36 percent versus 32 percent), though not for students (15 percent versus 14 percent). Clearly, more research is needed on the issue of the most effective form of invitation for Web surveys—and this may well differ for different populations of interest.

Other studies have manipulated such features of the email invitation as the sender's email address, the subject line, and the salutation. In general, the effects of these manipulations are quite weak, in part because they depend on the recipient getting, and in some cases opening and reading the email invitation. We believe a large part of the nonresponse in Web surveys occurs because the invitation never reaches the sample person.

To our knowledge, only one study (Smith and Kiniorski, 2003) has experimented with different email senders in the context of a volunteer panel, finding no effect of the manipulations. Similarly, we are aware of no study that has experimented with the way the intended recipient is addressed, although we would expect that individually-addressed emails would be more effective than invitations sent to generic email groups or undisclosed recipients.

A few studies have explored alternative subject lines for email invitations. Porter and Whitcomb (2005) found no effects of their manipulations on the proportion of sample members starting the survey among high-involvement subjects—those with a relationship to the institution conducting the survey. But for low-involvement subjects, a blank subject line achieved a higher click-through rate than a subject line that identified the purpose of the email (a survey) or the survey sponsor (university). This survey was conducted among high school students who had requested information about the university, and the finding may not hold for other populations. Trouteaud (2004) reported a five percentage point advantage of a "plea" subject line ("please help [Company Name] with your advice and opinions") over an "offer" subject line ("Share your advice and opinions now with [Company Name]"). Kent and Brandel (2003) found that a prize subject line ("Win a weekend for two") yielded a significantly *lower* response rate than a subject line that stated the email was about a survey (52 percent versus 68 percent); their sample consisted of members of a customer loyalty program.

We suspect that the relationship of the sender to the recipient may be an important factor in the effect of subject line manipulations—for example, in employee surveys, surveys of students or faculty, surveys of access panel members, and the like. This makes it difficult to generalize from these limited studies on subject lines in email invitations.

Several studies have explored design alternatives for the body of the email invitation, including the salutation, the signature, and the placement of the URL. In a survey of alumni, Pearson and Levine (2003) found a small but nonsignificant benefit of personalization. Heerwegh, Vanhove, Matthijs, and Loosveldt (2005) found significant effects of a personal salutation ("Dear [First name Last name]") over an impersonal salutation ("Dear student") in a survey of college students, with 64.3 percent and 54.5 percent logging into the survey, respectively (see also Heerwegh,

2005). In a series of studies, Joinson and his colleagues (Joinson and Reips, 2007; Joinson, Woodley, and Reips, 2007) explored both personalization and the status of the sender. They found that status of the sender affected response rates, with higher status senders getting higher response rates (see also Guéguen and Jacob, 2002). But Joinson and his colleagues also found that personalization is only effective when the sender is of high status. Furthermore, they found that personalization decreases perceived anonymity and hence may decrease disclosure (see also Heerwegh, 2005).

Finally, Kaplowitz and his colleagues (Kaplowitz et al., 2012) tested the length of the email invitation and the placement of the URL (top versus bottom) in a survey of university faculty, staff, and students. Contrary to expectation, they found that longer invitations resulted in higher response rates than shorter invitations, and that placing the URL near the bottom of the invitation yielded higher response rates than placing it near the top. They also found that the effect of these and other design manipulations on response rate varied between faculty, staff, and students.

Topic and sponsorship. Some researchers have worried that revealing the topic of the survey in the invitation may increase nonresponse bias; the low response rates and large number of invitations in opt-in panels may worsen this bias. So far, relatively little research has examined this issue.

In one recent exception, Tourangeau, Groves, Kennedy, and Yan (2009) conducted an experiment on topic-induced nonresponse bias; their study used members of two different online panels. They found that membership in multiple panels and a high individual participation rate were strong predictors of response to a follow-up survey, but that interest in the topic was not a significant predictor. More studies are needed to confirm this null finding pertaining to topic interest, but the only available evidence suggests that general online survey-taking behavior may have more impact on participation decisions than attitudes about the survey topic. The effects of the survey topic aren't always clear in surveys in other modes, either (Groves, Couper, Presser, Singer, Tourangeau, Acosta, and Nelson, 2006).

To our knowledge, no research has experimentally varied organizational sponsorship (e.g., government versus academic versus commercial) in online surveys, but we see no reason why the findings from other modes of data collection (see, e.g., Groves and Couper, 1998, Chapter 10) should not apply to Web surveys, producing higher response rates when the sponsor is a government agency or an academic researcher than when it is a commercial firm.

The number and type of contact attempts. Lozar Manfreda and colleagues' (2008) meta-analysis found a significant effect of the number of contacts on the differences in response rates between Web surveys and other modes (see Section 3.2). For the 23 studies which made only one or two contact attempts, the Web survey response rates were about five percentage points lower than the alternative mode. However, for those studies with three to five contact attempts, the difference was 16 percentage points; clearly, additional contact attempts produced greater benefits in other modes than they did in Web surveys. Shih and Fan (2008) found a similar effect of the number of reminders on response rates differences, with smaller differences for surveys with no reminders (four percentage points lower for Web) than with one or more reminders (14 percentage points lower for Web). While there is evidence suggesting that additional email reminders continue to bring in more respondents (see, e.g., Muñoz-Leiva, Sánchez-Fernández, Montoro-Ríos, and Ibáñez-Zapata, 2010), there does seem to be an overall pattern of diminishing returns. Although email reminders are virtually costless, continuing to send such reminders may backfire, hardening sample persons' resistance to future requests. The results also suggest that the value of an email contact attempt may not be as great as, say, a mail contact attempt, perhaps reflecting the lower likelihood that sample members will receive and read an email message.

Incentives. Relative to other strategies for increasing response rates in Web surveys, many studies have examined the use of incentives. Much of this work is summarized in a meta-analysis by Göritz (2006a; see also Göritz, 2010). Across 32 experimental studies, she found that incentives significantly increased the proportion of invitees who started the survey (with an average odds ratio for the incentive effect of 1.19). But what types of incentives are most effective? The general findings in the survey literature are that prepaid incentives are more effective than promised or conditional ones, and that cash incentives are more effective than alternatives such as in-kind incentives, prize draws, sweepstakes, loyalty points, and the like (see Church, 1993; Singer, 2002). Despite this, sweepstakes or loyalty-point incentives, conditional on completion, are popular in Web surveys, especially among volunteer panels.

There are several reasons why Web researchers prefer conditional incentives to prepaid ones and noncash incentives to cash. First, prepaid cash incentives cannot be delivered electronically; they require mailing addresses and entail more expensive processing and mailing of materials. Second, if the response rate is likely to be in the single digits (as is often the case), the return on investment may be low (but see Alexander, Divine, Couper, McClure, Stopponi, Fortman, Tolsma, Strecher, and Johnson, 2008, discussed below). Third, as Göritz (2006b) notes, the costs of sweepstakes are usually capped, since the size of the prize stays the same regardless of how many people participate. This makes it easier to manage survey costs. Although sweepstakes and loyalty points are attractive to the researchers, are they effective in encouraging response from sample persons?

Göritz (2006a) found that sweepstakes incentives produced higher response rates than no incentives in her meta-analysis of 27 experimental studies involving sweepstakes, most of them based on commercial panels. However, in a meta-analysis of six incentive experiments in a nonprofit (academic) panel, she found that offering a cash sweepstakes provided no significant benefit over no incentive at all (Göritz, 2006b). Thus, while sweepstakes may be better than nothing, at least for commercial panels, it is not clear whether they are better than alternative incentive strategies.

In one of the few studies comparing different types of incentives, Bosnjak and Tuten (2002) conducted an experiment in a survey among real estate agents and brokers for whom they had email addresses. They tested four incentive types: 1) $2 prepaid via PayPal with the first contact produced a 14.3 response rate; 2) $2 promised via PayPal upon completion produced a 15.9 percent response rate; 3) a prize draw for two $50 and four $25 prizes upon completion produced a 23.4 percent response rate; and 4) a control group with no incentive produced 12.9 response rate. One reason why the prize draw may have outperformed the prepaid and promised incentives is that cash was not used for the latter; for the PayPal incentive to be of value, one had to have a PayPal account. Another study (Birnholtz, Horn, Finholt, and Bae, 2004) compared 1) a mail invitation with $5 cash, 2) a mail invitation with a $5 Amazon.com gift certificate, and 3) an email invitation with a $5 Amazon.com e-certificate in a sample of engineering faculty and students at 20 universities. The study found the highest response rate (56.9 percent) for the cash incentive group, followed by the mail (40.0 percent) and email gift certificate groups (32.4 percent). This study suggests that cash outperforms a gift certificate (consistent with the earlier literature on survey incentives) and is also consistent with the studies showing an advantage of mail over email invitations.

Alexander and her colleagues (2008) conducted an incentive experiment as part of the recruitment effort for an online health intervention. Invitations to enroll online were sent by mail to members of a health maintenance organization. The experiment tested six different enrollment incentives: no incentive, prepaid incentives of $1, $2, or $5, and promised incentives of $10 or $20. The highest enrollment rates were for the three prepaid incentive groups, with 7.7 percent enrolling with the $5 incentive, 6.9 percent with the $2 incentive, and 3.9 percent with the $1 incentive. The promised incentives produced enrollment rates of 3.4 percent with the $10 promised incentive and 3.3 percent with the $20 promised incentive. The no-incentive group had a 2.7 percent enrollment rate. This provides further evidence in support of the effectiveness of prepaid incentives in online surveys. In terms of cost, the $5 prepaid group cost approximately $77.73 per enrolled case, the $2 prepaid group cost about $43.37, the $1 prepaid group $51.25, the no-incentive group $36.70, the $10 promised group $41.09, and the $20 promised group $50.94. Despite the relatively low enrollment rates, a small prepaid incentive (a $2 bill) proved cost-effective relative to the promised incentives, though not compared to no incentives at all.

This brief review suggests that incentives seem to work for Web surveys in pretty much the same way as in other modes of data collection and for pretty much the same reasons. Although it is impractical for Web panels to send mail invitations with prepaid incentives when they are sending tens of thousands of invitations a day, the combination of an advance letter, a small prepaid cash incentive, and an email invitation may be most effective for list-based samples.

3.5 NONRESPONSE IN MIXED-MODE SURVEYS

So far, we have focused on factors that affect response rates in stand-alone Web surveys. In this section, we examine how giving sample members a choice of modes for responding, including the Web as one of the options, affects the overall response rate for the survey. Because of the coverage and sampling issues reviewed in Chapter 2, many organizations—especially government statistical agencies concerned with broad population representation—are reluctant to use the Web as the only mode of data collection for their surveys and have used the Web as part of a mixed-mode strategy, most often in combination with mail. The goals of this strategy are to increase response rates in general and to increase the proportion of respondents completing the survey via the cheaper mode (Web).

There are two main approaches to combining modes, concurrent mixed-mode designs and sequential mixed-mode designs (de Leeuw, 2005). Concurrent designs offer two modes simultaneously; for example, a survey might send a paper questionnaire to sample persons or households, but might provide them with the opportunity to complete the survey online, giving them a choice of modes from the outset. Several studies have found that giving respondents such a choice does not increase response rates, but instead produces lower response rates than the mail-only approach. These studies are briefly summarized in Table 3.1. Eight of the ten studies show lower response rates when respondents are offered a Web option in a mail survey than when they are not given the Web option.

Why should giving someone the option of completing a survey by mail or Web produce lower response rates than offering only the mail option? There are several potential explanations for the drop in response rates. One line of argument is that sample members given a choice between mail and Web procrastinate, and this *procrastination* is what lowers the response rate. According to this account, sample members make a tentative decision to complete the survey online, throw the paper questionnaire away, but soon forget about completing the survey. In contrast, when the Web is not offered as an option, sample members are more likely to keep the paper questionnaire and the questionnaire itself serves as a physical reminder to complete the survey. A second possibility is that offering the Web option in a mail survey involves *incompatible modes*; that is, sample members are contacted in one mode (when they receive the mail questionnaire) and, although they may prefer to respond online, this involves switching modes. There are costs associated with the mode switch (e.g., going to the computer, remembering the personal ID number, entering a URL, etc.) and these costs may be too high for many sample members, who end up as nonrespondents. A third possibility is *implementation failure*. Some sample members may try to complete the survey online, but because of onerous login procedures or difficulty completing the online survey, they abandon the effort and also decide not to complete the paper survey either. Still another account involves the added *cognitive burden* associated with making a choice. Schwartz (2000) and related work suggests that adding options can paralyze people or simply increase the cognitive costs involved in deciding whether or not to respond to the survey at all (see also Iyengar and Lepper, 2000), leading to a failure to act. Research is underway to sort out these competing explanations, but the key lesson may be that simply offering a Web option to a mail survey may not always increase response rates.

TABLE 3.1. Response Rates from Mode Choice Experiments

Study	Brief Description	Response Rates
Griffin, Fischer, and Morgan (2001)	US households; American Community Survey (ACS) test; self-response rates	Mail only: 43.6% Web option: 37.8%
Brennan (2005)	Adults in New Zealand	Mail only: 40.0% Web option: 25.4%
Schneider et al. (2005)	US Census short form experiment; one group encouraged to do Web (telephone calling card enclosed); other not encouraged	Mail only: 71.4% Web option (no encouragement): 71.5% Web option (encouragement): 73.9%
Werner (2005)	College students in Sweden	Mail only: 66% Web option: 62–64%
Brøgger et al. (2007)	Adults 20–40 years old in Norway	Mail only: 46.7% Web option: 44.8%
Gentry and Good (2008)	Radio listener diaries, US households	Paper diary: 60.6% eDiary option: 56.4%
Israel (2009)	Users of the Cooperative Extension surveys in the United States	Mail only: 64.5% Web option: 59.2%
Lebrasseur et al. (2010)	Canadian census test; rates of self-completion	Mail only: 61.1% Web option: 61.5%
Smyth et al. (2010)	Address-based sample of a local area in the United States; mail preference group given option of Web in final mailing	Mail preference: 71.1% Web option: 63.0%
Millar and Dillman (2011)	College students in the United States.	Mail only: 53.2% Web option: 52.3%

More recent studies have examined sequential mixed-mode designs, in which sample members are initially approached in one mode, rather than being given a choice, but nonrespondents are followed up in a different mode. One example is a study of adults in Stockholm by Holmberg, Lorenc, and Werner (2010). They compared several different sequential strategies involving mail and Web. While overall response rates did not differ significantly across the five experimental conditions, Holmberg and his colleagues found that the proportion of respondents completing the survey online increased as the Web option was pushed more heavily in a sequential design. For example, when the first two mail contacts (following the advance letter) mentioned only the Web option, and the mail questionnaire was provided only at the third contact, the overall response rate was 73.3 percent, with 47.4 percent of the sample using the Web. In contrast, in the condition where the mail questionnaire was provided in the first contact, the possibility of a Web option was not mentioned until the second (reminder) contact, and the login for the Web survey was not provided until the third contact (along with a replacement questionnaire), the overall response rate was 74.8 percent but only 1.9 percent of the sample completed the Web version. Millar and Dillman (2011) report similar findings in study comparing a "mail push" approach with a "Web push" approach.

However, two other studies failed to find advantages for the sequential approach. Tourkin, Parmer, Cox, and Zukerberg (2005; see also Cox, Parmer, Tourkin, Warner, Lyter., and Rowland, 2007) tested a sequential mixed-mode design. In the control condition, respondents were only given the mail option. In one experimental condition, the invitation letter mentioned only the Internet option, but a mail survey was later sent to nonrespondents. In the other experimental condition, the invitation to complete the survey online mentioned the upcoming mail option. This was crossed with an incentive experiment, but averaging over the incentive conditions, the mail-only survey achieved a higher response rate (48.8 percent) than either Web-plus-mail version (45.4 percent when the mail option wasn't mentioned in the invitation letter and 42.4 percent when it was mentioned).

Cantor, Brick, Han, and Aponte (2010) tested a similar sequential design for a short screening survey. Half the sample was sent an initial invitation to a Web survey, with a follow-up mail questionnaire sent to the nonrespondents. This group was further split into two groups. One group received a color insert encouraging Web participation; the other group received no such encouragement. The other half of the sample was only offered the mail survey at both time points. The response rate to the mail-only group (34.3 percent) was significantly higher than either Web-plus-mail group (28.5 percent with the insert and 27.3 percent without it).

These mixed results (see also Lesser, Newton, and Yang, 2010; Smyth, Dillman, Christian, and O'Neill, 2010) show that there is much we still don't know about combining mail and Web effectively to increase participation. The variation in the findings across studies may reflect differences in the populations being studied, the nature of the request, the design of the choice or sequential mixed-mode approach, or other factors. Despite these mixed results, a number of National Statistical Institutes are providing a Web option for census returns with apparent success (in the sense of growing proportions of the population responding online). The success of these census efforts may suggest that the length of the form or questionnaire may be a factor in whether it is completed online or not. In addition, censuses tend to be heavily-promoted public events and are often mandatory, and these factors may play a role in the successful outcome. Much more research is needed into the conditions under which mixed-mode designs involving mail and Web will yield improvements in response rate or reductions in nonresponse bias.

3.6 FACTORS AFFECTING BREAKOFFS IN WEB SURVEYS

Having clicked on or typed in the URL and been taken to the survey's welcome page, some sample members continue to the end of the survey, but others quit at some point before they finish. The problem of breakoffs (also called abandonments or terminations) affects all types of Web surveys, whether they use probability or non-probability samples. Breakoffs occur in other modes of data collection, too. In interviewer-administered surveys (whether telephone or face-to-face), breakoffs are relatively rare and are usually treated as a form of unit nonresponse (especially if the breakoff occurs early in the survey) or as partial interviews (if a pre-determined set of questions is answered before the breakoff). The extent of breakoffs in mail surveys—sample persons starting the questionnaire but failing to complete it or mail it back—is not known.

Breakoffs are more common in automated self-administered modes, such as IVR and Web surveys, than in the interviewer-administered modes. Tourangeau, Steiger, and Wilson (2002) review a number of IVR studies that demonstrate that breakoffs are common in IVR surveys, especially during the switch from a live interviewer to the IVR system. Peytchev (2009) cites two unpublished meta-analyses of breakoffs in Web surveys, reporting median breakoff rates of 16 percent and 34 percent respectively. Galešic (2006) reported breakoff rates in Web surveys as high as 80 percent. In the last five studies the authors have conducted using opt-in panels, breakoff rates have ranged from 13.4 to 30.2 percent with an average of 22.4 percent. Still, breakoff rates aren't always high in Web surveys. The Internet surveys conducted among members of the HRS panel had breakoff rates of 1.4 percent in 2007 and 0.4 percent in 2009. That breakoff rates are generally much higher in IVR and Web surveys than in telephone or face-to-face surveys doubtless reflects the greater ease of ending an interaction with an automated system than with a live interviewer.

Most breakoffs appear to occur relatively early in the survey (often on the welcome page or very first question) and thus can be viewed as a form of unit nonresponse. These early breakoffs do not appear to depend on the difficulty of the items. However, the further the respondent gets through the survey, the more likely it is that the breakoff will be precipitated by specific questions that engender negative reactions from the respondents. For example, Peytchev (2009) argued that grids and pages with hard questions (those presenting substantial comprehension, judgment, or response mapping difficulties) were associated with higher levels of breakoff. Breakoffs are thus useful sources of information on questionnaire design problems in Web surveys and can be used as an indicator for evaluating the effect of different design options (as we do in later chapters).

There is limited research on survey (as opposed to instrument) characteristics that affect breakoffs. Göritz's (2006a) meta-analysis on incentives found that, in addition to increasing the proportion of people who start the survey, incentives significantly increased the proportion of people who finish it (mean odds ratio of 1.27, based on 26 experiments). This is hardly surprising, since most of the incentives in the 26 studies she examined were conditional on completing the survey.

Another design feature thought to affect breakoff rates is the length of the questionnaire. Crawford, Couper, and Lamias (2001) experimentally manipulated the length of the survey mentioned in the invitation. Sample members who were told that the survey would take 8 to 10 minutes were more likely to start the survey (67.5 percent) than those told it would take 20 minutes (63.4 percent). However, those in the 8-to-10 minute group who started the survey were more likely to break off (11.3 percent) than those in the 20-minute condition (9.0 percent), producing similar overall completion rates across the two conditions. (The survey had an actual median length of 19.5 minutes.) Galešic (2006) also varied the length of a Web survey experimentally. She found that compared with a 10-minute survey, the risk of breakoffs was 20 percent higher for those who got the 20-minute survey and 40 percent higher for those who got the 30-minute survey. In addition, she found that interest in the topic (which was measured at the start of each section) significantly lowered the risk of breakoff and that perceived burden significantly increased it.

Progress indicators are often thought to reduce breakoffs in Web surveys. We postpone until Chapter 6 a discussion of the research on progress indicators and their role in affecting breakoffs.

Many of the findings reviewed here and in our discussion of progress indicators in Chapter 6 can be explained by a model that assumes sample members make a tentative decision about whether to complete a Web survey based on their early experiences with the questionnaire, but may reconsider their decision if they encounter unexpected difficulties later on. For example, when a progress indicator is rigged to show rapid progress through the early questions, sample members are more likely to decide to finish the questionnaire than when the early feedback is discouraging (and they are more likely to stick to their initial decision in the face of difficult items later on). But this initial commitment to complete the questionnaire is only tentative; respondents may reconsider and break off when they realize that the items are harder or the questionnaire longer than they bargained for. Peytchev (2009) notes that section transitions often trigger breakoffs. Section headings may signal to respondents that many additional questions are coming. Similarly, in an IVR study using questions from the Long Form of the 2000 census, Tourangeau, Steiger, and Wilson (2002) found that respondents were likely to break off when they were asked to report about the next member of the household; apparently, at that point, it became obvious to the respondents just how long the survey was likely to take. This *sample-decide-reconsider* model of breakoffs underscores the importance of making the beginning of a Web survey relatively pleasant (e.g., by asking easy questions) and of avoiding or minimizing unpleasant surprises later in the questionnaire.

3.7 ITEM NONRESPONSE IN WEB SURVEYS

Like breakoffs, item nonresponse can often be a sign of poor question design. The level of item missing data is a function of several factors besides the question itself, including the overall design approach for the survey, the strategies it incorporates to minimize missing data, and numerous respondent characteristics (such as their motivation, interest, commitment, etc.).

The level of missing data can vary greatly in Web surveys, depending on several key design choices. For instance, a scrolling Web survey with no prompts for missing data may resemble a mail survey in terms of missing data rates. A paging survey where answers are required or missing answers are probed is likely to have missing data rates similar to an interviewer-administered computer-assisted survey. We discuss the differences between scrolling and paging designs in Chapter 4. Whether a "don't know" option is explicitly offered may also affect whether the questions are left unanswered. Given this dependence of the rate of missing data on basic features of the Web survey design, it is not surprising that the findings on rates of missing data in Web surveys versus other modes are inconsistent.

For example, Kwak and Radler (2002) reported significantly higher rates of missing data for a mail survey (an average of 2.47 percent of the items missing) than for a Web survey (an average of 1.98 percent missing) in a mode experiment among college students. By contrast, in an experiment involving a survey of agency employees, Bates (2001) reported significantly higher missing data rates for the Web version of the question than for the mail version for items about the organization and about personal experiences, but not for items on demographic and employment characteristics. Similarly, Denniston, Brener, Kann, Eaton, McManus, Kyle, Roberts, Flint, and Ross (2010) found higher missing data rates for Web questionnaires with skips (4.4 percent) or without skips (5.2 percent) than for a paper survey (1.5 percent); in this experiment, the surveys were administered to high school students in a group setting. Denscombe (2009) found *lower* missing data rates for a Web (1.8 percent for factual questions, 1.5 percent for opinion questions, and 6.8 percent for open questions) than for a paper (2.6 percent for factual, 2.7 percent for opinion, and 15.1 percent for open questions) version of a questionnaire administered to high school pupils. And Wolfe, Converse, Airen, and Bodenhorn (2009) found no differences in missing data rates between Web and mail surveys in an experiment with school counselors. Thus, across five studies, two find lower missing data rates on the Web, two find lower missing data rates on paper, and one finds no differences between the two modes. It is not clear why these studies come to such different conclusions about the differences between Web and paper questionnaires. In general, we suspect that when Web surveys are designed to resemble paper surveys (e.g., using scrolling designs, with no automatic skips or error messages), the missing data rates will resemble those of mail surveys but, that when the Web surveys are designed to take advantage of the interactive capabilities of the Web, missing data rates will be lower. We discuss these interactive capabilities in Chapter 6.

Requiring respondents to answer every question is one way to eliminate item missing data, but this may come at the price of increased breakoffs or other undesirable respondent behaviors, especially when respondents aren't given a non-substantive answer option, such as "No opinion." Requiring answers is common in market research surveys, whereas permitting nonanswers is common in academic surveys.

Couper, Baker, and Mechling (2011) experimentally varied whether answers were required or not, and whether respondents were prompted for answers to questions they left blank. They found that requiring answers eliminated missing data, but probing for missing answers had a similar effect without the coerciveness of requiring answers. In addition, they found slightly higher breakoff rates when answers were required (10.5 percent) than when prompting was used (9.4 percent) or when there were no prompts (8.2 percent), but none of these differences in breakoff rates reached statistical significance. In general, Couper and his colleagues found the effects of requiring answers to be small, perhaps because the survey was administered to members of an opt-in panel who were accustomed to surveys that required answers. Albaum and colleagues (2010) conducted a similar study using a sample of email addresses purchased from a vendor. They found that requiring answers significantly reduced item missing data (again, by design, to zero) but did not significantly affect breakoff rates. It could be that those who respond to Web survey requests have gotten used to surveys that require answers, which are common. More research is needed, especially on the potential trade-off between missing data and the quality of the responses when answers are required. Regardless of the evidence, forcing respondents to answer the questions may raise ethical concerns, particularly with Institutional Review Boards (IRBs) or ethics review committees, since it seems to contradict the principle of allowing people to decide whether to answer or not.

3.8 SUMMARY

The discussion of nonresponse in this chapter paints a pretty bleak picture for Web surveys, with lower response rates and higher breakoff rates than for more traditional modes of data collection. One reason that Web survey response rates may often be low compared to those of earlier modes is that Web surveys have not been around as long and we have not yet discovered the best techniques for increasing response rates. We suspect this is not the only explanation. An alternative possibility is the vast number of Web surveys being distributed. Web surveys have democratized the survey process. The rise in do-it-yourself Web survey tools means that almost anyone can design and deploy his or her own Web surveys. The proliferation of surveys makes it harder for potential respondents to distinguish good surveys from bad ones and legitimate survey requests from less worthwhile ones. Coupled with the general rise in email traffic, the rise in the number of Web surveys may mean that we have saturated the market. Evidence for this can be seen in the increasing number of survey requests to opt-in panel members and the corresponding decline in response rates. There may simply be too many surveys chasing too few respondents. The very qualities that led to the rapid adoption of Web surveys—their low cost and high convenience—may now be their downfall.

Another explanation may lie in the medium itself. Invitations by email are simply too easy to ignore, relative to, say, interviewer requests in person or over the telephone. There are signs that mail invitations to Web surveys are treated by sample members with greater seriousness—or at least are ignored less often—than invitations sent by email. Using some other method (such as mail) for follow-up—for example, in a sequential mixed-mode design—may also improve response rates to Web surveys. Ironically, one relatively effective approach for dealing the nonresponse problem in Web surveys may be to use other modes for communicating with sample members.

INTRODUCTION TO MEASUREMENT AND DESIGN IN WEB SURVEYS

Chapters 2 and 3 examined various types of non-observation errors in Web surveys, including coverage errors, sampling errors, and nonresponse errors. The representativeness of Web samples, especially their ability to represent the general population, remains a major source of concern. However, when it comes to observation or measurement errors, Web surveys have many attractive features that may give them an advantage over other modes of data collection. At the same time, because of the broad range of design options available with Web surveys and the relative novelty of the platform, there is the risk that poor design will lead to higher levels of measurement error than with more traditional modes. In this chapter, we present an overview of Web survey measurement and discuss the role of basic design decisions in minimizing observation errors. In the next three chapters, we cover more specific design issues in greater detail. Chapter 5 examines Web surveys as a visual mode of data collection, Chapter 6 examines Web surveys as an interactive mode, and Chapter 7 examines Web surveys as a method of self-administration.

Web surveys have a lot in common with other methods of data collection. For example, mail questionnaires are also both visual and self-administered. Much of what we have learned about design through Web-based experimentation applies to other modes of data collection as well; similarly, earlier findings on the effects of the layout and design of survey questions in both interviewer- and self-administered paper surveys apply to Web surveys, too. Relevant literature on Web site design (e.g., Lynch and Horton, 2001; Nielsen, 2000) may also apply—although one should exercise caution about the wholesale adoption of design principles intended for other purposes.[1] Yet Web surveys are also distinctive. They are characterized by their great design flexibility. They can be designed in many different ways, behaving at times like computer-assisted interviews and at other times like self-administered paper

---

[1] For example, Nielsen (http://www.useit.com/alertbox/application-mistakes.html) argues for the use of default options, which make sense in e-commerce, but not in surveys.

questionnaires. Understanding the range of design elements available and using them appropriately are key issues in Web survey design.

4.1 MEASUREMENT ERROR IN WEB SURVEYS

Measurement error involves a different type of inference problem from those discussed in Chapters 2 and 3. In those chapters, we examined how well Web samples represent their target populations. In this chapter, we begin to examine how well particular observations or measurements from a Web survey respondent characterize the corresponding true values for that respondent. The simplest mathematical model for measurement error breaks each observation (y_{iA}) collected from respondent i under a specific mode (mode A) into two components—the true score and the error:

$$(4.1) \quad y_{iA} = \mu_i + \varepsilon_{iA},$$

where μ_i is the true score for respondent i and ε_{iA} is error for that respondent under that mode of data collection. To estimate the level of measurement error using this expression, we need to know the true value. Deviations from the true value can arise from a number of sources, including the respondent, the interviewer (in interviewer-administered surveys), and the instrument (including question wording, order, format, or design elements). The focus here and in Chapters 5 through 7 is on the effects of the design of Web surveys on measurement errors.

In practice, we rarely know true values. Researchers often rely on alternative approaches to examine measurement error properties of a mode or a design. One common method is to examine differences in responses to alternative presentations of the same questions, and that is the approach we rely on most often in this book. In effect, the measurement error in Equation 4.1 is broken into two components, a systematic component (M_{ijA}) due to the method of presenting the question (indexed by j) and a residual component (e_{ijA}):

$$y_{ij} = \mu_i + M_{ijA} + e_{ijA},$$
$$\varepsilon_{ijA} = M_{ijA} + e_{ijA}.$$

The classic split-ballot experiments to examine question wording effects (e.g., Schuman and Presser, 1981) are examples of this approach. One of the advantages of Web surveys is that they make it easy to carry out randomization, giving researchers a powerful tool to explore measurement effects. Still, a key drawback of this approach is that, without knowing the true values, it is sometimes difficult to say which method of presenting the question is "better"—that is, which method actually reduces error.

Another approach to examine measurement error involves administering the same (or similar) measures to respondents at different times, to explore reliability of measurement. This approach has been employed to explore mode effects (e.g., mail versus Web), often involving repeated measurement using the same instruments (but different modes) administered to the same respondents at different times.

Whatever the approach used, researchers must often rely on indirect measures to evaluate measurement error. In Web survey design studies, these indirect measures of data quality include missing data rates, breakoff rates (potentially leading to increased nonresponse error), speed of completion, and subjective reactions by respondents. These all point to potential advantages of one design approach over another, without directly assessing measurement errors. So, in this chapter (and in the next three), we focus more on the measurement *process* than on measurement *error*, and explore how the design of Web surveys can affect both.

4.2 MEASUREMENT FEATURES OF WEB SURVEYS

Web surveys have several characteristics that affect the design of survey instruments and hence the resulting measurement error. None of these characteristics is unique to Web surveys, but each of them presents both opportunities and challenges for the Web survey designer.

First, perhaps the most striking feature of Web surveys is their rich visual character. This is a feature that has already been widely exploited by Web survey designers. Although other survey modes are visual, too—for example, pictures or images have been used in paper surveys—the ease with which visual elements can be incorporated into Web surveys is what makes the Web distinctive as a data collection mode. These visual elements include not only pictures, but colors, shapes, symbols, drawings, diagrams, and videos. The cost of adding a full-color image to a Web survey is trivial. In fact, Web surveys can allow multimedia presentation of the questions, including both sound and video. The richness of the medium brings many opportunities to enhance and extend survey measurement, and it is one of the most exciting features of Web surveys. Still, the broad array of visual and other enhancements also brings risks. Much of our research has focused on the visual aspects of Web survey design, and we explore this topic in greater detail in Chapter 5.

Second, Web surveys are computerized. Like computer-assisted personal interviewing (CAPI) and computer-assisted telephone interviewing (CATI), but unlike paper surveys, Web surveys allow a full range of advanced features to be used in questionnaires. Randomization (of question order, response order, question wording or format, etc.) is relatively easy in Web surveys. This is one reason why Web surveys have brought about a huge increase in the number of survey design experiments. Other aspects of computer-assisted interviewing that are easy to carry out in Web surveys but relatively hard to use in paper surveys include automated routing (conditional questions), edit checks, fills (inserting information from prior answers in the current question), and the like. All this means that the surveys can be highly customized to each individual respondent, based on information available from the sampling frame or from earlier questions in the survey. This permits the use of very complex instruments and complex measurement approaches, such as computerized adaptive testing. However, adding such complexity increases the need for testing, increases the chances of programming errors, and makes careful specification and testing of the instrument all the more important.

A third feature of Web surveys, which is related to their being computerized, is that they can be designed with varying degrees of interactivity—that is, to react based on the actions of the respondent. Conditional routing is one form of interactivity. Because Web surveys can be interactive, they can be designed to behave more like interviewer-administered surveys, for example, prompting for missing data, offering clarification, providing feedback, and the like. We discuss the interactive character of Web surveys in greater detail in Chapter 6 and also discuss interactivity in the context of scrolling versus paging designs in Section 4.3 below.

A fourth characteristic of Web surveys is that they are distributed, and the designers lack control over the final display of the questions. In the traditional computer-assisted modes, the technology is in the hands of the interviewer, and both the hardware and software are provided by (and under the control of) the survey organization. This means that the designers can control the look and feel of the survey instruments. In contrast, with Web surveys, designers have little control over the browser or the hardware the respondent uses to access and complete the survey. Increasingly, people are accessing the Web using a variety of mobile devices (such as smart phones or tablets) and these present new challenges for the Web survey designer. But the presentation of Web surveys can vary in many other ways too, because of the user's setting for the size of the browser, the security settings that affect whether and how JavaScript, Flash, or other enhancements work, or the connection type that determines the speed with which respondent can download or upload information online. While hypertext markup language (HTML) is standard across browsers and platforms, JavaScript (for example) does not always behave in the same way across different operating systems. While these variations give respondents great flexibility in terms of how, when, and where they access the survey instrument, they make it difficult or impossible to ensure a consistent look and feel to the questionnaire for all respondents to the survey.

Finally, Web surveys are self-administered. In this regard, they are like paper self-administered questionnaires (e.g., mail surveys) and computerized self-administered questionnaires (e.g., computer-assisted self-interviewing [CASI] or interactive voice response [IVR]). Self-administration has long been shown to be advantageous in terms of reducing effects related to the presence of an interviewer, such as social desirability biases. At the same time, the benefits of interviewer presence—such as in motivating respondents, probing answers, or clarifying questions—are also absent. From an instrument design perspective, this means that the instrument itself must serve these functions. Each questionnaire must also be easy enough for untrained or inexperienced survey-takers to complete. Chapter 7 examines the merits of Web surveys relative to other methods of self-administration and also explores the pros and cons of fostering a greater sense of social presence in Web surveys (for example, through the use of virtual interviewers).

Given the vast range of possibilities that the Web offers, Web survey designers face many design decisions—about the general design approach (scrolling versus paging) to adopt, the response or input formats to use for specific questions, navigation, and general layout and style elements. We address each of these topics in turn below.

4.3 CHOICE OF BROAD DESIGN APPROACHES

One of the first—and most important—choices Web survey designers face is whether to present all the questions in a single scrolling Web page or to present each question on its own page. There are many intermediate options along this continuum and few surveys adopt either extreme. For example, it is common to group related questions on a page (an approach called "semantic chunking" by Norman, Friedman, Norman, and Stevenson, 2001) or to break a long scrolling survey into several pages, one for each section. Figure 4.1 presents examples of a scrolling and paging design for the same survey. Some Web survey software—especially at the low end of the market—does not support paging approaches, and other software makes it difficult to control the layout of multiple-item pages. Clearly, the decision about the design approach should not be dictated by the software, but by the objectives of the survey and the content of the questions.

Despite the importance of this basic design decision, there is remarkably little research on the relative merits of the two approaches. There are several early unpublished comparisons of the two (see, for example, Burris, Chen, Graf, Johnson, and Owens, 2001; Clark and Nyiri, 2001; Nyiri and Clark, 2003; Vehovar, Lozar Manfreda, and Batagelj, 1999), but most of these had sample sizes too small to detect meaningful differences or used instruments that would not favor either approach. Thus, it is not surprising that these studies find no differences. Since then, this topic has received little research attention. To our knowledge, only one study has explored the design choice with a large enough sample to detect differences. Peytchev, Couper, McCabe and Crawford (2006) compared a scrolling design (with the survey divided into five sections) with a paging design (with one or more questions on a page) for a survey on drug and alcohol use among college students. They found no differences in unit nonresponse, breakoffs, and nonsubstantive answers (explicit refusals or "don't know" responses), and response distributions and key associations did not differ between versions. However, they did find significantly more item missing data and longer completion times in the scrolling version, which they attribute to the automated control of navigation and routing in the paging design.

In practice, survey researchers seem to prefer scrolling designs for short surveys with few skips or edits or for mixed-mode designs where the goal is to replicate a paper questionnaire. Overall, paging designs appear to be much more common; they give the researcher control over the order in which questions are presented, allow automated skips and routing, permit edit checks at the point of occurrence, and so on. The more complex the instrument and the more the designers want to control the interaction, the more likely a paging design will be employed.

(a) Scrolling design

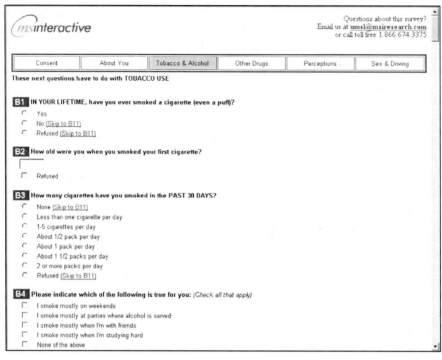

(b) Paging design

FIGURE 4.1. Examples of scrolling and paging designs (taken from Peytchev, Couper, McCabe and Crawford, 2006). The top panel shows a scrolling design; the bottom panel a paging design. (See color insert.) Reprinted with permission from Peytchev, Couper, McCabe and Crawford, 2006.

4.4 THE LOOK AND FEEL OF THE WEB SURVEY

Another set of decisions a designer faces relates to the "look and feel" of the Web survey. With all the visual and interactive features available, there are many different design options. These decisions may be faced for an individual survey or for all surveys conducted by an organization. In either case, we believe the survey designer should be an active participant in this process. Although they have much in common, designing a Web survey is not the same as designing a Web site. The designs serve different purposes and should encourage different types of user behavior.

Some of the elements a designer must consider include:

- Background and foreground design;
- Font or typeface;
- General layout and use of panes;
- Response requirements (forcing functions, requiring answers, etc.); and
- Navigation conventions.

Many of these design issues are discussed in greater detail in Couper (2008a, Chapter 4). We provide a brief overview here, focusing on those areas that have received the most research attention. We postpone our discussion of navigation conventions to Section 4.5.

Background/foreground design. One design decision relates to the choice of background colors, patterns, textures, or other presentation styles for each Web survey page. Paper questionnaires have typically been printed on a single color stock (usually white), although increasingly more colors are possible. For example, Dillman, Sinclair, and Clark (2003) report improvements in response rates in a 1990 census test with a design which included (among other things) a paper questionnaire printed with a light blue background with white answer spaces (see also Jenkins and Dillman, 1997). Subsequently, the 1995 National Census Test compared blue versus green census forms (again with white answer spaces), and found no significant differences in response rates (Scott and Barrett, 1996). Neither study reported any differences in data quality in or in perceived or actual completion times. The advent of Web surveys gives researchers access to potentially millions of different colors, yet the research on the effects (if any) of background color on data quality has been quite limited.

The choice of background/foreground colors has two potential implications for Web surveys. The first is its effect on legibility or readability. Insufficient contrast may make it difficult to read the survey and this effect can be exacerbated when the font size is small. While we have seen many examples of Web surveys that strain legibility, we know of no research on this topic. There are various guidelines and tools available to ensure sufficient contrast to facilitate reading online, and we can simply be prescriptive and say that these guidelines should be followed (see Couper, 2008a, pp. 164–167). Most authors favor black font on a white or light color (such as light blue or yellow) background. The second implication of the choice of background colors is the meaning that respondents may attach to the different colors (see, e.g. White, 1990) or the effect of these choices on how respondents answer the questions. Work by Schwarz and colleagues (see e.g., Novemsky, Dhar, Schwarz, and Simonson, 2007; Reber and Schwarz, 1999; Song and Schwarz, 2008a, 2008b) suggests that perceptual fluency—the ease of seeing and identifying a stimulus— can affect judgments; for example, higher levels of perceptual fluency can lead to more positive evaluations. Perceptual fluency may be affected both by background/ foreground contrast and by typeface or font size.

There are a few unpublished studies on the effect of background color in Web surveys. Pope and Baker (2005) compared white, blue, and pink backgrounds in a survey of college students. They found no significant differences in response rates or breakoff rates by background color. The actual and perceived survey times were slightly (but not significantly) lower for the blue than for the pink and white backgrounds, and these differences were larger for males than for females, suggesting that men were more negatively affected by the pink background. Baker and Couper (2007) tested white, blue, and yellow backgrounds in a consumer survey on energy use. The yellow background had a significantly higher breakoff rate (15.0 percent) than the blue background (10.8 percent) with white occupying a middle position (13.7 percent). However, background color had no significant effect on perceived or actual time of survey completion or on a variety of subjective evaluation items asked at the end of the survey. In another study, Hammen (2010) asked respondents about their preferred color for an Internet page; the largest proportion (31.1 percent) expressed no preference, but 29.5 percent preferred blue, with white being the next most popular option at 15.8 percent. She then tested white, blue, green, and red backgrounds in a Web survey and found no significant differences in breakoff rates. None of these studies reported any differences in response distributions by background color.

These three studies suggest that caution should be used in choosing background colors, but the effects are not generally large. The particular choice of a background color can be dictated by considerations of branding (i.e., matching the color scheme of the parent Web site or sponsoring organization), navigation (e.g., using different colors for different sections of the questionnaire; mapping different colors onto different actions), aesthetics, and other considerations. The evidence to date, though limited, seems to weakly favor a light neutral-colored background (e.g., light blue).

In addition to color, there are a wide variety of background visual elements that can be used in Web surveys, including textures, lines, shapes, and even images. As we show in Chapter 5, respondents tend to attribute meaning to these graphical elements. In the best case, they may distract the respondent from the task of answering the questions; in the worst, they may change the meaning of the questions. As Nielsen (2000, p. 126) argues, "Use either plain-color backgrounds or extremely subtle background patterns. Background graphic interfere with the eye's capability to resolve the lines in the characters and recognize word shapes."

To summarize, the background should be just that—background. The canvas on which the questions and response options are presented should be as neutral as possible, with the goal of focusing attention on the key survey tasks.

Typeface and font size. Another design issue that may affect readability of the survey questions and hence the quality of responses is the typeface and font size used. The literature on typeface is largely qualitative or descriptive (see, e.g., Lynch and Horton, 2001, Chapter 5; Schriver, 1997, Chapter 5; Spiekermann and

Ginger, 2003), and it tends to focus on reading large bodies of text rather than the relatively short questions and response options that are common in surveys. Typeface can affect the comprehension of survey questions by affecting their readability. But typeface can also convey emotional meaning, which could affect how questions are interpreted (see, e.g., Childers and Jass, 2002; McCarthy and Mothersbaugh, 2002; Novemsky et al., 2007). In general, though, as long as the font size is large enough to permit comfortable reading, and as long as the typeface is readily readable, the effect on survey response should be minimal. Further, the Web offers a potential advantage over paper instruments in that the respondents can adjust the font size setting in their browsers to facilitate comfortable reading. However, the designer must take care that permitting such flexibility does not cause other layout or design problems for any response scales, tables, or images that the survey includes.

Selective emphasis. A design decision related to the typeface involves how to emphasize certain textual elements. There are again many different possibilities, including boldface, underlining, capitalization, and color. For example, Crawford, McCabe, and Pope (2003) advocate the use of boldface for question text and regular type for the response options; they further advocate the use of blue for emphasis. There is some consensus in the Web site design literature (see, e.g., Nielsen, 2005) that color (especially blue) and underlining should *not* be used for emphasis, since these suggest linkable text in Web pages. While capitalization is not suitable for long bodies of text, it is appropriate for selective emphasis. Italicized text draws attention because of the contrast in shape from regular text, but is less readable than regular type. A common convention in Web surveys is to use italics for instructions, in part to convey the notion that they are not as important as the question text and may be ignored if not needed. If regular text is used for the questions, bold works for emphasis; otherwise, capitalization is effective. Again, they key is *selective* emphasis —too much emphasis will be counter-productive (see Lynch and Horton, 2001, pp. 132–133). Further, the use of text styles should be applied consistently throughout the instrument so that respondents can learn the meaning associated with different text elements.

Page layout and alignment. Another global decision a Web survey designer faces relates to the spatial arrangement of various elements on the screen. Because HTML is designed to facilitate a layout from left to right and from top to bottom, most designers adhere to this format, even in countries like China and Japan where vertical text may be more common in printed documents. For Western readers, and for most Internet users, the top left corner of the screen has a privileged position. The eye usually begins there when scanning Web pages (e.g., Nielsen and Pernice, 2010) and browsing activity is typically anchored to that point.

It is also common to use a header on each Web page. Headers can serve a branding or orienting function, reminding the respondent of key survey elements (topic, sponsor, etc.); they can also provide links for additional information (such as frequently asked questions, or FAQs). Research suggests that respondents quickly

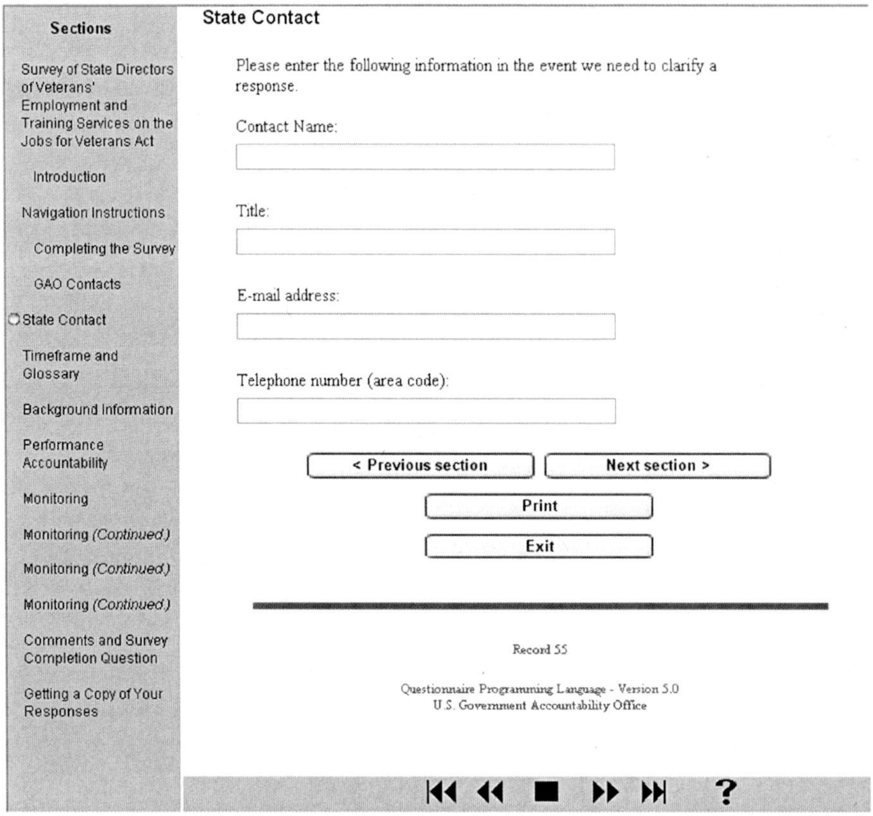

FIGURE 4.2. Use of panes in a survey from the US Government Accountability Office. The pane on the left allows respondents to switch sections; the pane at the bottom allows other movements through the questionnaire. (See color insert.).

get used to the header and ignore any information it contains. This phenomenon is known as banner blindness (Benway, 1998; Benway and Lane, 1998; Pagendarm and Schaumburg, 2001). Surveys that require that navigation or other information be displayed on every page often use a vertical navigation pane. This approach appears to be more common in establishment surveys and surveys conducted by government agencies. Figure 4.2 shows an example of a survey with a pane for moving to different sections of the questionnaire (on the left) and a pane for other movements through the questionnaire (at the bottom). The careful use of background and foreground color in these panes can help keep the respondent's attention on the key survey content.

Because different parts of the screen are more or less easily seen by respondents (see Section 5.3), it is important that the placement of the questions makes it easy for respondents to find the beginning of each question. Left-justifying the question text may help respondents locate where the question starts. With multiple questions on a page, question numbering or icons that serve to identify each question may also help guide the respondent.

There are several issues regarding the alignment and placement of the response options. One is whether the options should be arranged vertically or horizontally below the question. Some have argued that the latter approach better conveys the sense of a continuum. However, our own research (see Tourangeau, Couper, and Conrad, in press) shows no effect of the vertical or horizontal presentation of response options on response distributions, although response times are sometimes affected (see Chapter 5). Another issue is whether the input field (such as a radio button or check box) should be placed to the left or to the right of the label for the field. Arguments could be made for either position in paper surveys (see, for example, Dillman, 2007, pp. 123–124). The potential advantage for putting the input field on the right is that the skip instructions will be more visible and the labels are not obscured (for right-handed people) when the respondent answers. There is no compelling empirical evidence in favor of one over the other on the Web. In paging surveys, the skips can be handed automatically, eliminating the need for skip instructions. Further, in most Web surveys, a mouse or other indirect pointing device is used to select the answers, so that the respondent's hand does not obscure the response options (although, with the increasing adoption of touch screen devices, this may become an issue in the future). In HTML it is easier to place the input field to the left of the label, and this has become a common Web convention, so we recommend this position.

Still another alignment decision concerns the use of multiple columns. Arranging response options into several columns may reduce the need for vertical scrolling, but may lead respondents to believe that each of the different columns requires separate answers. Research by Christian, Parsons, and Dillman (2009) and Toepoel, Das, and van Soest (2009a) suggests that the arrangement of the response options into rows and columns affects response distributions. The order in which the options are read (whether by row or by column) is likely to be affected by how far apart the columns are relative to the rows. If the columns are visually distinct from each other, the respondent might read down the first column before starting on the next column. However, if the rows are more distinct, the respondent may read row-by-row. Web surveys do not have the same space restrictions as paper surveys and we see no need to use multiple columns. We agree with Christian, Parsons, and Dillman (2009, p. 420), who conclude that "presenting the options linearly in one column facilitates respondents' processing of the scale and encourages them to process the categories in the same order, making it easier to provide a response."

A final issue with the arrangement of response options is their relative spacing. We address this issue in more detail in Section 5.1 of the next chapter. In general, with regard to the broad design issues we have discussed here, our experience is that as long as sufficient readability is ensured and clear design conventions are followed, respondents adapt quickly to the specific design elements used in a survey. So, consistency of design may be more important than following any particular set of guidelines.

4.5 NAVIGATION CONVENTIONS

There are only a small number of actions a respondent usually performs in completing a survey, in addition to answering the survey questions. Yet, there are many different ways in which the tools used for navigation or movement through the instrument can be designed.

In scrolling surveys, the primary navigation tool is the scroll bar. This is an inherent feature of Web browsers over which survey designers have no control. The benefit of this is that most users are familiar with vertical scrolling of Web pages and require no guidance or instruction. The drawback is that the longer the Web page, the smaller the scroll bar, requiring more precise mouse movements from respondents and increasing the risk they will inadvertently miss an item.

In paging surveys, the process of moving from one page to the next is under greater designer control. Indeed, some Web survey vendors permit only forward movement, preventing users from going backwards in the instrument. Others use an automatic advance, with the next page being delivered as soon as a response option is selected (Hammen, 2010; Hays, Bode, Rothrock, Riley, Cella, and Gershon, 2010; Rivers, 2006). It is more common to have respondents press a "Next" (or "Continue" or a forward arrow) button to proceed after they have selected an answer. Requiring respondents to press the "Next" button may increase the time to answer and require extra mouse clicks, but some proportion of respondents make multiple selections in single-selection (radio button) items (see Heerwegh, 2003; Stern, 2008). We believe that using a "Next" button gives respondents the opportunity to check and reconsider their answers before proceeding. Another reason for including a "Next" button is that the automatic advance works only for single selection items, not for multiple-response questions, open-ended items, or pages with multiple questions.

So, "Next" buttons seem to be useful. What about "Previous" buttons? There is little research on this topic, but we believe giving the respondent an opportunity to go back and review or change a previous answer is likely to improve data quality. In our own surveys, we find that respondents generally do not use this function often, but when they do, it is often an indication that there was a problem understanding the earlier question that was only revealed by the follow-up question (for example, the respondent is routed to a question that does not apply to them).

If both a "Next" and a "Previous" button are included on each page of the survey, how should they be designed? There are at least three issues here: 1) whether to use the standard HTML action buttons or their graphical equivalents; 2) how to label the buttons; and 3) where to place them. We know of no research on the first topic, and our own unpublished research on the second suggests that the label (e.g., "Previous" versus "Back" versus "< – ") has little effect on performance. Couper, Baker, and Mechling (2011) experimented with the placement of the "Previous" and "Next" button (see Figure 4.3 below), and found little effect on breakoff rates or completion times, but did find effects on the level of use of the "Previous" button. Respondents were more likely to use the "Previous" button when it was to the right of and just as prominent as the "Next" button (panels (a) and (b) in Figure 4.3). Overall, Couper and his colleagues found some support for reducing the visual prominence of the "Previous" button, either by using a hyperlink instead or placing it below the "Next" button (panels (c) or (d)). This discouraged use of the "Previous" button—which often appears to be accidental when it is prominently displayed—and reduced completion times. These findings are consistent with Wroblewski's (2009) recommendation to place more frequently used action buttons on the left side of the screen.

4.6 CHOICE OF RESPONSE FORMATS

The design decisions we have discussed so far concern general issues that affect all pages or items in an instrument; the choice of response or input formats, by contrast,

(a) *Next* on left, *Previous* on right

Who in your household is responsible for paying your household's energy utility bills?

Select one.

- I am responsible for doing so
- Another member of my household is responsible for doing so
- Not applicable - someone who does not live in my household is responsible for doing so
- Not applicable - energy utility bills are incuded in rent or condominium fees the household pays
- Don't know

[Next]   [Previous]

(b) *Next* and *Previous* both on left, horizontal arrangement

Who in your household is responsible for paying your household's energy utility bills?

Select one.

- I am responsible for doing so
- Another member of my household is responsible for doing so
- Not applicable - someone who does not live in my househcld is responsible for doing so
- Not applicable - energy utility bills are included in rent or condominium fees the househod pays
- Don't know

[Next] [Previous]

(c) *Next* and *Previous* both on left, vertical arrangement

Who in your household is responsible for paying your household's energy utility bills?

Select one.

- I am responsible for doing so
- Another member of my household is responsible for doing so
- Not applicable - someone who does not live n my household is responsible for doing so
- Not applicable - energy utility bills are included in rent or condominium fees the household pays
- Don't know

[Next]
[Previous]

(Continued)

FIGURE 4.3. *(Continued)*

(d) *Next* and *Previous* both on left, hyperlink for *Previous*

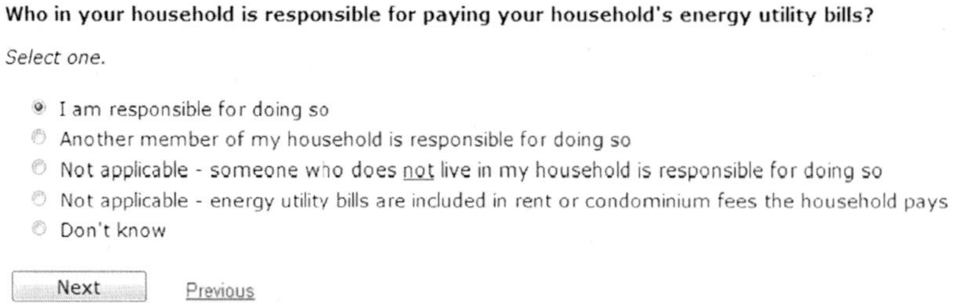

Who in your household is responsible for paying your household's energy utility bills?

Select one.

- ◉ I am responsible for doing so
- ○ Another member of my household is responsible for doing so
- ○ Not applicable - someone who does <u>not</u> live in my household is responsible for doing so
- ○ Not applicable - energy utility bills are included in rent or condominium fees the household pays
- ○ Don't know

    Next   Previous

(e) *Previous* and *Next* both on left (*Previous* first), horizontal arrangement

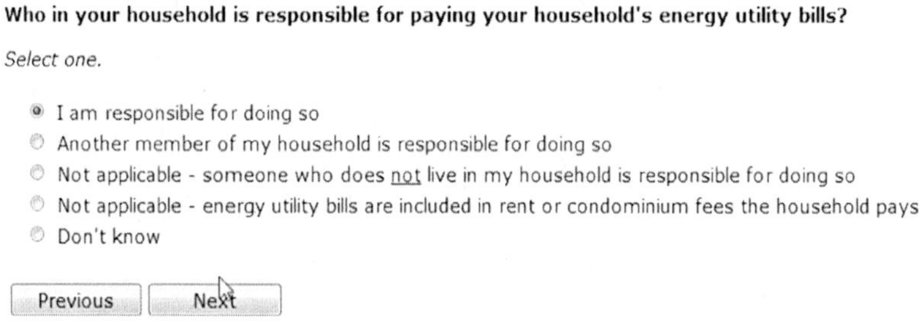

Who in your household is responsible for paying your household's energy utility bills?

Select one.

- ◉ I am responsible for doing so
- ○ Another member of my household is responsible for doing so
- ○ Not applicable - someone who does <u>not</u> live in my household is responsible for doing so
- ○ Not applicable - energy utility bills are included in rent or condominium fees the household pays
- ○ Don't know

    Previous   Next

FIGURE 4.3. Action button conditions from Couper, Baker, and Mechling (2011) study. The different conditions vary the placement and visual prominence of the "Previous" button. Reprinted with permission from Couper, M., Baker, R., and Mechling, *J. Survey Practice,* 2011.

is specific to individual items. As with the other design decisions we have covered, there are many alternatives for capturing responses in Web surveys. In paper surveys, the response options place no absolute constraints on the respondent (who can always check multiple options or write in an answer), but the input tools in Web surveys may serve both as visual guides to the respondent about how to answer and as devices for imposing conditions on the answers (Couper, 2008b). For example, radio buttons permit the selection of one and only one response. Drop boxes or select lists similarly constrain the selection to one of the available options. This feature of input tools has the advantage of restricting the respondent to the desired action, but it places greater burden on the survey designers to ensure that all possible options are available to the respondent and that the design does not inappropriately limit the options a respondent can choose.

The set of input formats available to the survey designer may be limited to those available in HTML and those that can be created using active scripting such as JavaScript, Java, or Flash. Within HTML, there are radio buttons (commonly used for single-response questions) and check boxes (used for multiple-response or check-all-that-apply items); there are drop boxes, which allow respondents to make single or multiple selections from a long scrolling list; and there are text fields and text areas, which allow respondents to enter unformatted responses. Many Web survey software systems have their own menu of selection tools. Using active scripting, the format of response options is almost limitless, including visual analog scales or slider bars (e.g., Couper, Tourangeau, Conrad, and Singer, 2006; Funke, Reips, and Thomas, 2011), drag-and-drop (e.g., Delavande and Rohwedder, 2008), card sort methods, map-based input, and so on. The extent to which these interactive features add value—either for the survey researcher in terms of better measurement or for the respondent in terms of greater enjoyment or smoother flow—is still a matter of debate. Software vendors whose products include these features and market research companies promoting their competitive advantage trumpet the benefits of such tools, but careful research contrasting these input tools with the more standard HTML approaches is still mostly lacking. We discuss research on one input tool—slider bars—in Chapter 6 (see Section 6.2.3).

There are two key issues for the survey designer in the selection of input formats. The first is the choice of the appropriate tool for a particular question; the second is how best to design that tool to facilitate the task of providing a response. Both decisions should exploit affordances—the notion that the shape of an object should somehow suggest how the object is to be used. Gibson (1979) first introduced the idea of affordances, arguing that visual perception involved the recognition of affordances. But Norman's (1988) classic *The Design of Everyday Things* popularized the concept and applied it to the design of interfaces. Both radio buttons and check boxes "afford" clicking, but the former permits only a single selection from a set while the latter acts as an on-off switch for each item in the set. Of course, this difference between the formats may not be apparent to inexperienced users. We continue to see examples of Web surveys where the input tool does not match the intended task. However, there is little research examining the effect of the type of selection tool on the number, quality, and completeness of responses.

In one study, Couper, Traugott, and Lamias (2001) contrasted radio buttons with text boxes for a series of questions about the race/ethnicity of the respondent's friends, classmates, etc., where the task was to enter a number from 1 to 10 for each of five groups. The text boxes allowed respondents to give invalid (out-of-range) responses, while the radio button version prevented them from giving such answers, producing significant differences in both the proportion of invalid responses and the rate of missing data (including DK/NA responses). Further, the size of the text box also affected responses, with a longer box eliciting more invalid responses than a short box. However, the text boxes made it easier for respondents to make the five numbers sum to ten (as they were instructed to). Thus, although the text entry box made it easier for respondents to avoid answering the question and failed to prevent out-of-range or otherwise unusable responses, the radio button format made it harder for respondents to make the numbers add up as requested. In part, the text boxes revealed the difficulty of the underlying task, which was not so apparent in the radio button version.

Heerwegh and Loosveldt (2002) compared radio buttons with drop boxes for a series of questions. They found no effect of format on completion rates, on nonsubstantive responses, or on missing data. They did not examine substantive distributions.

However, they did find that radio buttons required more time to download, affecting respondents with slower Internet connections. This is likely to be less of a concern given the prevalence of high-speed Internet connections today. Healey (2007) also compared radio buttons with drop boxes and reported findings similar to those of Heerwegh and Loosveldt; the input format did not significantly affect survey completions, the number of nonsubstantive answers, or overall completion times. Again, Healey did not examine substantive distributions between versions. However, drop boxes in Healey's study led to slightly higher item nonresponse and longer response times per item. Furthermore, those who used the scroll mouse to complete the survey (about 76 percent of respondents did so) were prone to change answers accidentally in the drop box condition, a phenomenon that may have been responsible for some of the inconsistencies found in the 2009 Canadian Census test (Lebrasseur, Morin, Rodrigue, and Taylor, 2010).

Couper, Tourangeau, Conrad, and Crawford (2004a) examined response order effects using three different formats: a series of radio buttons, a drop box, and a scroll box (with a partial list of the response options visible). They found that the magnitude of the response order effects depended on the format used to display the items, with significantly bigger order effects in the scroll box version. Their findings suggest that while reading order produces primacy effects in visually presented measures, the effect is exacerbated when a respondent action is required to see the last few options in the list. Respondents were much more likely to select one of the options visible from the outset than to scroll to view and select one of the other response options. We discuss this study further in Section 5.3 in the next chapter.

Aside from these studies, there are few empirical tests of alternative response formats. Much more research has focused on the *design* of such input tools; we review this work in Chapter 5.

4.7 GRID OR MATRIX QUESTIONS

Whether the survey uses a scrolling or paging design, a design issue for many surveys is whether to group items that share a common set of response options into a grid or matrix. The use of grid questions is common practice in Web surveys, whether in market research, academic, or government settings. Yet, the research on grid questions suggests that, although grids may reduce completion time, the format may also increase breakoffs, missing data, and measurement error. Whether this means that grids are inherently problematic or that they are often poorly designed is the focus of current research.

Research on grids can be grouped into two categories, the first comparing questions in grids to questions in other formats and the second exploring the effects of alternative grid designs on respondent performance on the grid questions. We first examine the research on grids versus other methods for presenting the items. A summary of these studies is presented in Table 4.1.

TABLE 4.1. Studies on Grids versus Alternative Designs

Study	Sample and design	Key Findings
Couper, Traugott, & Lamias (2001)	U.S. college students; five items in one grid versus five separate pages; 11 items in three grids (four, four, and three per page) versus 11 separate pages; n = 665	• Grids significantly faster ($p<.05$) • Significantly less missing data in grids ($p<.01$) • Inter-item correlations not significantly different
Bell, Mangione, & Kahn (2001)	General population volunteers recruited on Web sites in the U.S.; Grid versus expanded format (item by item on same page) for each scale of the SF-36; n = 1,464	• Response times not significantly different • Inter-item correlations not significantly different
Tourangeau, Couper, & Conrad (2004)	Members of U.S. opt-in panel; eight agree-disagree items on seven-point scale; items in one grid versus two grids (four items each) versus eight separate pages; n = 2,568	• Significant linear trend of inter-item correlations ($p<.01$): One grid > two grids > separate items • Significant ($p<.01$) trend in differentiation: One grid < two grids < separate items • Significant ($p<.001$) trend in completion time: One grid < two grids < separate items
Yan (2005)	Members of U.S. opt-in panel; six items in one grid versus six items on same page in item-by-item format versus six separate pages; also varied instructions on relatedness of items; n = 2,587	• Inter-item correlations not significantly different • Perceived relatedness not significantly different
Toepoel, Das, & van Soest (2009b)	Probability panel in the Netherlands; 40 agree-disagree items on five-point scale; items in one grid versus four grids (ten items in each) versus ten grids (items in each) versus 40 separate pages; n = 2,565	• No effect of format on mean score or variance • Inter-item correlations not significantly different • Significant ($p<.01$) increase in missing data as number of items on page increases • Significant ($p = .006$) decrease in time as number of items on page increases • Significantly ($p<.001$) lower evaluations as number of items on page increases

(Continued)

TABLE 4.1. *(Continued)*

Study	Sample and design	Key Findings
Callegaro, Shand-Lubbers, & Dennis (2009)	Probability-based panel in the U.S.; ten items on five-point scale; grid versus single item per screen (collapsing across other conditions); n = 1,419	• Faster completion time for grid (median = 45 seconds) than single items (median = 70 seconds) • Inter-item correlations not significantly different • Correlations between reverse-worded items and rest of scale not significantly different • No significant differences in subjective enjoyment

Couper, Traugott, and Lamias (2001) examined a five-item knowledge measure (with the items on one page in a grid or on five separate pages) and an 11-item attitude measure (with the items in three grids or on 11 separate pages). The grid version took significantly less time to complete (168 seconds on average for the 16 items) than the item-by-item version (194 seconds). The inter-item correlations (as measured by Cronbach's alpha) were slightly but not significantly higher for the grid versions of the scales. The researchers also found significantly lower rates of item missing data (DK or NA responses) in the grid version.

In another early experiment, Bell, Mangione, and Kahn (2001) contrasted a grid version of the SF-36 health questionnaire with an item-by-item version (with all items on the same page). Completion time for the item-by-item version was slightly longer than for the grid version (5.22 versus 5.07 minutes), but the difference was not statistically significant. They found no differences in inter-item correlations (again using Cronbach's alpha).

Tourangeau, Couper, and Conrad (2004) compared eight agree-disagree items presented in three formats: 1) all the items on a single page in one grid, 2) four items in each of two grids presented on separate pages, and 3) each item on a separate page. Respondents took significantly less time to answer in the grid format (60 seconds on average) than when each item was on a separate page (99 seconds). They also found a significant linear trend in the alpha coefficients across the three conditions, with inter-item correlations increasing as the grouping of items increased. However, they found that respondents who got the items in a grid showed less differentiation in the answers—that is, they were more likely to choose the same response option for all items. Further, the part-whole correlations for two reverse-worded items were weaker in the grid version, suggesting that respondents were less likely to notice the reverse wording when the items were in a grid. A reanalysis of these data by Peytchev (2005) using structural equation modeling suggests that the increased correlations indicated higher measurement error rather than increased reliability of measurement. These results suggest that the faster completion times may come at the cost of suboptimal responding.

Yan (2005) explicitly tested whether putting items in a grid encouraged respondents to see them as more highly related. She assigned respondents to one of three versions of a set of six loosely-related items: 1) one item per page, 2) all six items on the same page in an item-by-item approach, and 3) the six items in a single grid. She also manipulated the introduction to the six items, with one introduction suggesting all the items came from the same source and another suggesting they came from different sources. The effect of the layout on the inter-item correlations (Cronbach's alpha) was not statistically significant. In a follow-up question asking respondents how related they thought the items were, she again found no significant effect of layout.

Toepoel, Das, and van Soest (2009b) compared four versions of a 40-item arousal scale, with one, four, ten, or 40 items per page. They found no effect of format on the arousal index scores and only modest effects on inter-item correlations. However, item missing data increased monotonically with the number of items on a page. Using grids reduced the time to complete the set of items, but also lowered scores on respondents' subjective evaluations of the questionnaire.

Finally, Callegaro, Shand-Lubbers, and Dennis (2009) tested two subscales of the SF-36 health questionnaire in grid versus single-item-per-page versions, also varying the shading of rows. They report median response times of 45 seconds for the grid groups and about 70 seconds for the single item per screen groups. The inter-item correlations (Cronbach's alpha) did not differ significantly by version nor did the reverse-worded items show weaker correlations in the grid conditions. Further, they found no significant differences in the perceived difficulty or self-reported enjoyment of respondents across the versions.

Perhaps the clearest finding from these studies is that grids reduce the time it takes for respondents to complete a set of items. Four of the six studies find significant reductions in response times with grids. Tourangeau and his colleagues also find significantly higher inter-item correlations with grids, but none of the other studies replicates this finding. The studies also disagree about the impact of grids on item nonresponse. One study reports significantly lower item nonresponse when the items are in a grid format (Couper, Traugott, and Lamias, 2001), but another finds higher item nonresponse with longer grids (Toepoel, Das, and van Soest, 2009b). These inconsistencies across studies may be explained by a number of factors, such as the topics or populations in the study, whether the items asked about behaviors or attitudes, whether any of the items were reverse-worded, the number of items (rows) in the grid, the number of response options (columns), and so on.

Grids remain popular despite research suggesting they may be problematic for respondents, and researchers are exploring how the design of grids can be improved to mitigate their negative effects while still taking advantage of their virtues; we discuss this work in Section 6.2.5. Taken together, these studies suggest that the complexity of grids may be an important factor contributing to their negative effects on survey breakoffs, item missing data, and respondent satisfaction. If grids are to be used, making them simpler—whether by reducing the number of items (rows) in the grid, by splitting the questions (reducing the number of columns), or by using visual feedback to guide respondents as they answer grid questions—may reduce some of their negative effects.

4.8 SUMMARY

There is a long history of research on the wording of survey questions. More recently, attention has turned to other aspects of questionnaire design, particularly in Web surveys where there are so many design options available and where the respondents interact directly with the instrument rather than though a trained interviewer. Given the vast number of design options, it is not surprising that there is still much work to be done to understand when, how, and why the different options may affect the answers obtained in Web surveys. Much of the research done so far has examined differences in item missing data rates, completion times, or response distributions. Assumptions need to be made about which designs yield more accurate data or improve validity. Further, relatively little has been done to explore the reliability of measurement under different design conditions.

Many of the experiments described in this chapter—and in the next three chapters—are based on studies of college students or of members of non-probability panels. The former are likely to be quite adept at using the Internet and to respond well to unexpected designs. The latter generally get large numbers of survey requests, often from different vendors using different layouts and designs. These veteran respondents may have become inured to design variations because of their exposure to a wide array of good and bad Web survey designs. It is, therefore, important to replicate findings about Web survey design with members of probability panels. We have done this with the Knowledge Networks and FFRISP panels; similarly, Toepoel and her colleagues (2009a, 2009b) have done this using the CentERpanel. These replications give us greater confidence that the results we summarize here generalize across other groups with different Web survey experiences or different motivations (see also Toepoel, Das, and van Soest, 2008, 2009c). But we should remain wary about the possible influence of the samples in our studies on the effects—as well as the lack of effects—that we find. It is impossible to completely separate concerns about measurement error from concerns about representativeness and population inference.

Regardless of the shortcomings in the evidence, it seems clear that careful attention to the design details may improve the quality of the answers obtained and may reduce breakoffs and missing data in Web surveys. There is no simple recipe for achieving an effective Web survey design, and researchers still have great flexibility in designing Web surveys so long as they stay within some broad limits. Still, the evidence presented in this chapter suggests that the overall design of the instrument should receive as much attention as the content.

/// 5 /// THE WEB AS A VISUAL MEDIUM

Although other modes of data collection, including traditional paper self-administered questionnaires, rely on the visual channel to communicate with survey respondents, Web surveys often incorporate more visual material (for example, color or photographs) than paper surveys typically do, and they also sometimes incorporate types of visual material (such as video clips) that paper surveys cannot include. The need to move the mouse from one screen location to another may also make the position of the item on screen or the distance between two items more salient in Web surveys than in paper questionnaires. Because of these differences, the visual features of Web surveys are likely to have more impact on the respondents and their answers than the visual features of traditional paper questionnaires, although visual design issues are clearly important for paper questionnaires, too (Christian and Dillman, 2004; Jenkins and Dillman, 1997; Redline, Dillman, Dajani, and Scaggs, 2003). This chapter examines the impact of the web's visual characteristics on the format and content of the answers that respondents provide. The impact of visual information may not be all-or-none and, accordingly, we examine the importance of a variable we call "visibility"—that is, the level of visual prominence of information on screen.

5.1 INTERPRETING VISUAL FEATURES OF WEB QUESTIONNAIRES

Although Web panelists can be very experienced survey respondents, even experienced survey respondents are often unclear about how they are supposed to respond to specific questions. The work of Schober and Conrad (e.g., Conrad and Schober, 2000; Schober and Conrad, 1997; Suessbrick, Schober, and Conrad, 2000) indicates that there is often considerable variability in how respondents interpret the terms in survey questions. Schober and Conrad focused on the interpretation of the *words* in the question. There is also a good deal of evidence that respondents are often unclear about the meaning of the response options and that they may rely on incidental cues in deciding what the options are supposed to mean (for a review, see Schwarz, 1996).

Interpreting response scales. To cite one example of this uncertainty, Schwarz and his colleagues have demonstrated that the numbers attached to the response scale (for example, –5 to +5 versus 0 to 10) can affect respondents' answers by shaping their understanding of the scale (Schwarz, Grayson, and Knäuper, 1998, Experiment 1; Schwarz, Knäuper, Hippler, Noelle-Neumann, and Clark, 1991; see also O'Muircheartaigh, Gaskell, and Wright, 1995, and Tourangeau, Couper, and Conrad, 2007). Other studies have shown that the visual representation of the response options may affect their relative popularity. A response scale in the shape of a ladder suggests that the options are supposed to be roughly equal in popularity; by contrast, a scale in the shape of a pyramid suggests that the options at the top are supposed to be chosen less often than those at the bottom (Smith, 1995; see also Schwarz, Grayson, and Knäuper, 1998, Experiment 2).

Because Web survey design exploits such a wide range of visual features, respondents may be particularly likely to use visual features of the questions or response options as supplementary information to help them pin down the meaning of the question or the potential answers.[1] Many survey items use partially labeled response scales for attitudinal items and the respondents may have difficulty in assigning precise meanings to the scale points, particularly those that are not labeled verbally. It seems likely that respondents generally begin with expectations about response scales as they decide how to use them in communicating their answers. For example, in the absence of conflicting information, they may assume that the scale options are supposed to represent equally spaced points on the underlying dimension of judgment. We refer to this expectation as the *presumption of equal spacing*. Similarly, when the scale is clearly bipolar (say, one endpoint is labeled "Very strongly agree" and the other endpoint is labeled "Very strongly disagree"), respondents may assume that the scales points are intended to represent points that are symmetrically arrayed around a neutral midpoint on the underlying continuum. We refer to this as the *presumption of symmetry* (which applies only to bipolar scales).

Of course, the verbal labels on the scale points may confirm or disconfirm these expectations. In addition, the spacing of the scale points may affect respondents' understanding of the conceptual range that each option is supposed to represent. The spacing of the scale points in Figure 5.1 below (which features a fully labeled scale) suggests that the scale points do *not* represent equal conceptual intervals. Instead, respondents may see the neutral option as conceptually further from the "Somewhat agree" and "Somewhat disagree" options than those options are from the "Strongly agree" and "Strongly disagree" options, respectively. As we shall see, however, the verbal labels often take interpretive precedence over visual cues like spacing.

---

[1] As Tourangeau, Rips, and Rasinski (2000; see Chapter 2) argue, the meaning of the question is inextricably linked to the meaning of the response options, because someone hasn't fully understood the question unless he or she correctly identifies the set of possible answers (what Tourangeau, Rips, and Rasinski refer to as the question's "uncertainty space").

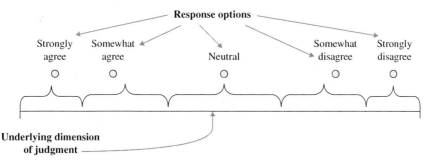

FIGURE 5.1. The top portion of the figure displays a scale that varies the spacing of the response options; the space taken up by the middle option seems wider than the space given to the other four options, suggesting that it represents a larger portion of the underlying dimension of judgment than the other four options do. The bottom portion displays the underlying dimension of judgment, in this case, agreement and disagreement. The brackets indicate the mapping from the options to a portion of the underlying dimension.

Heuristics for interpreting scales in Web surveys. We (Tourangeau, Couper, and Conrad, 2004, 2007) argue that respondents apply five heuristics that help them interpret the response scales in Web and other visual surveys. Each heuristic assigns a meaning to some visual feature of the response scale or of the item itself. Here are the five heuristics:

- Middle means typical or central;
- Left and top mean first;
- Near means related;
- Like (in appearance) means close (in meaning); and
- Up means good.

According to the first heuristic, the visual midpoint of a scale plays a special role in establishing the meaning of other scale points. As the presumption of symmetry implies, the midpoint of a bipolar scale will be taken to represent the conceptual midpoint of the underlying dimension—that is, the neutral point or the numerical midpoint. When the underlying dimension is unipolar, respondents may assume it represents the midpoint in another sense—the population median or mode (see, for example, Schwarz and Hippler, 1987). We (Tourangeau et al., 2004, Experiment 3) show that, when the visual midpoint does not coincide with the conceptual midpoint of the scale (say, because the scale options aren't evenly spaced), the distribution of the answers changes. Figure 5.2 below shows one of the items we used in that study. The scale option corresponding to midpoint of the probability scale ("Even chance") has been displaced to the left of the visual midpoint of the scale. Respondents who received this scale were more likely to choose one of the options from the low probability end of the scale than respondents who got a scale with equally spaced options and with "Even chance" at the visual midpoint. Respondents apparently inferred that options like "Possible" and "Unlikely" represented probabilities closer

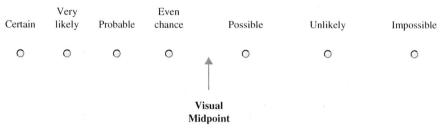

During the next year, what is the chance that you will get so sick that you will have to stay in bed for the entire day or longer?

FIGURE 5.2. A scale with unevenly spaced response options; the point that presumably corresponds to the conceptual middle point of the dimension of interest ("Even chance") is to the left of the visual midpoint of the scale. Adapted with permission from Tourangeau, Couper, and Conrad (2004).

to 50 percent when the options were not evenly spaced (as in the figure) than when they were.

The second heuristic ("Left and top mean first") refers to the expectation that the response options will follow some logical order, typically progressing from one end of the relevant dimension to the other, beginning with the leftmost option (when the options are arrayed horizontally) and moving in order to the rightmost, or beginning with the top option (when the options are arrayed vertically) and moving to the bottom. We (Tourangeau et al., 2004, Experiment 4; see also Toepoel and Dillman, 2008) demonstrated that, when the order of the answer options was inconsistent with this heuristic, response times were much slower than when the order of the options was consistent with it. In addition, another experiment showed that, with unfamiliar items, respondents inferred the value of the item on the dimension of interest from the values of more familiar items nearby (Tourangeau et al., 2004, Experiment 5; see Figure 5.3 below). For example, respondents were asked to decide which hotels in a list of hotel chains were expensive. They were more likely to classify the Clarion Inn as expensive when it came right after two expensive hotel chains than when it came immediately after two inexpensive ones. Respondents apparently inferred that the hotels were arrayed in some logical order (e.g., from the most to least expensive) and gave ratings to the unfamiliar Clarion Inn that were consistent with this inference. In fact, the Clarion Inn is a budget hotel chain. Further, the impact of the position of the unfamiliar item within a list on respondent's judgments about the item depended on how well the remaining items did in fact seem to follow a logical progression—that is, the more that the other items seemed to be arrayed in an order, the more they affected respondents' judgments about the unfamiliar items.

The "Near means related" heuristic refers to the tendency for respondents to infer a conceptual relation between two items based on their physical proximity. In an experiment examining the application of this heuristic, we (Tourangeau et al., 2004, Experiment 6) compared three methods for presenting a series of items. Eight agree-disagree items on dietary issues were presented a) in a grid on a single screen, b) in two

Do you consider the cost of these hotels or hotel chains to be EXPENSIVE OR INEXPENSIVE?

(Please select an answer for each item)

	Expensive	Inexpensive
Ritz-Carlton	○	○
Hyatt Hotel	○	○
Clarion Inn	○	○
Courtyard	○	○
Holiday Inn	○	○
Days Inn	○	○
Motel 6	○	○

Next Screen ==>		<== Previous Screen

Do you consider the cost of these hotels or hotel chains to be EXPENSIVE OR INEXPENSIVE?

(Please select an answer for each item)

	Expensive	Inexpensive
Ritz-Carlton	○	○
Hyatt Hotel	○	○
Courtyard	○	○
Holiday Inn	○	○
Days Inn	○	○
Motel 6	○	○
Clarion Inn	○	○

Next Screen ==>		<== Previous Screen

FIGURE 5.3. The impact of the position of an item within a list. In the top grid, Clarion Inn appears in the third position, among more expensive hotels; in the bottom grid, Clarion Inn appears last, among the less expensive chains. Respondents were more likely to rate Clarion Inn as expensive when they received the top grid.

grids on two screens, or c) as individual items on eight adjacent screens. The correlations among the eight items were highest when all eight were presented in a single grid and lowest when the items appeared on eight separate screens (for similar findings, see Couper, Traugott, and Lamias, 2001). Respondents apparently expected the items to be more similar to each other when they appeared together in one grid. In addition, they were more likely to overlook the fact that a couple of the items were worded in the opposite direction from the other six when all eight items appeared in a single grid. When the items were in a grid together, respondents seemed to expect the items to be very similar and didn't feel a need to read them very carefully. Another possibility is that grids encourage satisficing. Grids are common in both Web and paper questionnaires and the findings here suggest that they can have unintended consequences for the answers. Still, a number of studies (summarized in Table 4.1) suggest that grids do not generally increase the correlations among the items relative to other formats, and the jury is still out on overall impact of the grid format on data quality.

The fourth heuristic ("Like in appearance means close in meaning") refers to the tendency for respondents to infer conceptual similarity between two items

How much do you favor or oppose avoiding "fast food?"

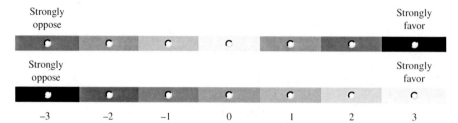

FIGURE 5.4. Two formats for response scales. In the top scale, the options differ in both hue and brightness. The options on the left side of the scale are shades of red; those on the right side are shades of blue. In the bottom scale, the options are all shades of blue and vary only in brightness. (See color insert.) Adapted with permission from Tourangeau, Couper, and Conrad (2007).

or response options based on their similarity in appearance. For example, when the two ends of the response scale are shades of the same hue, respondents may infer that the two extremes are closer conceptually than when the two ends of the scales are shades of the different hues. As a result, their answers may shift, reflecting the greater conceptual distance when scales involve two, rather than one, hue (Tourangeau et al., 2007). Figure 5.4 shows examples of two scales we compared experimentally (Tourangeau et al., 2007). If the use of two colors emphasizes the difference between the extreme scale values, respondents whose opinion is positive may select answers closer to the positive end of the scale ("strongly favor" in the figure) to indicate greater subjective distance from the negative end of the scale whose extremity has been emphasized. We found that responses were displaced to the "Strongly favor" end of the scale when the top scale (which featured two hues) was used as compared to the bottom scale (with a single hue). We observed similar (though more marked) displacement to that end of the scale when the scale points also had numerical labels that ranged from –3 to +3 as opposed to 1 to 7 (see Figure 5.5 below). Color apparently works like other features of the question in affecting respondents' understanding of the underlying response scale. The use of colors can introduce another problem—not everyone sees color the same way, and the various forms of colorblindness can be related to other respondent characteristics, such as their sex.

The final heuristic we described ("Up means good") involves inferring something about the value of an item from its position on the screen. We argue that vertical position and desirability are often linked metaphorically (e.g., heaven is above, hell below; upswings are good, downswings bad; an upbeat mood is positive, a downbeat mood negative; and so on; see Carbonell, 1983). This link may be the basis for expecting that good things will be positioned above bad things. In a laboratory experiment done by Meier and Robinson (2004), participants were quicker to classify positive words (*brave, loyal, hero*) as positive when they appeared near the top of the computer screen than when they appeared near the bottom. The reverse was true for negative words (*bitter, clumsy, crime*)—participants classified them as negative

(a)

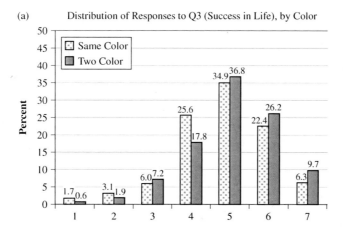

Distribution of Responses to Q3 (Success in Life), by Color

(b)

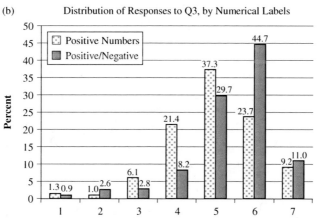

Distribution of Responses to Q3, by Numerical Labels

FIGURE 5.5. The graph in panel a shows the percent distribution of responses by color (same color or two colors) for the condition in which only the end points of the scale were labeled (as in Figure 5.4 above) and no numerical labels were used; the graph in panel b shows the percent distribution of responses by numerical labels, collapsing across color conditions. Q3 asked respondents to evaluate their success in life; higher numbers indicate greater success in life. Reprinted with permission from Tourangeau et al., 2007.

more quickly when they appeared near the bottom of the screen than near the top. Apparently, the participants expected the positive words to be up screen (and the negative ones to be down), and they were slower to respond when these expectations weren't met. According to Meier and Robinson:

> The results of our studies provide evidence for an automatic association between affect and vertical position. These findings suggest that, when making evaluations, people automatically assume that objects that are high in visual space are good, whereas objects that are low in visual space are bad. The results of these studies extend prior work...in suggesting that affect is grounded in sensorimotor perception. (Meier and Robinson, 2004, page 247)

TABLE 5.1. Studies of the Position of the Items on Screen

Study	Topic	Position Manipulation/Other Factors
Study 1	Doctors, HMO managers, Congress, the scientific community	• Item first vs. second on the screen • Order and orientation of response options
Study 2	Six food items (riboflavin, niacin, antioxidants, flour, allspice, cornstarch)	• Item to be rated above or below rating scale • Order of response options
Study 3	Six food items (as in Study 2)	• Item to be rated above or below rating scale • Order of response options
Study 4 Replicated in two consecutive months	Six food items (as in Study 2)	• Second item on screen near top or middle of screen • Order and orientation of response options
Study 5	Six food items (as in Study 2) Six physician specialties (Pediatrician, gynecologist, internist, endocrinologist, nephrologist, urologist)	• Item first or second on screen • Second item on screen near middle or bottom of screen

In a series of experiments, we (Tourangeau, Couper, and Conrad, in press) found results in a Web survey that were similar to those of Meier and Robinson. Respondents were faster to rate various health-related entities (such as HMOs) when the good end of a vertically arrayed rating scale was up than when the good end was down; by contrast, the order of the response options didn't affect response times when the options were arrayed horizontally. Additional experiments showed that respondents rated food items (such as *riboflavins* and *corn starch*) more favorably when they were positioned near the top of the screen than when they were positioned toward the middle. Table 5.1 summarizes the main features of these studies. Study 4 in the table was based on a national area probability sample whose members were provided with a computer and Internet access if they could not otherwise participate.

A meta-analysis showed that overall, a higher position on screen led to more favorable ratings for an item. Figure 5.6 displays the effects sizes from the six experiments. The effect size was the difference between the mean rating for an item (such as *riboflavin*) when that item appeared higher or lower on the screen divided by the pooled standard deviation of the ratings; positive effects indicated more favorable ratings for higher positioned items. We (Tourangeau et al., in press) found a significant overall effect for the position of the item, with a mean effect size of about 0.08. As can be seen from the figure, the vertical position of the item on screen had a small but consistent effect on the ratings it received.

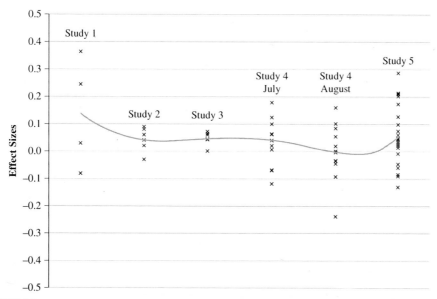

FIGURE 5.6. The graph displays the effect sizes from each experiment examining the impact of the position on item on screen. The effect size is the mean difference between the ratings for the item when it was displayed at the top of the screen and when it was displayed lower down on the screen divided by the pooled standard deviation of the ratings.

The hierarchy of interpretive cues. This work supports the idea that respondents are often unclear about how to use rating scales (especially when they are not fully labeled) and that respondents draw on a hierarchy of cues to help them decide what each scale point means. Verbal labels seem to take precedence over other cues; numerical labels receive the next highest priority; and cues like spacing and color are used only when these higher priority cues are absent or weak. For example, when every scale point was verbally labeled, the color of the rating scale points had little impact on the ratings (Tourangeau et al., 2004); similarly, the results displayed in Figure 5.5 show that the numerical labels have a stronger effect on the ratings than the scale color does

Five experiments conducted by Toepoel and Dillman (2008) provide further evidence that verbal cues, particularly labels on each scale point, can reduce the impact of visual cues. For example, their fifth experiment replicated a result we reported (Tourangeau et al., 2007) that the impact of color on responses to a rating scale was eliminated when every option was verbally labeled. Fully labeled scales were also less affected by the spacing of the response options and by the grouping of the items (that is, on a single screen or across multiple screens) than scales in which only the end points had verbal labels.

Entering open-ended responses. Our later work extends these ideas, showing that respondents may also be unsure how to deal with questions that call for open-ended (but highly circumscribed) answers, such as numerical estimates, dollar amounts, or dates (Couper, Kennedy, Conrad, and Tourangeau, 2011). With such questions, one issue for the respondents is how to format their answers. Similar issues arise in many Web applications, where credit card numbers, addresses, telephone numbers, or other information must be entered in a format that is consistent with the program requirements.

Several experiments have examined the use of various methods intended to help respondents enter dates in the desired format. Table 5.2 summarizes the results of three experiments by Christian, Dillman, and Smyth (2007) and two additional experiments by us (2008) that compare various formats for items intended to collect information about dates. Several conclusions emerge from these experiments. First, even without any hints about the intended format for the answer, respondents often provide dates in MM/YYYY format. In the studies by Christian, Dillman, and Smyth (2007), almost 90 percent of the respondents gave their answers in that format when the question read "When did you begin your studies at Washington State University" and the entry box provided no further clues about the desired format (Christian et al., 2007, Survey 2). That percentage didn't change much when the item read "What month and year did you begin your studies . . . ?" Clearly, there are strong non-survey conventions about the appropriate format for dates. Second, providing a verbal or graphical label for a text box affects the format of the answers. When the entry boxes is labeled "Month" rather than "MM" respondents are much more likely to spell out the name of the month and less likely to provide it in numeric form. Respondents' answers seem to mimic the format of the label. Third, making the month box half the length of the year box increased the proportion of respondents giving an answer in the intended numerical format (compare the top two rows in the first panel of Table 5.1; the difference between 55 percent and 63 percent is statistically significant).

The best solution may be not to require that the respondents enter their answers at all—drop boxes seem to be better than any of the open-ended response formats for collecting dates (Couper et al., 2011). Drop boxes produce the highest percentage of correctly formatted answers and they yield them more quickly than any of the open-ended formats. (All of the formats produce some missing data and this explains why the drop box conditions didn't have 100 percent correctly formatted answers.) All designs but the drop box require respondents to interpret the visual hints and generate compatibly formatted answers; the drop box reduces the task to recognizing the desired value in a list. Note also that all of the designs except the drop box can be implemented in paper. The drop box requires an interactive medium like the Web (see Chapter 6) and so its superiority represents an advantage for Web over paper administration.

We (Couper et al., 2011; Experiment 2) also looked at open responses to items asking for (whole) dollar amounts. When asked about dollar amounts, respondents were more likely to give answers in the desired format when the text box had a dollar sign to the left and a decimal point followed by two zeroes to the right. These graphical hints made it clear that the questions sought amounts in whole dollars. Fuchs (2009) reports a similar finding. Respondents completing a paper questionnaire were more likely to provide exact answers rather than round values when the question included a label than when it didn't ("_____ students" vs. "_____"). Answer boxes also seemed to promote exact answers (as compared to blank lines).

TABLE 5.2. Percent of Correctly Formatted Responses, by Experiment and Condition

Paper/Study	Conditions	Percent Correctly Formatted (n)
Christian, Dillman, and Smyth (2007)—Survey 1	[ ] [ ] Month Year	55% (367)
	[ ][ ] Month Year	63% (351)
	[ ] [ ] MM YYYY	91% (438)
	[ ][ ] MM YYYY	88% (435)
Christian et al. (2007)—Survey 2	[ ] [ ] Month Year	45% (423)
	[ ] [ ] MM YYYY	87% (426)
	Verbal only ("When...?")	89% (393)
	Verbal only ("In what month and year...?")	87% (426)
Christian et al. (2007)—Survey 3	MM YYYY [ ] [ ]	94% (351)
	[ ] MM [ ] YYYY	96% (379)
	MM [ ] YYYY [ ]	93% (352)
Couper, Kennedy, Conrad, and Tourangeau (2011)— Experiment 3	**In what month and year did you last see a medical doctor?** [ ]	74% (2,182)
	In what month and year did you last see a medical doctor? Month: [ ] Year: [ ]	95% (2,160) (42% give numeric response; 53% spell out the month)
	Drop Box	98% (2,220)

(Continued)

TABLE 5.2. *(Continued)*

Paper/Study	Conditions	Percent Correctly Formatted (n)
Couper et al. (2011)— Experiment 4	**What is your date of birth?**	
	(Please enter the date in MM/DD/YYYY format)	83% (585)
	What is your date of birth?	
	(Please enter the date in MM/DD/YYYY format)	91% (616)
	What is your date of birth?	96% (616)
	MM DD YYYY	
	Drop box	98% (583)

In general, the size of the entry box provides a cue to the desired format for the answer, but it is a relatively weak one, that mainly affects the length of narrative open-ended responses (Couper et al., 2011; see also Smyth, Dillman, Christian, and McBride, 2009, who find an effect for the size of the entry box on narrative responses, but only for respondents who sent back the questionnaire relatively late in the field period).

5.2 THE IMPACT OF IMAGES

As we noted earlier, Web surveys make it easier to display photographs, pictures, and other visual material to the respondents than other modes of data collection do, but relatively little research has examined the effects that such material may have on the data that are ultimately collected. Although many Web surveys use images largely as a kind of decoration to provide a more attractive interface for the respondents, images are sometimes an integral part of the question, helping respondents to identify the particular object they are being asked about (see Couper, Tourangeau, and Kenyon, 2004, on task versus stylistic elements in survey questionnaires). Even when images are intended merely as embellishment, they can still affect the response process for a given item, shaping the respondent's understanding of the question or altering the specific considerations the respondent takes into account as he or she formulates an answer. In general, images are likely to be influential contextual stimuli and can have effects on responses similar to those of prior questions (see Tourangeau and Rasinski, 1988, and Tourangeau, Rips, and Rasinski, 2000, Chapter 7, for reviews of the literature on question context effects). Two types of effects are commonly found in question order experiments—assimilation effects (in which the answers to the later questions move in the direction of the earlier answers) and contrast effects (in which the answers to the later questions move in the direction opposite to those given earlier).

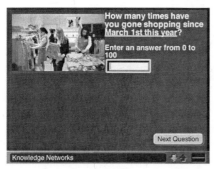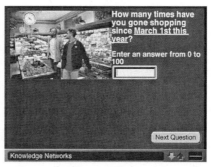

FIGURE 5.7. Two images used by Couper, Tourangeau, and Kenyon (2004). The left side shows shopping at a clothing store, a low frequency exemplar of the category of shopping; the right side shows shopping at a grocery store, a higher frequency exemplar. Some respondents got one photograph and some got the other. Other respondents in the experiment got both of these images or neither of them. (See color insert.) Reprinted with permission from Couper, Tourangeau and Kenyon, 2004.

Couper, Tourangeau, and Kenyon (2004) conducted an experiment that varied the content of the photographs that accompanied each of six survey items. Each item asked respondents how often they did something, such as attending a sporting event during the past year or going on an overnight trip during that period. The photographs (for an example, see Figure 5.7 below) depicted some instance of the category of interest. The pictures were chosen to represent either low or high frequency exemplars of the target category. One group of respondents was presented only the high frequency exemplars and a second group received only low frequency exemplars. In addition, respondents in two other experimental treatments got neither image or they got both the high and low frequency examples. For all six items, which images respondents received had statistically significant effects on their answers. The overall trend was for respondents who got the high frequency exemplars to report higher frequencies than those who got the low frequency exemplars; the differences between the high and low frequency groups were significant for four of six items.

Open-ended responses indicated that the instances shown in the pictures affected their construal of the target category. For example, two respondents explained their answers to a question about how often they went shopping as follows:

> What kind of shopping you were looking for was not defined because my number of times would be different depending on what type. I took it as how many times for leisure.
> Thought shopping meant clothes from the picture. If you include food shopping— went about ten times.

The first respondent didn't receive either photograph and the second one received a photograph that showed people shopping for clothes.

The study by Couper, Tourangeau, and Kenyon found that answers were moved in the direction of photograph—that is, an assimilation effect. That assimilation effect probably reflected the impact of the picture on how respondents interpreted the category of interest and on the specific memories they recalled in answering the question. We (Tourangeau, Conrad, Couper, and Ye, 2011) did two more studies that found assimilation effects like the one reported by Couper, Tourangeau, and Kenyon (2004). In these studies, respondents got photographs depicting examples of different categories of food; respondents who got pictures of foods that are generally eaten frequently (such as *cheese* and *butter*) reported eating more servings of foods in the target category (*dairy products*) in a typical week than those who got pictures of foods eaten less often (*frozen yogurt* and *sour cream*). We argue that respondents base their food frequency estimates on the small set of category members that come to mind and that the pictures change which examples respondents consider as they formulate their estimates. When the pictures showed frequently consumed examples, the frequency estimates went up; when they showed infrequently consumed examples, the frequency estimates went down.

These studies (Tourangeau et al., 2011) also suggest that, in general, pictures may narrow the interpretation of the category of interest. One of our studies compared visual examples (pictures) with verbal examples. Pictures are necessarily concrete. It is easier to depict "an apple" than "a fruit." Words, by contrast, can vary in their level of generality. We found the respondents tended to report eating more servings of foods in the target category on average when they got verbal examples than when they got pictorial examples, even though we tried to choose verbal and pictorial examples that were on the same level of generality (see Tourangeau et al., 2011).

Tourangeau, Couper, and Steiger (2003) demonstrate an additional context effect produced by the images that preceded a set of survey questions. In these studies, the Web questionnaire periodically displayed photographs and textual messages from one of the investigators as respondents worked their way through the survey. For example, in one experiment, roughly a third of the sample got a picture and messages from the female investigator ("Hi! My name is Darby Miller Steiger. I'm one of the investigators on this project. Thanks for taking part in my study."). Another third got a picture and messages from one of the male investigators; and the remainder got screens with the study logo. A later replication of this study compared the study logo with photographs featuring the female investigator. In both experiments, respondents answered a series of questions about women's roles; the respondents who got the pictures of a woman gave more feminist responses than those who got the picture of a man or the study logo. A photograph of an attractive, professional-looking woman may have triggered pro-women reactions, shifting the answers to the questions on women's roles in a feminist direction.

To summarize, the studies by Couper et al. (2004a), Tourangeau et al. (2011), and Tourangeau et al. (2003) all demonstrate assimilation effects from the presentation of images, with the pictures seeming to affect how respondents interpret the questions (Couper et al., 2004) or what they retrieve as they formulate their answers (Tourangeau et al., 2011; Tourangeau et al., 2003).

Visual contrast effects. Another line of work suggests that images can serve as a standard of comparison affecting the judgments that respondents make. In these studies, the object of judgment—the respondent's own health—is contrasted with

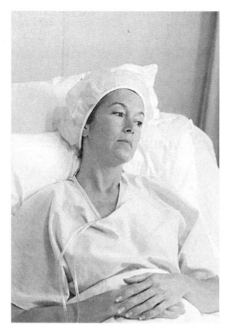

FIGURE 5.8. Photographs used by Couper, Conrad, and Tourangeau (2007). Respondents received one or the other picture in a Web survey. The pictures were presented on the same screen near a question about the respondent's own health, in the header of that screen, or on the screen just prior to the health item. (See color insert.)

the person depicted in a photograph. These experiments (Couper, Conrad, and Tourangeau, 2007) displayed photographs either of a woman in a hospital bed or a young woman jogging as part of a Web survey (see Figure 5.8 for the photographs we used). In addition, the experiments varied the position of the picture (putting it on the screen preceding the target question, on the same page just to the left and above the target question, or in the header at the top of the same screen with the target question). We examined the effects of the content and placement of the pictures on respondents' ratings of their own health. We predicted a judgmental contrast effect—that is, we thought respondents would rate their own health as worse when they got the picture of the jogger and as better when they got the picture of the sick women. Table 5.3 displays the key results from the three experiments. In all three, the expected contrast

TABLE 5.3. Mean Ratings of Respondent's Health, by Study and Experimental Condition

Position of Picture	Study 1		Study 2		Study 3	
	Fit Woman	Sick Woman	Fit Woman	Sick Woman	Fit Woman	Sick Woman
Prior Screen	3.29	2.93	–	–	–	–
Header	3.14	3.29	3.37	3.23	3.66	3.60
Question Area	3.30	3.05	3.41	3.25		
Small image					3.73	3.61
Large image					3.66	3.55

Note: Lower numbers indicate higher levels of self-rated health.

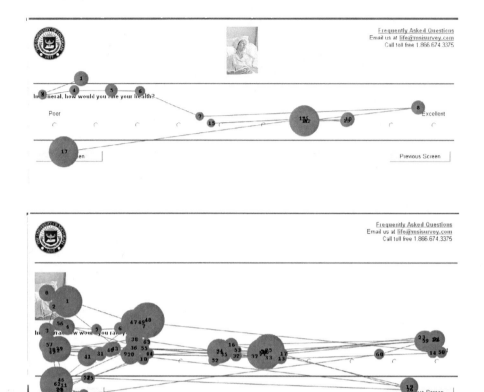

FIGURE 5.9. Gaze plots for two respondents in an eye-tracking study. In the top panel, the respondent never fixates on the photograph, which was presented in the header section of the Web page; in the bottom panel the respondent does look at the picture, which appears just above the question. (See color insert.)

effects were found and, in all three, the effects of the content of the picture were statistically significant. Although there was an apparent reversal in the first experiment when the pictures appeared in the header, this reversal didn't replicate in the second and third studies. Still, the effect of the pictures seems weaker when they are in the header, probably due to "banner blindness" (Benway, 1998; Benway and Lane, 1998), or the tendency for Web users to ignore material in the header of a Web page.

A follow-up study by Tourangeau, Couper, and Galešic (2005) used eye-tracking to examine how the placement of the picture affected the time respondents spent looking at it. When the picture appeared in the header respondents often ignored it. Figure 5.9 shows the gaze plots for a respondent who never fixated on the photograph when it was presented in the header and for a second respondent who fixated on the photograph when it was presented next to the question. Overall, respondents fixated less often on the picture and fixated for less overall time on average when the picture was presented in the header than when it was presented next to the question. This study also found some evidence that the contrast effect produced by the picture was confined to the respondents who fixated on it; among respondents who never fixated on the picture, there was some evidence of an assimilation effect.

5.3 THE CONCEPT OF VISIBILITY

The findings on the placement of images support the larger point that not all information on a Web page is equally visible—that is, equally likely to be noticed and attended to by respondents or other users. If the banner blindness hypothesis is generally true, then information in the header of a Web page is less visible than information in other locations. There may also be a general gradient of visibility from the top left portion of the screen (just below the header) to the bottom right. This gradient may reflect how users scan the information on a Web page. Nielsen (2006) tracked the eye movements of more than 200 users as they scanned different Web pages. Overall, their eye movements followed an F-shaped pattern. Users typically started at the top of the page, scanned horizontally to the right side, moved further down the left side of the page, scanned over to the right again, moved down the page further, and so on. Their horizontal scans to the right tended to become progressively shorter, creating the appearance of an F. This pattern of scanning material on Web pages implies that the top left corner is the most visible area on a Web page and the bottom right corner the least visible.

Response formats. Online surveys use a variety of response formats, including boxes for text entry, check-all-that-apply items, grids, and so on, but two of the most common are radio buttons and dropdown boxes (see Chapter 4). With both dropdown boxes and radio buttons, the different options may differ systematically in their visibility.

Consider dropdown boxes. When there is a long list of possible answers, dropdown boxes often display only a subset of them, and the respondent must scroll up or down to see the remaining options. Clearly, the options displayed initially are more visible than the hidden options and, thus, more likely to be selected. Even when the question uses some other response format, the options may not all be equally visible. With options displayed in radio button format, respondents seem to pay greater attention to the earlier options and less attention to the later ones (for example, see Figure 5.10 below, taken from Galešic, Tourangeau, Couper, and Conrad, 2009).

These differences in the level of attention respondents give to the different options can lead to response order effects. Response order effects are common in surveys (see Holbrook, Krosnick, Moore, and Tourangeau, 2007, for a recent analysis of response order effects in telephone surveys). These effects refer to changes in the popularity of a response option according to its position in the list of possible responses. The effects generally take one of two forms—sometimes options are more popular when they come at the beginning of the list (primacy effects) and sometimes they are more popular when they come at the end (recency effects). Primacy effects predominate in surveys that rely on the visual channel, including Web surveys. One account for response order effects is based on two main assumptions: First, respondents process the options they consider first more deeply than those they consider later and, second, they are more likely to select an option that they have thought about more deeply than ones to which they have given less thought.[2] This diminishing attention to later options partly accounts for the greater popularity of the options that respondents attend to first. In visual surveys, respondents are likely to consider the options in the order in which they are presented, whereas in auditory surveys they are likely to begin by considering the last option they heard (Krosnick, 1999).

One of our studies explored how the relative visibility of the response options might affect the size of the primacy effects in a Web survey (Couper, Tourangeau, Conrad, and Crawford, 2004). This study compared three response formats— radio buttons (a format that displays all the options on screen from the outset), a dropdown box that didn't display any of the options initially but required respondents to click to see them, and a dropdown box that showed five of the options initially but hid the other five (see Figure 5.10). We examined responses to two items, one asking about breakfast cereal (that item is the one shown in Figure 5.10) and a similar item asking about car purchases. Besides varying the response format, the experiment also varied the order of the response options. Roughly half the respondents got the options for the cereal item in the order shown in the figure, beginning with "Protein" and ending with "Vitamin E;" the remainder got these options in the opposite order. Regardless of the order of the other options, "None of the above" always came last. The experiment for the car item followed a similar design.

To assess the impact of the order of the response options, we examined the percentage of respondents who selected an option in the group of answers from "Protein" to "Fiber." Table 5.4 displays the key results from the experiment. With all three response formats, there were primacy effects; that is, in all three formats, respondents were more likely to choose one of the options in this group of answers when they were the first five options presented than when they were the last five. But the order effect was largest in the drop box condition in which only the first five options were visible from the outset. The options that were visible from the outset in that condition were chosen 27 percent more of the time than those which were not initially visible. The results were similar, though less dramatic, for the experiment involving the item on cars (see Couper et al., 2004b, for details). For both items, the interaction between the response format and response order variables was highly significant.

Response order and visibility. Nielsen's eye-tracking results indicate that there may be a general falloff in visibility as one proceeds from top to bottom of the screen

---

[2] There are two reasons why respondents might be prone to select the options that they think about more deeply. First, they may simply have a low threshold for selecting an option. For example, they may pick the first option that they consider that seems like an acceptable answer (rather than the best answer) and stop processing once they find such an answer. Or they may tend to think of reasons for selecting an option (exhibiting a "confirmatory bias") rather than reasons for rejecting it; the options considered first would have an advantage, according to this account, because respondents have less working memory capacity to generate reasons for selecting the later ones—their minds are cluttered with reasons for selecting the options they've already considered. Krosnick (1999), Sudman, Bradburn, and Schwarz (1996), and Tourangeau, Rips, and Rasinski (2000, Chapter 8) all present more extensive theoretical discussions of response order effects.

(a) Drop Box Version of the Item with Five Options Visible

(b) Drop Box Version of the Item with No Options Visible, Before Clicking

(c) Drop Box Version of the Item with No Options Visible, After Clicking

FIGURE 5.10. Two versions of an item about breakfast cereal. The top portion of the figure (panel a) shows the drop box that made five of the options visible initially but hid five more options; the middle panel (b) shows the conventional drop box format before the respondent clicked to reveal the options; and the bottom panel (c) shows the drop box after the respondent clicked. Respondents could also select a "None of the above" option (which is hidden in both drop box conditions). Reprinted with permission from Galešic et al., 2009.

TABLE 5.4. Percentage of Respondents (and Sample Sizes) Choosing Selected Answers, by Response Order and Format

Order of Options	Radio Buttons	Drop Box – None Visible	Drop Box – Five Visible
Protein to Vitamin E	61.4 (395)	60.0 (422)	67.6 (433)
Vitamin E to Protein	50.4 (433)	54.9 (437)	40.2 (440)
Difference	11.0	5.1	27.4

Note: The percentages refer to the proportion of respondents choosing one of the options from "Protein" to "Fiber." These were the first five options in the one order condition and the second five in the other.

and from left to the right. (Of course, it is also possible that a similar falloff occurs with printed pages.)

Do the successive response options in a list of response options show decreasing visibility as well? A study by Galešic, Tourangeau, Couper, and Conrad (2009) suggests that there is a gradient of visibility across response options displayed vertically. They tracked the eye movements of respondents as they completed a Web survey. The respondents fixated less often and for less total time on the later response options than on those near the beginning of the list. Figure 5.11 displays the eye-tracking results for two more or less typical respondents. Both of the respondents fixated more often on the options near the top of the list (in the color version of the figure, the red areas indicate more fixations; the green areas, fewer) than on those at the bottom, even though the second respondent (whose fixations are displayed in the bottom panel of the figure) selected an option from the second half of the list. Overall, both the total number of fixations and

(a) Fixations for a respondent who choose an answer from the first half of the options

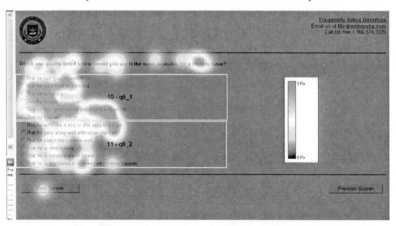

(b) Fixations for a respondent who choose an answer from the second half of the options

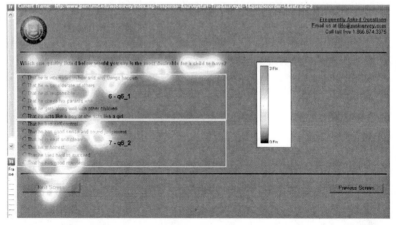

FIGURE 5.11. "Hot spot" display of fixations for a respondent who chose an option from the first six of the options presented (top panel) and for one who chose an option from the second six (bottom panel). (See color insert.)

the total fixation time were significantly greater on average for the response options in the first half of the list of options than for those in the second half.

These results on response format and response order suggest that two determinants of the visibility of a response option are whether the respondent has to do something to make the option appear on screen (as with the drop boxes) and where the option appears within the list of response options. The greater the effort required to see an item, the less visible it is; the further down an option is on the list of options, the lower its visibility.

The visibility of definitions. Research on the use of definitions in Web surveys also illustrates the importance of the visibility of information on screen. Survey items often contain terms that are unfamiliar to the respondents or that are used in some specialized way in the survey. A good deal of evidence suggests that respondents often misunderstand survey questions (e.g., Belson, 1981; Suessbrick, Schober, and Conrad, 2000). One possible solution is to provide definitions for the key terms in the questions. The trick is getting respondents to notice and read the definitions. Survey respondents may not think they need the definitions, particularly when the question asks about a seemingly familiar concept. Tourangeau, Conrad, Arens, Fricker, Lee, and Smith (2006) showed that respondents pretty much ignored the relatively technical definition of the term "disability" that was presented in the survey and relied instead on their everyday sense of that term. Such findings make it clear that it may be important not only to offer definitional help to respondents but to get them to read and apply that help.

Conrad, Couper, Tourangeau, and Peytchev (2006; see also Peytchev, Conrad, Couper, and Tourangeau, 2010) compared several methods by which respondents could access definitions experimentally. In these studies, relatively few respondents bothered to access the definitions, but they were more likely to access them if access was easy. In terms of visibility, the interfaces line up in the following order: 1) definitions always on screen (requiring only eye movements from the respondents); 2) rollovers (requiring only a movement of the mouse); 3) one-click (requiring both moving the mouse and clicking on the term); 4) two-click (requiring both mouse movements and two clicks); and 5) click-and-scroll (requiring movements of the mouse and at least two clicks). Not surprisingly, respondents seemed to pay more attention to definitions when they were more visible. We present a more detailed discussion of the issue of presenting definitions in Chapter 6.

Conclusions. Respondents to Web surveys (or Web users, more generally) are more likely to use information that they can see easily than information that is hidden or that requires some action before it becomes fully visible. The research on respondent's use (and non-use) of definitions argues for the general conclusion that the less visible information is the less likely it is to be processed by respondents. And, as the work of Gray and Fu (2004) shows, users often refuse even to make eye movements in order to see helpful information, rendering that information essentially invisible.

The visibility of information is likely to be affected by a large number of additional variables (see, for example, Ware, 2004), including at a minimum:

- The information's position on the page, as in the "banner blindness" phenomenon (see Benway, 1998; see also Nielsen, 2006);

- The information's position in a list of items (for example, a list of response options; Couper, Tourangeau, Conrad, and Crawford, 2004);
- Inherent characteristics of the item, such as its size, brightness, contrast with the background, and whether it moves or changes (Ware, 2004).

5.4 SUMMARY

The Web expands the visual possibilities for surveys far beyond those offered by traditional paper questionnaires. This chapter reviewed the evidence about how respondents are affected by the visual character of Web questionnaires. Respondents use visual cues like spacing and color to help them assign meanings to scale points. In addition, the position of an item within a list of response options or its position on the screen may affect the ratings the item receives. Respondents bring various assumptions to bear in using rating scales, such as the presumptions that the scale options follow one another in some logical order, that they are equally spaced, and that in a bipolar scale they are arrayed symmetrically around the midpoint. Respondents also use visual and graphical cues (e.g., the number of entry boxes and the associated labels) to help them decide how to format open-ended responses, such as dates or dollar amounts. Both types of cues seem to be useful in getting respondents to put their answers in the desired format. Clearly, scales should be designed to be consistent with their associated visual cues and with the heuristics respondents apply in interpreting them. For example, if researchers intend for the options to be equally spaced and symmetrical, they should make sure the options are displayed that way on screen.

Web surveys make it relatively easy for surveys to incorporate photographs, graphics, and other images, and these can be powerful contextual stimuli that affect how respondents construe the questions, what they consider in formulating their answers, and the standards they apply as they make judgments. There is no reason to think that images are any less influential than prior questions in shaping respondents' answers and, as a result, the images incorporated into a survey need to be chosen very carefully or avoided altogether if they are not clearly useful.

The position of information on screen is one of several variables that affect its visibility, or the likelihood that respondents will notice and attend to it. Certain areas of the screen, like the banner, are less likely to be attended to and there may be a general gradient of visibility from the top left of the screen to the bottom right. Respondents are much less likely to see and use information if they have to perform some action to render it visible.

Still, the fact that information is highly visible doesn't guarantee that respondents will use it in the way the researchers intended. Indeed, as the color studies indicate, visible information can backfire, misleading respondents about what the researchers intended (see also Redline, Tourangeau, Couper, and Conrad, 2009). More generally, survey respondents adopt the presumption of interpretability (Clark and Schober, 1991)—that is, they expect visual material to be meaningful and relevant. As a result, they try to interpret visual cues, and the interpretations they come up with may or may not coincide with what the researchers meant. Images, color, and other visual material that isn't essential to the purpose of the question should be carefully tested to ensure that they don't mislead respondents or should be avoided altogether.

(a) Scrolling design

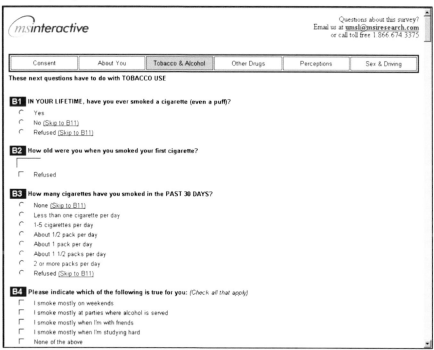

(b) Paging design

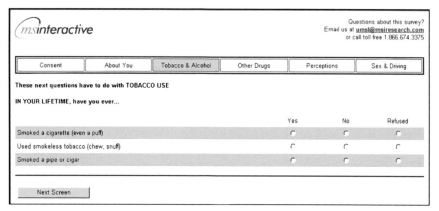

FIGURE 4.1. Examples of scrolling and paging designs (taken from Peytchev, Couper, McCabe and Crawford, 2006). The top panel shows a scrolling design; the bottom panel a paging design. Reprinted with permission from Peytchev, Couper, McCabe and Crawford, 2006.

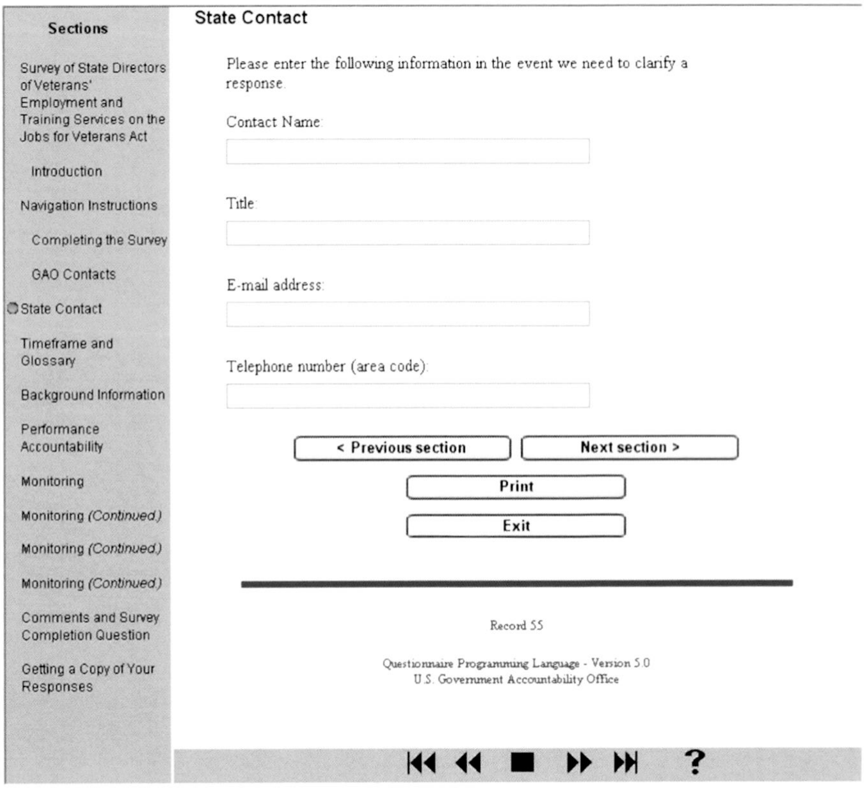

Sections

Survey of State Directors
of Veterans'
Employment and
Training Services on the
Jobs for Veterans Act

Introduction

Navigation Instructions

Completing the Survey

GAO Contacts

State Contact

Timeframe and
Glossary

Background Information

Performance
Accountability

Monitoring

Monitoring *(Continued)*

Monitoring *(Continued)*

Monitoring *(Continued)*

Comments and Survey
Completion Question

Getting a Copy of Your
Responses

State Contact

Please enter the following information in the event we need to clarify a
response.

Contact Name:

Title:

E-mail address:

Telephone number (area code):

[< Previous section]   [Next section >]

[Print]

[Exit]

Record 55

Questionnaire Programming Language - Version 5.0
U.S. Government Accountability Office

FIGURE 4.2. Use of panes in a survey from the US Government Accountability Office. The pane on the left allows respondents to switch sections; the pane at the bottom allows other movements through the questionnaire.

How much do you favor or oppose avoiding "fast food?"

FIGURE 5.4. Two formats for response scales. In the top scale, the options differ in both hue and brightness; in the bottom scale, they vary only in brightness. Adapted with permission from Tourangeau, Couper, and Conrad (2007).

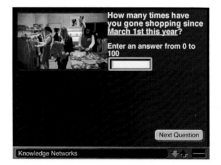

FIGURE 5.7. Two images used by Couper, Tourangeau, and Kenyon (2004). The left side shows shopping at a clothing store, a low frequency exemplar of the category of shopping; the right side shows shopping at a grocery store, a higher frequency exemplar. Some respondents got one photograph and some got the other. Other respondents in the experiment got both of these images or neither of them. Reprinted with permission from Couper, Tourangeau and Kenyon, 2004.

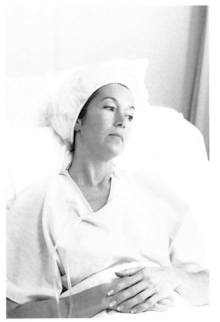

FIGURE 5.8. Photographs used by Couper, Conrad, and Tourangeau (2007). Respondents received one or the other picture in a Web survey. The pictures were presented on the same screen near a question about the respondent's own health, in the header of that screen, or on the screen just prior to the health item.

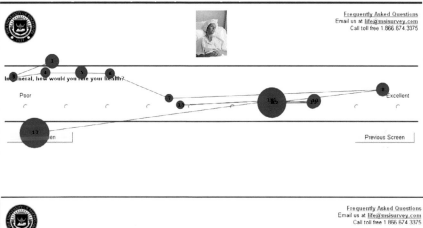

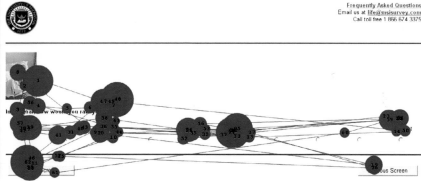

FIGURE 5.9. Gaze plots for two respondents in an eye-tracking study. In the top panel, the respondent never fixates on the photograph, which was presented in the header section of the Web page; in the bottom panel the respondent does look at the picture, which appears just above the question.

(a) Fixations for a respondent who choose an answer from the first half of the options

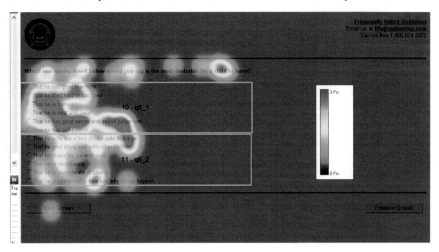

(b) Fixations for a respondent who choose an answer from the second half of the options

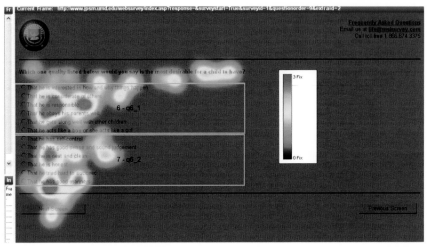

FIGURE 5.11. "Hot spot" display of fixations for a respondent who chose an option from the first six of the options presented (top panel) and for one who chose an option from the second six (bottom panel).

Thinking of all of the time that you use the Internet, what percentage of the time do you spend on the following activities? Please do not count the same activity categories more than once.

Please be sure your answers add up to 100%.

Your answers do not add up to 100%. Please revise your answers so that they add to 100%.

75	EMAIL - composing and reading messages
	NEWS - reading newspapers and news magazines; include weather, sports, and financial information
10	RETRIEVING INFORMATION - for example, with a search engine like Google
	INSTANT MESSAGING and CHATTING
	COMMERCE - buying and selling merchandise, stocks, services, etc.; do not include purchases for travel.
	TRAVEL PLANNING - transportation and lodging information; reservations, purchases, getting maps and directions
	VIDEO and MUSIC - downloading or streaming music, radio, movies, etc.; do not include time spent viewing downloaded files
	PLAYING GAMES - with remote players or at game sites; do not include time spent playing games downloaded from a web site.
	TAKING A COURSE - distance learning; only include time spent actually on line.
	OTHER
85	TOTAL

🔒 🌐 Internet

FIGURE 6.3. Constant sum-item with running tally and server-side feedback. The items in Conrad, Couper, Tourangeau, Gale**š**ic, and Yan (2009) displayed one form or feedback or the other.

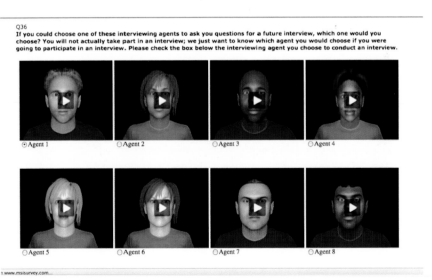

FIGURE 6.6. Choice of virtual interviewer. Respondents were required to click on each virtual interviewer to see and hear it present a survey introduction (Conrad, Schober and Nielsen, 2011). Reprinted with permission from Conrad, Schober & Nielsen, 2011.

FIGURE 6.7. Video-recorded interviewer from Fuchs and Funke (2007).

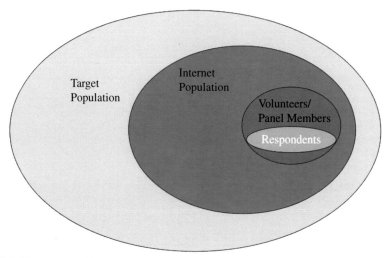

FIGURE 8.1. The largest ellipse represents the target population; the smallest ellipse, the respondents to a particular Web survey. The intermediate ellipses represent the subset of the target population with Web access and the population members who join the Web panel from which the respondents are drawn. The difference between the target and the Internet populations constitutes coverage error. The difference between the Internet population and the volunteers or panel members constitutes selection bias. The difference between the volunteers/panel members and the respondents to the survey constitutes nonresponse error.

INTERACTIVE FEATURES AND MEASUREMENT ERROR

The Web is an unusually diverse and rich survey mode. In fact, it's not a single mode at all but a multimodal communication medium. This gives survey designers many options. They can present questions textually as in a paper questionnaire; they can add visual images (which are possible with paper but easier and cheaper with online questionnaires); they can present questions via recorded speech; or they can design the questionnaire so that a video-recorded interviewer presents the questions, giving the survey the feel of a face-to-face interview. The similarity of Web and interviewer administration is increased when the Web questionnaire takes some action in response to what the respondent does or doesn't do. For example, a Web survey can offer to clarify the question if the respondent is inactive for a given interval. This can give the questionnaire a feeling of animacy and intentionality that makes the respondent's experience qualitatively different from the experience of filling out a static paper or Web questionnaire.

This chapter examines the possibilities for exploiting the Web's interactive capabilities for survey data collection. There are several possible reasons for including interactive features in Web questionnaires. First, as with many evolving technologies, Web survey designers sometimes build in interactive features simply because they can. Consider animated question text that arrives character by character or rotates in three dimensions. Designers might use such techniques to add visual interest to the questionnaire or to make the task more fun for respondents. Second, sometimes the Web counterpart of a technique used in more static modes is inherently interactive. For example, visual analog scales (e.g., a 100-point scale on which the respondent indicates his or her opinion) have been used for some time in paper questionnaires. In the Web realization of visual analog scales, respondents typically manipulate a slider bar to register their answers; this produces an animated display of the pointer (and sometimes a numerical value) moving in synch with respondents' mouse movements. Third, some techniques can really only be implemented in online questionnaires because of their interactive character. For example, it is possible in a Web survey to allow respondents to choose an animated, virtual interviewer with particular characteristics, such as specific age, race, or gender. There is little precedent for this kind of choice with human interviewers (although see Catania, Binson, Canchola, Pollack, Hauck, and Coates, 1996, for an exception). A final reason for building interactive questionnaires is to test whether phenomena found in other modes are also observed in Web surveys when similar conditions are created through interactivity. For example, Fuchs (2009) examined whether the gender of video-recorded interviewers asking questions affects answers to gender-related questions as the gender of human interviewers does.

Web survey designers sometimes try to exploit the interactive capabilities of the Web to decrease measurement error, reduce breakoffs, or produce some other desirable outcome. For example, it is relatively easy to make definitions of key question terms available to respondents with a mouse click or a rollover. Definitions-on-demand can help respondents understand questions that might otherwise confuse them and thus increase response accuracy (Conrad, Schober, and Coiner, 2007). In addition, Web questionnaires can be programmed to offer help when the respondent shows evidence of confusion; this also improves comprehension and response accuracy (Conrad et al., 2007). Interactive features can also be used to discourage respondent behaviors associated with poor data quality. For example, the questionnaire can present messages to respondents who answer very quickly ("speeders"), asking them to take more time. These interventions have been shown to slow respondents down (Conrad, Couper, Tourangeau, and Zhang, in preparation).

The problem is that interactive features do not necessarily have their intended effects. Sometimes, as with definitions, respondents just don't use the feature very often. In other cases, the feature backfires. As we shall see in Section 6.2, this often happens with progress indicators. This chapter reviews what we know about the effectiveness of various interactive features that have been tried in Web surveys, assessing their impact on completion rates, measurement error, and other outcomes related to survey error.

6.1 DIMENSIONS OF INTERACTIVITY

As a preliminary matter, it will be useful to explore what we mean by interactivity. Interactive features include *dynamic* features—that is, features that involve some kind of movement or change in what is displayed to the respondent. They also include features that are *responsive* to user actions. The most complete form of such responsiveness involves turn-by-turn interactions as in telephone speech dialogue systems (in which the user speaks, the system speaks, the user speaks again, and so on). In Web survey interactions, however, there are often just one or two respondent turns (e.g., the respondent clicks a radio button and then clicks on the "Next" button); interactivity, as we use the term, does not require extended exchanges. Some responsive features in a Web survey may be invoked by intermittent respondent behaviors; for example, a help feature may be triggered when the user's actions indicate she or he is having difficulty. Such features are responsive in that they are initiated by particular respondent actions. Many features of automated questionnaires in general—not just Web-based questionnaires—such as skips, fills, edit checks, conditional branching, and so on—are responsive, and these are often implemented in Web questionnaires. Nonresponsive dynamic features change what is displayed irrespective of what the user does. Responsive features take action contingent on particular user actions; they are also dynamic in that some change results from their actions.

We also distinguish between features that simulate attributes or behaviors of humans and those that do not. For example, human interviewers can detect respondent comprehension difficulty, so simulating this ability in a Web questionnaire gives it human-like character. Conversely, computers can easily maintain running tallies of answers, and they do this with greater accuracy than human interviewers; as a result, we consider this feature to be machine-like. We make this distinction between *human-like* and *machine-like* features because human-like interactions may change the experience of completing a Web survey, making it more like the experience of an interview.

These two dimensions—responsiveness and humanness—define a space of interactive features. The impact of a given feature on measurement may be affected by its position in this space. For example, responsive and human-like features may be particularly effective at improving respondents' performance. Consider a prompt to slow down and think more. Respondents may attend to such prompts because the prompts are clearly triggered by one of their actions and because the prompts reflect an evaluation of their behavior of the sort typically made by another human.

A video recording of an interviewer asking survey questions is not responsive; the video file plays regardless of what the respondent does and does not change based on the respondent's actions. But the content of the video is certainly identifiable as a human interviewer so the feature is *dynamic* and *human-like*. Other features are much like the video-recorded interviewer just mentioned but do not display content that looks or sounds like a human interviewer. We classify these as *dynamic* and *machine-like*. One example is the display of video vignettes rather than text to provide information to respondents before they make an evaluation. One study (Heinberg, Hung, Kapteyn, Lusardi, and Yoong, 2010) presented vignettes to respondents in which a couple talked over a financial decision and one member of the couple explained key concepts to the other. The investigators then tested the respondents on their understanding of the financial concepts. The video vignette approach was effective for communicating content to respondents but did not seem to improve their task performance. But a *reactive* and *machine-like* feature, such as automatic tallies, is likely to improve respondent performance by carrying out the arithmetic.

6.2 RESPONSIVE, MACHINE-LIKE FEATURES

We begin our examination of interactivity in Web surveys by looking at features that are responsive and machine-like. We focus on five such features—progress indicators, running tallies, visual analog scales, interactive grids, and on-demand definitions.

6.2.1 Progress Indicators

Many Web questionnaires present one or two questions per page, with respondents submitting their answers to advance to the next page. A potential drawback to the paging approach is that it gives respondents no indication of how much of the questionnaire they have completed and how much is left (Peytchev, Couper, McCabe and Crawford, 2006; see also Chapter 4). To compensate for the absence of this information, designers sometimes include *progress indicators,* such as a graphical bar that increases in length as the respondent completes more of the questionnaire or that provides textual feedback (e.g., "13 percent completed") on respondent progress. Progress indicators are *responsive* because they change as respondents advance from page to page; they are *machine-like* because they communicate information that interviewers usually do not convey (aside from occasional unscripted comments such as "we're almost done"). The assumption seems to be that respondents want to be informed about their position in the questionnaire and that providing this information will increase the likelihood they will finish it.

Early studies. The early empirical evidence on the effects of progress indicators is mixed. Couper, Traugott and Lamias (2001) found no difference in completion rates when progress indicators were used versus when they were not used but suggested that the potential benefits of progress indicators might have been offset by the extra download time required to display the graphical feedback, given the slow Internet connections of the day. A related study by Crawford, Couper, and Lamias (2001) controlled for download time and found a *lower* completion rate when progress indicators were used than when they were not. They observed that many of the breakoffs occurred on open questions, apparently because typing in an answer is more burdensome than selecting one from a set of fixed options. In a follow-up experiment, they dropped the open questions and observed a modest but reliable increase in completion rates with a progress indicator. So, these early studies suggest that progress indicators can increase completion rates, reduce them, or have no impact.

Subsequent work shows that the effects of progress indicators on completion rates depends on several other variables, including the actual and expected length of the questionnaire, the rate of apparent progress, the frequency of feedback, and the difficulty of the questions. Depending on the combination of these attributes, progress indicators can increase or reduce breakoffs. A key finding emerging from this work is that progress indicators boost completion rates when they provide encouraging feedback but depress them when they provide discouraging feedback.

Expected and actual length. Consider the length of the questionnaire. Evidence that one is moving quickly through the questionnaire should be more encouraging than evidence of slow progress. With a relatively short questionnaire, a progress indicator will generally communicate to respondents that they are making good progress toward completing the task and this should lead to fewer breakoffs than no progress indicator. With a long questionnaire, however, a progress indicator may communicate just how long the task is likely to last and this may well increase breakoffs relative to no progress indicator. Yan, Conrad, Tourangeau, and Couper (2011) demonstrated this interaction between the presence of a progress indicator and the length of the questionnaire by comparing the breakoff rate for a questionnaire with 101 items to the breakoff rate for a questionnaire with 155 items; the longer questionnaire included the 101 items that made up the shorter one, plus 54 additional items. With the shorter questionnaire, 9.8 percent of respondents broke off with a progress indicator but 12.2 percent broke off without one. With the longer questionnaire, the pattern was reversed: 15.8 percent of respondents broke off without a progress indicator but 17.3 percent broke off with one.

Whether progress seems to be fast or slow may depend on how long the respondent expects the survey to take. Such expectations are known to affect how long the task *seems* to take (e.g., Boltz, 1993). In the early study by Crawford, Couper, and Lamias (2001), respondents were told the task would last either 8 to10 or 20 minutes. The presence of a progress indicator generally lowered completion rates in that study, but this effect was more extreme when respondents were told the task would last 20 minutes. Presumably, those who started the survey even though they expected it to last 20 minutes felt particularly misled when the progress feedback indicated the survey might take even longer. The mismatch between the promised and actual duration primarily reflected the first few questions in the questionnaire, which required open responses; these items accounted for about 20 percent of all the items but 50 percent of the *time* respondents would ultimately spend on the survey. Thus, if a respondent extrapolated from the early items, the estimated duration would exceed the duration in the invitation, promoting breakoffs.

Yan and her coauthors (2011) demonstrated a similar phenomenon experimentally. In this study, the researchers manipulated respondents' expectations about the duration of the questionnaire by either under- or overstating the likely duration in the invitation email. Specifically, they invited panel members to respond to the short or long version of the questionnaire described earlier. For the short questionnaire, the understated duration was 5 minutes and the overstated duration was 25 minutes; for the long questionnaire, the corresponding durations were 10 and 40 minutes. Half of the respondents were given progress feedback and half were not, creating a two (questionnaire length) by two (promised duration) by two (progress indicator) design. The breakoff rates are displayed in Figure 6.1. Progress indicators reduced breakoffs (8.2 percent) relative to no progress indicators (12.1 percent) when the invitation promised a short task and the questionnaire was in fact short (rightmost pair of bars in Figure 6.1), suggesting that when respondents expect a low-effort experience and the feedback is consistent with these expectations, they are less likely to break off than their counterparts who do not get any feedback. So, in this case, progress indicators helped. In contrast, progress indicators did not help when respondents expected a long task and the progress feedback confirmed these expectations

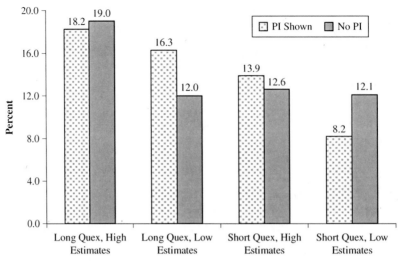

FIGURE 6.1. Breakoff rates for eight experimental conditions in Yan et al. (2011). The study varied both the actual length of the questionnaire and the expected length; in addition, it varied whether a progress indicator was displayed (solid bars) or not (bars with dots). Reprinted with permission from Yan et al., 2011.

(leftmost bars): there was no advantage to progress indicators under these conditions and, in fact, the breakoff rate was nonsignificantly higher with a progress indicator (16.3 percent) than without one (12.1 percent). For these last two experimental conditions, breakoffs occurred reliably earlier on average when respondents were shown a progress indicator than when they were not, further suggesting that progress feedback can serve as a disincentive to continue when it confirms negative expectations. In the remaining conditions, in which the length of the questionnaire was overstated, the progress indicator had no apparent effect on breakoffs.

Progress indicators don't necessarily intensify the effects of violated duration expectations. Heerwegh and Loosveldt (2006) invited respondents to take part in a survey of "approximately 20 to 25 minutes" or one that was "as short as possible." The actual duration was between 36 and 40 minutes. Neither the stated duration nor the progress bar variables affected completion by themselves or in combination. What we don't know is whether progress indicators might have helped if the experimenters had overstated the actual duration but clearly progress feedback did not help when the duration was understated.

Rate of apparent progress. It is possible that the speed of progress matters more early in the questionnaire than later on because, as we argue in Chapter 3, respondents decide whether to complete the task based on their early experiences in the questionnaire. To explore this idea, we (Conrad, Couper, Tourangeau, and Peytchev, 2005, 2010) manipulated two different progress indicators to communicate either rapid or slow progress early on. When the early progress was quick, later progress was slow; when the early feedback was slow, progress got faster later in the questionnaire. We referred to the first of these as fast-to-slow and the second as slow-to-fast progress indicators. A third indicator displayed constant speed progress feedback throughout the questionnaire. When the early feedback indicated rapid progress, fewer respondents broke off (11.3 percent) than when the early feedback indicated slow progress (21.8 percent). Encouraging news early in the questionnaire had a couple of other positive effects in this study. When the feedback indicated rapid early progress, respondents rated the questionnaire to be more interesting and they judged it to take less time than when it indicated slow progress early on. This last finding underscores the impact of early feedback on respondents' subjective experience because the questionnaire actually took longer for the group whose early feedback indicated quick initial progress. In the study by Heerwegh and Loosveldt (2006), a fast-to-slow progress indicator led to lower missing data rates than no progress indicator.

The enduring effects of early progress feedback was confirmed in a survival analysis by Matzat, Snijders, and van der Horst (2009), who looked for evidence that the likelihood of breakoff varied across 25 "check points" distributed through the questionnaire. They used progress indicators similar to the ones used by Conrad and his colleagues (Conrad et al., 2005, 2010), and found no evidence that the impact of early feedback was diminished later; slow-to-fast progress increased breakoffs equally across the questionnaire. Encouraging early feedback can also reduce the proportion of respondents who break off when they encounter difficult questions. In our study, respondents answered either a closed or open form of a question about automobile ownership; the closed question presented an easier response task than the open version. Breakoffs were very rare for the closed version of the question irrespective of the type of progress indicator, and they were relatively common for the open version for all of the progress indicators, except the one that moved quickly in the beginning. It seems the benefits of early encouraging progress feedback include not only reduced breakoffs and an improved subjective experience but also a kind of inoculation against the effects of difficult response tasks.

Given that some questions are more difficult to answer than others, it might be better to calculate progress in terms of overall effort rather than the number of questions. In the study by Crawford and his colleagues (2001), respondents spent disproportionally more time on the early than the later questions because the early ones required open text responses, whereas the later items were closed questions. As a result, the feedback (which was based on questions completed) provided an unnecessarily discouraging picture. This suggests that progress feedback might be more accurate and potentially more encouraging if it characterizes task completion in more relevant units than the number of questions or pages completed. Typical completion time would be a reasonable surrogate for total effort and could be derived from pretest data.

Frequency of progress information. Because survey designers may not know whether progress feedback will be perceived as encouraging or discouraging—this will depend on the many factors we have been discussing—it would be ideal to display progress feedback in a way that maximizes the benefits of encouraging information and minimizes the costs of discouraging information. It might be possible to achieve this by displaying the feedback intermittently. If the information is *discouraging*, presenting it on every page might well be experienced as a drum beat of bad

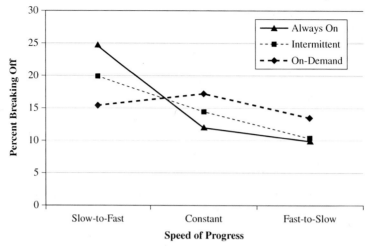

FIGURE 6.2. Breakoffs as a function of frequency of progress feedback and speed of progress. Reprinted with permission from Conrad, Couper, Tourangeau and Peytchev, 2010, Experiment 2.

news, intensifying the experience of slow progress. However, less frequent presentation of bad news might reduce its impact on completion rates. Moreover, even if it is slow, progress will be more evident when several questions intervene between each display than when the feedback is presented on each page. Thus, frequent presentation of discouraging feedback might increase breakoffs relative to less frequent presentation.

Presenting *encouraging* feedback on an intermittent schedule might also increase completion rates. If respondents find the display of progress on every page to be encouraging, then the larger changes between intermittent displays should be at least as motivating as more frequent feedback.

Conrad and his colleagues (2010) tested the effect of three frequencies of progress feedback for three speeds of early progress. More specifically, they displayed feedback information on every page ("Always On"), at each of the twelve section breaks ("Intermittent"), or very rarely ("On-Demand" feedback that respondents almost never accessed). They also computed progress so that the early feedback was encouraging (Fast-to-Slow), discouraging (Slow-to-Fast), or neutral ("Constant speed"). The results are presented in Figure 6.2. When discouraging feedback (left side of the figure) was presented all the time (Always On) breakoffs were at their highest; when the feedback was presented intermittently (Intermittent) or very rarely (On Demand), breakoffs decreased. This suggests that the costs of discouraging progress feedback can be reduced by presenting it less frequently. In contrast, encouraging information (right side of the figure) led to the lowest levels of breakoffs whether the feedback was presented all the time, intermittently, or very rarely, suggesting that encouraging feedback is highly motivating at any frequency of presentation. Thus, from this study (Conrad et al., 2010), it appears that intermittent feedback reduces the costs of discouraging feedback on completion rates without affecting the benefits of encouraging feedback.

Dynamic progress indicators. The progress indicators we have discussed so far are only minimally responsive because they are incremented in exactly the same way for all respondents as they advance from one page or question to the next. This is possible because the questionnaires in these studies did not have skip patterns—that is, everyone got all of the questions. This simplifies the calculation of progress because the total number of questions is the same for all respondents at all points in the questionnaire. But skip patterns are routine in practice and they can lead to large jumps in progress between items if the total number of questions possible is still used as the denominator for calculating the percent completed. The progress indicator might seem to lurch forward relative to the smaller, more uniform increments prior to the skip. Heerwegh and Loosveldt (2006, p. 200) report exactly this kind of discontinuity. Even worse, questionnaires with a lot of skip patterns can create a false sense of slow progress early if the respondent will skip a lot of the later questions.

Kaczmirek (2009) proposed a method for smoothing such discontinuous change by spreading it over the remaining pages in the questionnaire. When the respondent skips over several questions, Kaczmirek's "dynamic" approach recalculates the total number of pages and the current page number, taking into account that the questionnaire is now effectively shorter. Imagine that the skip pattern in a 30-item questionnaire advances the respondent four questions, from question 4 to 8. Under the usual approach, the respondent would have moved from the 13 percent to 27 percent complete—a large jump compared to the 3 percent increments prior to the skip. But under the dynamic approach, the question to which the respondent was routed would be redefined as question 5 (instead of 8) and the total number of questions reduced to 26. Based on Kaczmirek's algorithm, the progress feedback would change from 13 percent complete to 17 percent with increments of about 4 percent from that point forward. Kaczmirek tested the dynamic calculation of progress and found that it led to almost 6 percent fewer breakoffs than the static approach. Although this difference was apparently not significant, it suggests there may be benefits to the dynamic approach to calculating progress. In Kaczmirek's study, there was just one skip, but in a complex production survey there may be many skip patterns producing numerous possible paths through the questionnaire. Unless progress is calculated dynamically, the feedback might seem to advance sporadically without any apparent reason for the size of the change.

Summary of progress indicator studies. Table 6.1 presents a summary of the published findings on progress indicators and breakoff rates. Callegaro, Villar, and Yang (2011) carried out a meta-analysis of the studies in Table 6.1 and a few additional unpublished studies. Their conclusions are largely in line with our characterization of the research so far. First, constant-speed progress indicators do not reduce breakoffs and, if anything, they increase them, though not significantly. Second, they also find that across studies, fast early progress reduces breakoffs and slow early progress increases them relative to no progress indicator. The importance of feedback early in the questionnaire is consistent with the sample-decide-reconsider model of breakoffs proposed in Chapter 3 (see Section 3.6), which assumes that respondents

TABLE 6.1. Breakoff Rates and Progress Indicators, by Study and Experimental Conditions

Study	Conditions	Breakoff Rate (n)
Couper, Traugott, and Lamias (2001)	Progress Indicator	10.1 (378)
	No Progress Indicator	13.6 (376)
Crawford, Couper, and Lamias (2001)	8–10 Minutes	
	Progress Indicator	32.2 (486)
	No Progress Indicator	27.8 (487)
	20 Minutes	
	Progress Indicator	30.6 (437)
	No Progress Indicator	23.1 (425)
Healey, Macpherson, and Kuijten (2005)	Progress Indicator	14.3 (490)
	No Progress Indicator	13.3 (481)
Kaczmirek (2009)	Continuous Progress Indicator	22.9 (205)
	Dynamic Progress Indicator	16.8 (190)
	Accelerating Progress Indicator	17.0 (194)
	No Progress Indicator	14.1 (170)
Matzat, Snijders, and van der Horst (2009)	Slow-to-Fast Indicator	
	Long Questionnaire	11.0 (342)
	Short Questionnaire	15.6 (278)
	Constant Indicator	
	Long Questionnaire	13.1 (297)
	Short Questionnaire	10.4 (299)
	Fast-to-Slow Indicator	
	Long Questionnaire	9.0 (367)
	Short Questionnaire	11.1 (243)
	No Progress Indicator	
	Long Questionnaire	10.5 (279)
	Short Questionnaire	6.4 (355)
Conrad, Couper, Tourangeau, and Peytchev (2010)		
Experiment 1	Slow-to-Fast Indicator	21.8 (530)
	Constant Indicator	14.4 (562)
	Fast-to-Slow Indicator	11.3 (532)
	No Progress Indicator	12.7 (1,563)
Experiment 2	Slow-to-Fast Indicator	
	On-demand	15.4 (324)
	Intermittent	19.9 (276)
	Always on	24.8 (295)
	Constant Indicator	
	On-demand	17.2 (290)
	Intermittent	14.4 (340)
	Always on	12.0 (359)
	Fast-to-Slow Indicator	
	On-demand	13.5 (326)
	Intermittent	10.4 (327)
	Always on	9.9 (323)
	No Progress Indicator	14.3 (335)

(Continued)

TABLE 6.1 (*Continued*)

Study	Conditions	Breakoff Rate (n)
Yan, Conrad, Tourangeau, & Couper (2011)	Progress Indicator	
	Long Q'aire/High Estimate	16.3 (447)
	Long Q'aire/Low Estimate	18.2 (461)
	Short Q'aire/High Estimate	13.9 (267)
	Short Q'aire/Low Estimate	8.2 (669)
	No Progress Indicator	
	Long Q'aire/High Estimate	12.0 (207)
	Long Q'aire/Low Estimate	19.0 (237)
	Short Q'aire/High Estimate	12.6 (135)
	Short Q'aire/Low Estimate	12.1 (339)

make a tentative commitment to complete a questionnaire based on their early experiences with the survey. Rapid early progress may be an important cue that the survey will be easy to finish. The conclusions reached by Callegaro and his colleagues are also consistent with the findings in Table 6.1—progress indicators by themselves do not appear to lower breakoffs, they may increase breakoffs when they offer discouraging news, and they only clearly reduce breakoffs when they offer unusually positive feedback (as with the Fast-to-Slow indicators or a very short questionnaire).

Overall, then, encouraging feedback can reduce breakoff rates and produce other desirable outcomes. Still, there are two important caveats. First, there are many null effects in the literature, studies in which progress indicators had no effect on completion or other measures; these are not listed in the table. We did not include them because it's hard to know exactly why there was no effect in most of these studies; it often isn't clear whether the feedback encouraged or discouraged respondents. Many other variables seem to determine the effects of progress indicators, and depending on their values progress indicators can help, hurt, or have no impact. The second caveat is that in production surveys, the feedback given to respondents should be *accurate*. The studies that used variable-speed progress indicators used them to shed light on the process by which respondents decide to continue a questionnaire or to break off, not as a practical method to be applied in production surveys. As far as we know, no one advocates giving misleading feedback to respondents in non-methodological studies. Still, the method used to take skip patterns into account (or ignoring skip patterns) may create a misleading impression of the rate of progress for some respondents.

There may be better designs for progress indicators than those that are currently used. It is typically assumed that the question or page is the appropriate unit of progress, but sections of the questionnaire or other larger units might be appropriate. Yan and her colleagues (Yan et al., 2011) compared section-level progress feedback (e.g., "25 percent of section 2 out of 12 sections") to global feedback ("18 percent completed"); they found no difference between the two. Still, simple graphical bars that are filled as more questions are completed or percent-complete figures are not the only possible designs for progress indicators and other designs might change the way respondents experience the feedback.

6.2.2 Running Tallies

One thing that computers do better than people is arithmetic, so it makes sense to automate the calculations required for certain numerical responses in Web surveys. It's common in self-administered surveys to ask respondents about quantities associated with each component of an overall activity, where the component quantities must add up to some overall total—a "constant sum." For example, respondents might be asked about the percent of their overall grocery expenditures allocated to dairy, poultry, fish, other meats, fresh produce, breads and baked desserts, and all other foods; the individual percentages must sum to 100 percent. One reason survey researchers present constant-sum items is to explore how a total quantity is distributed across its parts. It has also been suggested that the quality of the individual estimates (the parts) is improved relative to isolated judgments because of the context provided by the other estimates (e.g., Szoc, Thomas, and Barlas, 2010). A potential problem with constant-sum items is that the individual components might not add up to the constant sum. It is relatively easy to program a Web survey to display a running tally so that respondents can quickly check whether the components do in fact add up to the target. Running tallies are responsive in the sense that the tally is updated as the respondent enters each new quantity; they are machine-like in that computers can easily compute and display the total but it is difficult for people to do this.

Running tallies seem likely to promote responses that add up to the constant sum, but that doesn't mean the component quantities are more *accurate* than they would have been without such feedback. Well-formed answers—those that add up to the requisite total—are clearly preferable to ill-formed responses, which are necessarily incomplete or incorrect; but if respondents simply adjust their answers to hit the target sum without attempting to answer more accurately, there will be little benefit from promoting well-formed answers.

To determine how displaying arithmetic feedback affects the well-formedness of constant sum responses, Conrad, Couper, Tourangeau, Galešic, and Yan (2009) asked respondents to report the percent of time typically spent on each of nine Internet activities. They compared the results under three feedback conditions—when a running tally was presented, when a message was generated by the server after the respondent submitted the answers if they didn't add up to the constant sum, and when no feedback was presented (see Figure 6.3). A running tally led to well-formed responses 96.5 percent of the time, server-side feedback led to well-formed responses 93.1 percent of the time, and no feedback led to well-formed responses only 84.8 percent of the time. The running tally produced these high levels of well-formed responses in less time (88.8 seconds) than the server-side feedback (98.8 seconds); it's likely that respondents receiving server-side feedback spent additional time revising their answers after they got the feedback.

In a follow-up study, Conrad and his colleagues (2009) presented a constant-sum item about daily time use in which the component answers (taking care of household members, eating, and shopping) were supposed to add up to 24 hours. Again, both a running tally and server-side feedback produced higher percentages of well-formed

Thinking of all of the time that you use the Internet, what percentage of the time do you spend on the following activities? Please do not count the same activity categories more than once.

Please be sure your answers add up to 100%.

Your answers do not add up to 100%. Please revise your answers so that they add to 100%.

75	EMAIL - composing and reading messages
	NEWS - reading newspapers and news magazines; include weather, sports, and financial information
10	RETRIEVING INFORMATION - for example, with a search engine like Google
	INSTANT MESSAGING and CHATTING
	COMMERCE - buying and selling merchandise, stocks, services, etc.; do not include purchases for travel.
	TRAVEL PLANNING - transportation and lodging information, reservations, purchases, getting maps and directions
	VIDEO and MUSIC - downloading or streaming music, radio, movies, etc.; do not include time spent viewing downloaded files.
	PLAYING GAMES - with remote players or at game sites; do not include time spent playing games downloaded from a web site.
	TAKING A COURSE - distance learning; only include time spent actually on line.
	OTHER
85	TOTAL

FIGURE 6.3. Constant sum-item with running tally and server-side feedback. The items in Conrad, Couper, Tourangeau, Galešic, and Yan (2009) displayed one form or feedback or the other. (See color insert.)

answers than no feedback; in addition, the estimates under these forms of feedback were closer to time use estimates from the American Time Use Survey. Conrad and his coauthors interpreted this as evidence that feedback improved the validity of the answers. They also found similar benefits from a running tally with the constant-sum question presented at the end of the questionnaire. That item asked respondents about the time they spent on each section of the questionnaire; the estimates for each section were supposed to add up to the total time spent on the questionnaire. The running tally (there was no server-side feedback in this experiment) led to both more well-formed and more accurate responses. So, it appears that this type of interactive feedback increases the proportion of answers that add up to the target total and increases the accuracy of the answers.

6.2.3 Visual Analog Scales

Rating scales have been used to collect information on subjective judgments since the earliest days of social and psychological research. When presented visually, the scale can be designed as a series of discrete points, such as a seven-point scale or a feeling thermometer running from 0 to 100; alternatively, the scale can be designed as a continuum on which the respondent selects a location on an unnumbered dimension. We refer to the first of these as discrete response scales, the second as visual analog scales (VAS). Discrete response scales are used far more often than visual analog scales in survey research; however, VAS's are widely used in health and medical research and in market research settings (Couper, Tourangeau, Conrad, and Singer, 2006). They may be attractive for surveys because, in principle, they allow respondents to express their position with more precision than discrete scales do; in addition, the numerical labels on a discrete scale can affect the interpretation of the scale points (e.g., Schwarz, Knäuper, Hippler, Noelle-Neumann, and Clark, 1991). Web surveys can incorporate VAS's that allow respondents to manipulate a graphical slider to register their position on the continuum.

In a Web survey experiment, Couper and his colleagues (2006) compared two versions of a VAS to four discrete scales with radio buttons at each option and two additional discrete scales requiring respondents to type in the number corresponding to the scale point they selected. One of the VAS's displayed the numerical value of the respondent's current choice; this value changed as the respondent moved the slider over an otherwise unnumbered continuum. The other VAS did not display any numerical feedback. The discrete scales varied in whether they had a midpoint and in whether the points had numerical labels. Respondents were given eight short vignettes about people with a particular attribute (e.g., athletic ability, a drinking problem) and were asked to indicate the degree to which this attribute was due to genetics or the environment. The extremes ("100 percent Genes," "100 percent Environment") and midpoint ("50 percent Genes, 50 percent Environment") were labeled in all of the scales.

They didn't find many measurement advantages for the VAS. Breakoffs and item non-response for the eight experimental items were both higher for the VAS formats than for the other formats and response times were longer. Some of the performance problems from the VAS might have been related to downloading the Java applet for the slider (or to having a compatible version of Java installed and enabled), but the effects persisted across the items even though the download problem should affect only the first of the items. There was no difference between the VAS and the other scales in the distribution of answers to the eight questions. There was one possible advantage for the VAS: respondents selected the middle option less often with the VAS than other scale formats.

Still, it is possible that VAS's increase the predictive validity of the data. Thomas (2010) explored this possibility by asking respondents to rate a behavior such as "Ate Mexican Food" on nine dimensions such as "good-bad," "like-don't like," "important to me-not important to me," and then used these ratings to model the frequency of the behavior in the last 30 days and the likelihood of the behavior in the next 30 days. The respondents made their ratings on one of three VAS's (continuous, five segments, 100 segments) or one of two discrete rating scales (fully labeled or just the end points labeled). Thomas found better predictions for the continuous and 100-segment VAS's and the fully labeled discrete scale than for the five-part VAS and the discrete scale with just the end points labeled. He interpreted these results as indicating general comparability between the answers collected with VAS's and those collected with discrete scales; that is, he did not provide a strong endorsement of VAS's.

Funke, Reips and Thomas (2011) report additional evidence that data quality from VAS's is no better than that from discrete scales in Web surveys. They presented respondents with either discrete scales (radio button) or VAS's, displayed vertically or horizontally. Respondents rated two abstract product concepts on scales whose end points were labeled "Very Negative" and "Very Positive." The VAS's led to higher breakoffs and slower response times than the discrete scales, especially for respondents with less formal education. Orientation had no discernible impact on the answers. Overall, then, the current literature provides no compelling reason to use VASs in Web surveys other than that it can be done.

6.2.4 Interactive Grids

Grids or matrix items allow designers to display multiple questions that share the same response options on a single page. Grids usually present the items or statements as the rows of the grid and the response options as the columns; the cells in the grid are used to indicate the answers to the questions (see panel (a) of Figure 6.4). Placing multiple questions on one page conserves screen space and visually reinforces the relationship between the items (see Chapter 5), including the fact that they share a single response scale. A downside of the grid format is that it may promote non-differentiation or straightlining, in which respondents select the same response option for every (or nearly every) item. The grid format may also promote item nonresponse, if respondents inadvertently lose their place in the grid and skip a row. Selecting the same options or missing an item is less likely when every item is presented on its own page.

One way to make it clearer to respondents which items they have completed is to change the appearance of each row as the respondent selects an answer for that item. Galešic, Tourangeau, Couper and Conrad (2007) experimented with two types of visual change when the respondent selected an answer: (1) the font in which the item was displayed was grayed out (Figure 6.4 (b)), or (2) the row corresponding to the item was grayed out (Figure 6.4(c)). Both of these interactive formats significantly reduced item nonresponse relative to the conventional, static grid format (Figure 6.4(a)). There was a small increase in response time for the interactive designs that the authors attributed to a "surprise" when the change first occurred, but no effect of changing the display on straightlining.

It is possible that highlighting the mouse position—the specific cell in the grid—while it hovers prior to selection will help more than highlighting the selected row. Kaczmirek (2011) compared item nonresponse when feedback was provided for the item (row) or a particular response for an item (cell), either before or after the respondent selected an answer. The pre-selection, cell-level feedback led to 2.6 percent *fewer* complete responses than a control grid with no highlighting, but post-selection, row-level feedback helped, increasing the proportion of complete responses by 3.9 percentage points. Kaczmirek suggests that the cell-level pre-selection feedback is visually distracting, leading to higher levels of item nonresponse. With more complex grids, both horizontal and vertical feedback may help reduce item nonresponse. Couper, Tourangeau, and Conrad (2009) found that when one column in a grid required a judgment about the frequency of consuming a particular food and the next column required a judgment about the usual quantity consumed, both row and column feedback led to higher completion rates.

While the conventional format for simple grids almost always places items in rows and response categories in columns, it is possible to array the items as columns and the response categories as rows. How does interactive, visual feedback work under these circumstances? Galešic and her colleagues (Galešic, Tourangeau,

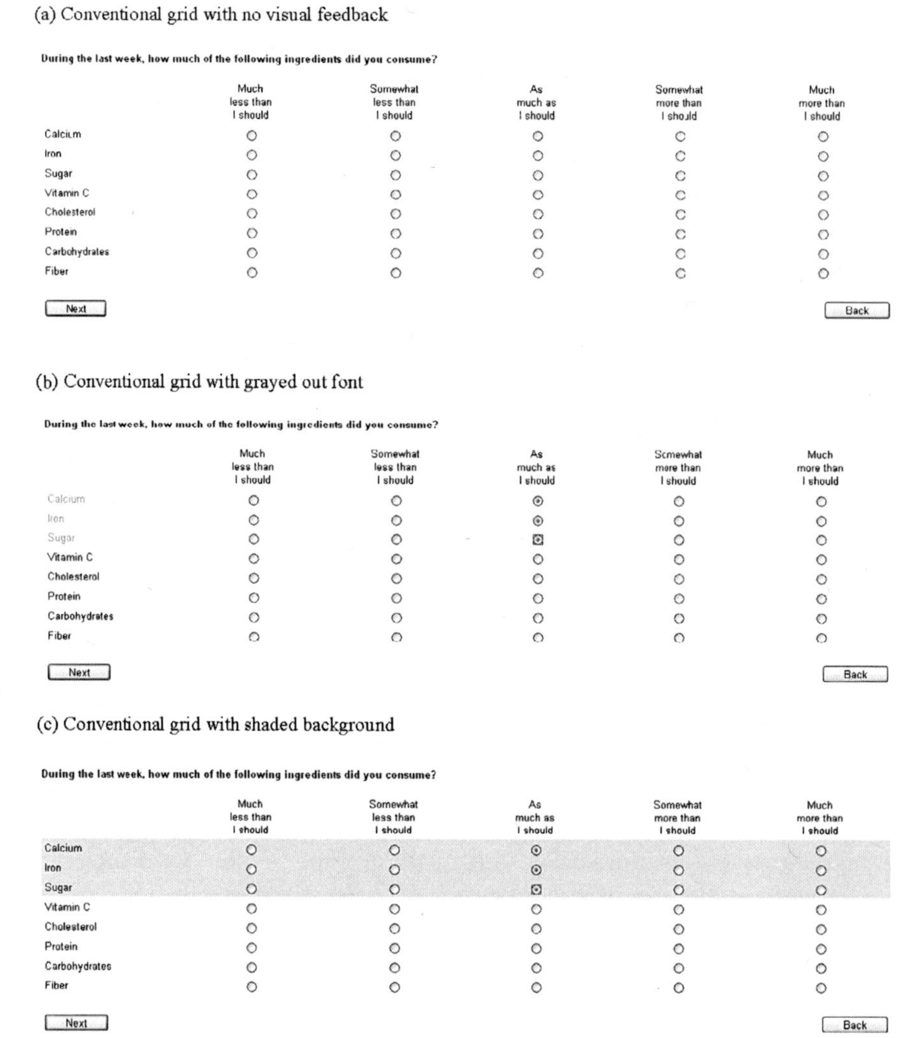

(a) Conventional grid with no visual feedback

During the last week, how much of the following ingredients did you consume?

	Much less than I should	Somewhat less than I should	As much as I should	Somewhat more than I should	Much more than I should
Calcium	○	○	○	○	○
Iron	○	○	○	○	○
Sugar	○	○	○	○	○
Vitamin C	○	○	○	○	○
Cholesterol	○	○	○	○	○
Protein	○	○	○	○	○
Carbohydrates	○	○	○	○	○
Fiber	○	○	○	○	○

[Next]   [Back]

(b) Conventional grid with grayed out font

During the last week, how much of the following ingredients did you consume?

	Much less than I should	Somewhat less than I should	As much as I should	Somewhat more than I should	Much more than I should
Calcium	○	○	⊙	○	○
Iron	○	○	⊙	○	○
Sugar	○	○	⊡	○	○
Vitamin C	○	○	○	○	○
Cholesterol	○	○	○	○	○
Protein	○	○	○	○	○
Carbohydrates	○	○	○	○	○
Fiber	○	○	○	○	○

[Next]   [Back]

(c) Conventional grid with shaded background

During the last week, how much of the following ingredients did you consume?

	Much less than I should	Somewhat less than I should	As much as I should	Somewhat more than I should	Much more than I should
Calcium	○	○	⊙	○	○
Iron	○	○	⊙	○	○
Sugar	○	○	⊡	○	○
Vitamin C	○	○	○	○	○
Cholesterol	○	○	○	○	○
Protein	○	○	○	○	○
Carbohydrates	○	○	○	○	○
Fiber	○	○	○	○	○

[Next]   [Back]

FIGURE 6.4. Grids used in Galešic, Tourangeau, Couper, and Conrad (2007). The top panel (a) shows a grid with no visual feedback, the middle panel (b) shows a grid with items grayed out as they are completed, and the bottom panel shows (c) a grid with shaded rows as items are completed.

Couper, and Conrad, 2007) examined this issue by changing the font or the background of columns as the respondent answered the corresponding question. The results were identical to those under the more conventional orientation, except there was an overall increase in item nonresponse under the reverse grid design, probably reflecting its nonconventional character.

Overall, then, the evidence suggests that providing visual feedback about which items respondents have completed reduces item nonresponse rates, but has little effect on straightlining. Combining vertical and horizontal feedback increased item nonresponse in the Kaczmirek study (which used simple grids), but vertical feedback decreased item nonresponse in the study by Couper and his colleagues (which used more complex grids) and increased completion in the reverse design grids in the study by Galešic, and her coworkers. It is probably a mistake to think about the feedback in terms of rows and columns per se; instead, Web survey designers should consider what aspect of the task is likely to be facilitated by interactive feedback. If the feedback clarifies which questions have been answered and which ones remain, it seems to help. Otherwise, feedback may just distract or confuse respondents.

6.2.5 Online Definitions

Enabling interviewers to define survey concepts *as needed* (that is, when respondents ask for clarification or when interviewers believe it will help) promotes the correct interpretation of the questions and, consequently, more accurate answers (Schober and Conrad, 1997; Conrad and Schober, 2000; Schober, Conrad, and Fricker, 2004). This approach, which has been called *conversational interviewing*, can result in non-uniform question wording because some respondents receive definitions but others do not, but it improves response accuracy without wasting the time of respondents who probably don't need clarification. This approach fits well with Web page design, where it is common to link content together so that users can obtain more detail by following the links.

Several studies have examined the benefits of providing definitions in online surveys (Conrad, Couper, Tourangeau and Peytchev, 2006; Conrad, Schober, and Coiner, 2007; Peytchev, Conrad, Couper, and Tourangeau, 2010; Tourangeau, Conrad, Arens, Fricker, Lee, and Smith, 2006). Table 6.2 summarizes this research on definitions in Web surveys. An important lesson from these studies is that respondents do not request clarification as often as they need it. One reason for this low use of definitions is that respondents may not realize they need clarification; they may assume they understand the question as intended even when they don't. Another possibility is that the actions involved in getting definitions, while easier than asking an interviewer, still involve more effort than many Web respondents are willing to invest. Web users in general—not just Web survey respondents—are notoriously impatient. For example, they don't read but tend to scan text on Web pages and they are unlikely to scroll to view content that is not immediately visible (Nielsen and Loranger, 2006). More generally, computer users tend to avoid minor movements, even eye movements, to obtain information that would enhance their performance (Gray and Fu, 2004). Web survey respondents may display similar reluctance to expend effort on nonessential components of a task, but muddle through based on their prior understanding of the concepts. In addition, respondents may be reluctant to obtain help by clicking on a link because this can result in unpredictable behavior. Some links open a new tab, some replace the current page with a new page on a completely different site, making it difficult to get back to original page, and some open smaller windows on the page being viewed. All of this can make people reluctant to click a link when they are in the middle of a task.

To test the impact of motor effort on requests for definitions, Conrad, Couper, Tourangeau and Peytchev (2006) conducted two experiments. In both, the authors

TABLE 6.2. Studies on the Use of Definitions in Web Surveys

Study	Variable	Main Finding	Setting, Type of Sample
Conrad et al. (2006), Exp. 1 and 2	*Effort* (number of actions required to obtain clarification)	Relatively few *R*s request any definitions but, among those who do, *R*s request more definitions with one click than with two and with a rollover than with one click	Web, volunteer panel (replication with probability panel)
Conrad et al. (2006), Exp. 1	*Informativeness* (degree to which definitions change how Rs think about key concept in question)	*R*s request more definitions if informative, but only if definitions can be obtained with little effort (e.g., one click)	Web, volunteer panel
Peytchev et al. (2010), Exp. 1	*Technicality* of words in question	*R*s more likely to request definitions for technical terms	Web, volunteer panel
Tourangeau et al. (2006), Exp. 2	*Technicality* of words in question	*R*s more likely to redisplay definition when terms are technical	Web, volunteer panel, responses based on vignettes
Peytchev et al. (2010)	Inclusion in question text ("*always-on*")	*R*s consult definitions more when they are always on than when they require a rollover; length of definition affects response time more when requested with a rollover than always on	Web, volunteer panel
Galešic et al. (2009), Exp. 3	Inclusion in question text ("*always-on*")	*R*s consult definitions more when they are always on than via rollover, but when they do request via rollover they read more; the longer they view the definition, the greater the effect on their answers	Laboratory (with eye-tracking), convenience sample
Tourangeau et al. (2006), Exp. 2	Default presentation of definition followed by option of requesting definition again	After default presentation of definition, *R*s were asked to make judgments based on the definition; *R*s who requested (by clicking) the definition a second time spent more time answering and were more accurate than *R*s who did not request additional display	Web, volunteer panel, responses based on vignettes

asked opt-in Web panelists to evaluate the amount of different food and nutrients they consumed and made definitions of the relevant terms available through interfaces that required different levels of effort. The experiments also varied the usefulness of definitions. Some respondents got definitions that included surprising or counterintuitive information, such as the information that French fries should be counted as vegetables; others got definitions consisting of information the respondents probably already knew, such as *beer* is "a fermented extract of barley malt, with or without other sources of starch, flavored with hops, and containing more than 0.5 percent alcohol by volume." Respondents received one kind of definition or the other.

In the first experiment, respondents could obtain definitions through interfaces that required one or two clicks or through a click-and-scroll interface that required a varying number of clicks, usually more than two. Overall, only 13.8 percent of respondents requested any definitions, indicating their overall unwillingness to invest the necessary effort to get definitions. But the respondents who did obtain definitions gave answers that differed from those who did not, suggesting that they read and applied the definitions in making their judgments about the food items. Among respondents who requested at least one definition, the number of requests varied with the number of clicks required to make a request; respondents who got the one-click interface requested an average of 2.5 out of four definitions; this dropped to 1.5 with the two-click and the click-and-scroll interfaces. The usefulness of the definitions mattered, but only when the definitions could be obtained with one click. Respondents who got the useful definitions (and the one-click interface) requested 3.7 out of four definitions on average versus 1.7 for those who got the definitions that were not useful (and the one-click interface). Even when respondents could see the informational value of definitions, the number of minor actions (moving the mouse, clicking it) required to display them seemed to be a key consideration in whether to request a definition. And when more than one click was required, respondents rarely requested more than one definition whether it was useful or not.

In the second experiment, Conrad and his colleagues (2006) examined an even less demanding interface than the one-click approach, a mouse rollover. Respondents requested definitions substantially more often, and more respondents requested at least one definition with rollovers than with either the one- or two-click interface. Overall, 36.5 percent of respondents accessed at least one definition via a rollover versus 8.9 percent and 6.5 percent with the one- and two-click interfaces, respectively. Some of the rollover requests may have been unintentional; respondents may have inadvertently triggered the display of the definition by moving the mouse too close to a term for which a rollover definition was available. Still, respondents seemed to consider the definitions that were displayed when they answered. The distributions of answers differed reliably when respondents obtained useful (versus non-useful) definitions with rollovers, which would only have happened if they read the definitions. The takeaway from these two experiments is that when it comes to using an interactive feature that is not essential to completing the questionnaire but that improves the quality of answers, respondents may be deterred by relatively small amounts of effort; they are also sensitive to small differences in effort between one interface and another.

Ease of use isn't the only variable affecting whether respondents request definitions. Respondents are more likely to request a definition when they are aware that they need help; thus, they are more likely to seek a definition for unfamiliar or technical terms. In the first experiment reported by Conrad and his colleagues (Conrad et al., 2006, Experiment 1), respondents requested definitions for technical terms like "polyunsaturated fatty acid" more often than for non-technical terms like "dairy." It's easy to believe one understands everyday words like dairy in the sense they are intended, even when one knows they might be used in a special way in the survey. Tourangeau, Conrad, Arens, Fricker, Lee and Smith (2006, Experiment 2) asked respondents to read a definition and then to apply that definition in judging whether people they read about in short vignettes should be classified as disabled or whether they should be counted as residents of the place they were staying. Respondents could click to see the definition again as they read each description. Most of them didn't bother. Overall, only 20 percent of the respondents requested a definition, but they were more likely to do so when the question used a technical term ("enumeration unit") instead of the corresponding everyday term ("residence"). Nonetheless, ease of use seems to trump respondents' awareness that they are not familiar with a term in the question when it comes to requesting clarification. In Study 1 by Conrad and his colleagues (2006), the number of requests for definitions of technical terms decreased reliably as the number of clicks required increased.

Getting a definition with a rollover involves less effort than with a mouse click, but even less effort is required if respondents can simply move their eyes. Presenting definitions as part of the question text allows respondents to read the definitions if they want to and to skip them if they don't need clarification. Does this approach increase the use of definitions? Peytchev, Conrad, Couper, and Tourangeau (2010) compared definitions presented as part of the question text to definitions accessible via rollovers. The main finding was that respondents reported consulting definitions presented in the question text more often (60.7 percent) than definitions accessible via rollover (35.6 percent). When respondents did get definitions with a mouse action (that is, with slightly more effort), they read them at least as carefully as when the definitions were included in the question—the length of the definitions affected response times more when respondents requested them with a mouse rollover than when the definitions were included in the question text. An eye-tracking study reported by Galešic, Tourangeau, Couper and Conrad (2007) provides additional evidence that respondents read the definitions they explicitly request relatively carefully. Respondents in their study were more likely to look at definitions presented with the question text, but they spent more time looking at definitions they had requested via a rollover. Regardless of how the definition was displayed (with the question or on request), the more time respondents spent looking at the definitions, the more it affected their answers. For example, the definition of herbal supplements mentioned that they can "protect cells against aging, improve sexual performance and reduce stress" but it mentioned this near the end of the definition. The more time respondents spent reading this definition, the more they reported consuming *much less* than they should. In the study by Tourangeau and his colleagues (Tourangeau et al., 2006), all respondents got a definition at the outset, but respondents who clicked to see the definition again as they made their judgments took more time and gave more accurate answers.

Taken together, these studies suggest that reducing the effort required to access definitions will increase the chance that respondents will consult the definitions; as a result, putting a definition on screen may be the best method for conveying it. Still, it may not be practical to provide on-screen definitions for every item in a long survey or when space is at a premium. In addition, it is unclear whether the level of effort needed to access the definitions affects how carefully respondents attend to them. There are at least two possibilities here: a) respondents who are motivated enough to click or roll over a definition are already motivated enough to read it carefully and apply it in answering, or b) having invested some effort to get a definition, respondents may, as a result, be more inclined to process it carefully. And, of course, both explanations could be true. Another approach to delivering definitions is to program the questionnaire so that it can volunteer clarification when a respondent seems to need it, much as a human interviewer might do; we return to this in the next section on human-like interactive features.

6.3 HUMAN-LIKE INTERACTIVE FEATURES

The second group of interactive features we discuss in this chapter are features that have a human-like quality. Some are merely dynamic; for example, a video of a human interviewer asking questions is human-like but does not typically respond to the actions of the respondent. Others are also responsive, for example, virtual, animated interviewers that offer clarification when the respondent seems confused. Many of these features are intended to approximate behaviors that live interviewers might perform—for example, probing for additional answers or offering help when the respondent seems to need it. We discuss three such features—interventions to slow down fast respondents, probes for additional answers to open-ended questions, and clarification offered to respondents who seem to be having difficulty with a question. Then, we examine the use of humanized survey interfaces, such as animated human faces to administer the questions, in which interviewer or interviewing agents are visually depicted.

Interactive interventions to reduce "speeding." One behavior that may bode ill for response quality is "speeding." This refers to answering too quickly—too quickly to have read the question, let alone to have given the answer much thought. It is possible that Web interactivity can be used to reduce this kind of behavior. Web questionnaires can be designed to prompt respondents who give unreasonably fast answers, offering them the opportunity to revisit the question on which they were caught speeding and answer it again after giving it more thought. Conrad, Tourangeau, Couper, and

Kennedy (2009) and Conrad, Tourangeau, Couper, and Zhang (2011, in preparation) have tested this approach. These studies asked respondents seven frequency questions (e.g., "How many overnight trips have you taken in the past 2 years?") or seven numeracy questions (e.g., "If the chance of getting a disease is 10 percent, how many people out of 100 would be expected to get the disease: 1, 10 or 20?"). If respondents answered in less time than the expected reading time, they got a prompt: "You seem to have responded very quickly. Please be sure you have given the question sufficient thought to provide an accurate answer." The prompt has human-like character in that it mimics the presence of an intelligent agent, even though the intervention results from an automated check on response time.

Did this intervention lead to slower or more accurate responses? Across several studies, prompting respondents whenever they were "caught speeding" reduced subsequent speeding episodes and slowed overall response times compared to a no-prompt control group. For the numeracy questions, prompting both slowed respondents and increased their accuracy, but the improvement in accuracy was apparent only for respondents with intermediate levels of education. The impact of the intervention on response times also seemed to be restricted to certain respondents; some respondents—"hard-core speeders"—never slowed down even after being prompted four or more times. The prompt for speeding positively affected other behaviors besides speeding. Respondents who had been prompted exhibited less straightlining on a subsequent grid item—they were less likely to select the same response option for all the items—than their counterparts in the no-prompt condition.

The intervention seemed to help without driving people away. There were very few breakoffs across the seven test items and never more than about a one percentage point increase in breakoffs with the prompt.

Probing for additional open-ended answers. As in other modes, open questions in Web surveys can add richness relative to closed questions and yield answers that were not anticipated by the researchers. One type of open question asks respondents to list one or more instances of a concept (for example, "What are the most important problems facing the country today?"). When interviewers ask this type of question, they routinely probe for additional answers ("Anything else?"). Web surveys that include such questions usually provide a response box for respondents to type in their answers (see Chapter 5) and the respondents' entries are typically accepted without evaluation. Web questionnaires could, however, simulate human interviewers in probing for more response content when respondents submit their initial answers. Probing should increase the number of ideas or themes in the response and this may lead to more complete answers.

Holland and Christian (2009) tested the effects of such probes. They asked students two open questions about their interests (for example, "What countries and topics are you interested in within Latin America and/or the Caribbean Region?"). Half of the students were probed for additional answers ("Are there any other countries or topics that you are interested in within Latin America and/or the Caribbean Region?") and half were not. The respondents who were probed gave answers that were, on average, modestly but reliably longer than answers without probing (12.1 versus 10.0 words). In a later study, Oudejans and Christian (2010) asked respondents from a Dutch probability panel four questions about life in the Netherlands. When respondents were probed, their answers included more topics and more words. The effect of probing was larger when the question text emphasized the importance of the question.

So, interactive probing had the expected effect across two studies with very different samples. Still, the effects were small when they were found and they were not present for all items. More importantly, the effects were attenuated as more questions were probed; in both studies, the difference between probed and unprobed answers was not significant for the last question that was probed. Respondents may find later probes intrusive or annoying or may simply ignore them.

Encouraging substantive answers. "Don't know" and other non-substantive responses are often considered evidence of shortcuts in the response process and reduced data quality (e.g., Krosnick, 1991). Much as an interviewer might attempt to obtain a substantive answer when the respondent declines to answer, a Web questionnaire can present a statement such as "We would very much like to have your answer to this question. If you would like to choose one of the proposed answers, please select 'Back.'" DeRouvray and Couper (2002) tried exactly this intervention and it reduced the frequency with which respondents selected "decline to answer."

Offering clarification. Requesting a definition by clicking highlighted question text is like asking an interviewer for help, only easier perhaps. However, even with a low effort interface such as a rollover (see 62.5), respondents may not request clarification every time they need it. Fortunately, Web questionnaires can offer (or just provide) a definition when the respondent's behavior indicates confusion, much as conversational interviewers might offer definitional help when they think it might be useful. One indication of possible comprehension difficulty is inactivity; a Web questionnaire can be programmed to offer help when the respondent has not produced any input (clicking, typing, etc.) for a relatively long period of time.

Conrad, Schober, and Coiner (2007) conducted a laboratory experiment that compared "respondent-initiated" clarification, in which respondents requested clarification by clicking, and "mixed initiative" clarification, in which the respondent could request clarification by clicking or the questionnaire offered clarification when respondents were inactive for more than a fixed amount of time. In two experiments, respondents answered a set of behavioral questions based on fictional scenarios; the scenarios described complicated or straightforward situations. For example, the question "How many people live in this house?" was potentially ambiguous when it was presented with a complicated scenario that described a family of four with a child who stays in a college dormitory most of the time. The corresponding straightforward scenario described a family whose members all sleep at home. The definition instructed respondents to "not count any people who would normally consider this their (legal) address but who are living away on business, in the armed forces, or attending school (such as boarding school or college)," resolving the ambiguity in the complicated scenario.

In the first experiment, most respondents could obtain definitions by clicking on highlighted question text; a control group could not. When they answered based on complicated scenarios, respondents who could not obtain definitions were accurate on an average of 40.9 percent of the questions; when they could obtain clarification, their accuracy improved to 67.5 percent in the respondent-initiated condition and to 66.4 percent in the mixed-initiative condition. (The mixed-initiative condition was in effect also respondent-initiated, because the inactivity threshold was long enough that respondents who got help typically had asked for it before help was triggered by their inactivity.) When respondents were warned they might get the answers wrong if they didn't consult the definitions, they requested definitions very frequently (73 to 87 percent of the time depending on the condition); respondents who were merely alerted to the availability of definitions requested them much less frequently (between 15 and 32 percent of the time). In a similar study with telephone interviews (Schober and Conrad, 1997), respondents requested definitions much less often than they did in the Web study. A simple motor action like clicking on a term may be easier than formulating and making a verbal request. However, unless they were made aware of the benefits of clarification, Web respondents rarely requested it.

In their second experiment (Conrad et al., 2007), Conrad and his colleagues tailored how quickly the system offered clarification in the mixed-initiative condition based on the respondent's age. One group of respondents was offered clarification after a fixed period of inactivity; in a second group, the period of inactivity triggering the offer of help was longer for older respondents than for younger ones on the assumption that cognitive aging generally slows response times for older respondents. Mixed-initiative clarification improved accuracy relative to respondent-initiated clarification only, and it helped even more when the threshold for offering clarification reflected the respondents' age. For complicated scenarios, respondents were accurate on an average of 24 percent of the questions when they could not obtain clarification; in the respondent-initiated clarification group, they were accurate 35 percent of the time; in the mixed-initiative clarification group with the same (generic) threshold for everyone, they were accurate 48 percent of the time; and in the mixed-initiative group with thresholds tailored to the respondent's age group (group-based), they were accurate 58 percent of the time. Accuracy on the complicated scenarios was highest when the definition was always displayed (see Figure 6.5), although this produced the lowest levels of satisfaction.

Animated faces in the user interface. The capabilities of the Web make it possible to display animated human-like forms in the user interface. These forms can be video recordings of human interviewers or animated interviewing agents (which we call "virtual interviewers"). Although video-recorded interviewers are dynamic, it is hard to make them responsive. To create responsive recorded interviewers would require recording interviewer actions for all possible respondent actions and developing software to determine which video file to present in a given situation. Virtual interviewers can also be either dynamic (that is, pre-recorded so they present questions irrespective of the respondent's behavior) or responsive (able to react to what

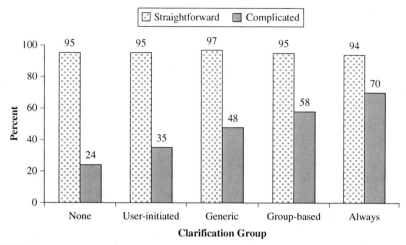

FIGURE 6.5. Response accuracy across five initiative conditions in Conrad et al.'s Experiment 2 (2007). The dark bars present the results for the straightforward scenarios; the dotted bars, for the complicated scenarios.

respondents do or say in real time). Whether they are recorded or virtual humans, these "interviewers" can, in principle, ask spoken questions. When the "interviewer" is recorded, it has no ability recognize respondent input, so respondents are typically required to enter their answers by clicking or typing, as in a typical browser interface. In contrast, responsive interviewing agents can, in principle, recognize respondents' verbal input—whether spoken or textual—and react to the input. Because the underlying software for virtual interviewers of this sort involves natural language processing, they have really only been simulated to date.

It is not clear at this point whether video-recorded or virtual interviewers add value to Web surveys. They may reintroduce social desirability biases and interviewer effects, potentially undermining some of the advantages of Web over interviewer administration. We return to these potential drawbacks of moving, talking faces in the interface in Chapter 7. However, there are several reasons why researchers might design online questionnaires with moving, human-like faces that ask the questions. These include:

1) *Increased engagement*: A moving, talking face might attract and hold respondents' attention, increasing the likelihood they will complete the questionnaire and do a careful job.

2) *Question comprehension*: Respondents might find it easier to understand spoken questions when they can see the face that is producing them; in addition, respondent comprehension may be improved when a video-recorded interviewer asks spoken questions accompanied by text as compared to presentation in one channel only (Fuchs and Funke, 2007, p. 66).

3) *Choice*: In principle, respondents can choose an "interviewer." With virtual interviewers, the range of choices is vast and respondents can potentially

configure a virtual interviewer so that it meets their specifications. Interacting with an "interviewer" they have chosen might motivate respondents to answer more conscientiously and to disclose more sensitive information than reporting to an interface over whose design they had no control.

There is some evidence on these potential advantages of including human-like faces in the interface. Turning first to the engagement hypothesis, more realistic virtual interviewers have been shown to increase respondent engagement relative to less realistic versions of the same virtual interviewers; this does not show, however, that respondents would be even less engaged without any virtual interviewer asking the question. Conrad, Schober, Jans, Orlowski, Nielsen and Levenstein (2008) manipulated the realism of a responsive virtual interviewer, comparing virtual interviewers that displayed facial movements that faithfully replicated the facial movements of a human actor on which the virtual interviewer was modeled with virtual interviewers that exhibited less realistic facial movements. Respondents who interacted with the more realistic virtual interviewer produced more verbal and visual backchannels (e.g., said *uh huh* and nodded as the virtual interviewer was speaking); in addition, they smiled more often and for longer durations while the virtual interviewer was speaking. Such "backchannels" are often interpreted as evidence the listener is paying attention to the speaker and understanding what he or she is saying (e.g., Clark and Schaefer, 1989; Duncan and Fiske, 1977; Goodwin, 1981; Schegloff, 1982). Listener smiles have been shown to serve similar purposes (e.g., Brunner, 1979). Still, these findings do not directly test the hypothesis that virtual interviewers increase completion rates; the study by Conrad and his colleagues was a laboratory study, where breakoffs are rare, and it did not include a comparison to an interface without a virtual interviewer.

Did virtual interviewers improve comprehension of the survey questions? Conrad and his colleagues (Conrad et al., 2008) report that a virtual interviewer, which was able to recognize respondents' confusion and provide clarification accordingly, increased the accuracy of respondents' answers compared to a virtual interviewer that only repeated the questions and used other neutral probes. Because automation of these skills involves challenging speech recognition and dialog design problems, the authors simulated these capabilities using a "Wizard of Oz" approach (e.g., Oviatt and Adams, 2000), in which a human experimenter monitored respondents' speech and presented relevant video recordings of the virtual interviewer, bringing human, as opposed to artificial, intelligence to the interaction. Nonetheless, respondents believed they were interacting with an autonomous software agent. Whether the comprehension benefits would be just as great with speech but no visible agent or simply with a textual, browser-based design (as in Conrad, Schober, and Coiner, 2007) remains to be seen.

What about the possible benefits of offering respondents a choice of interviewers? Conrad, Schober, and Nielsen (2011) presented respondents with an array of eight virtual interviewers (see Figure 6.6). Respondents clicked on each one to see

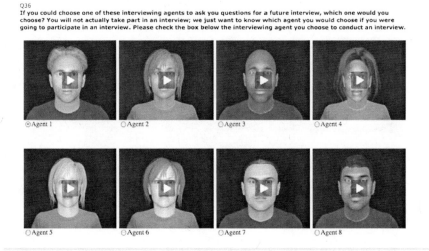

Q36
If you could choose one of these interviewing agents to ask you questions for a future interview, which one would you choose? You will not actually take part in an interview; we just want to know which agent you would choose if you were going to participate in an interview. Please check the box below the interviewing agent you choose to conduct an interview.

Agent 1   Agent 2   Agent 3   Agent 4

Agent 5   Agent 6   Agent 7   Agent 8

www.msisurvey.com

FIGURE 6.6. Choice of virtual interviewer. Respondents were required to click on each virtual interviewer to see and hear it present a survey introduction (Conrad, Schober and Nielsen, 2011). (See color insert.) Reprinted with permission from Conrad, Schober & Nielsen, 2011.

and hear it present an introduction to a hypothetical future survey; each respondent had already completed an interview with a virtual interviewer to which he or she had been assigned. The results suggest respondents have clear preferences for certain computer-animated interviewers. After they chose a virtual interviewer, respondents were asked to explain their choice. Common explanations cited the virtual interviewer's voice or appearance. Although the virtual interviewer's race was rarely mentioned explicitly, it seemed to be a factor; 80 percent of black respondents chose a black virtual interviewer; white respondents were more evenly split about the race of virtual interviewers they chose.

Despite these possible advantages of introducing moving, talking faces into the questionnaire, there are potential drawbacks as well. First, all the activity in the interface might distract respondents and reduce the amount of thought they give to their answers. Second, by introducing so many cues of humanness, designers might create the feeling that someone else is there, a sense of "social presence" (Short, Williams, and Christie, 1976; Tourangeau, Couper, and Steiger, 2003). The latter is of particular concern because it might potentially undermine the advantages of self-administering sensitive questions (Kreuter, Presser and Tourangeau, 2008; Tourangeau and Yan, 2009). If it feels like an interviewer is present, respondents might be as reluctant to disclose potentially embarrassing information as they are when a human interviewer asks the questions.

The evidence to date about video-recorded and virtual interviewers suggests that respondents react to them in ways that are reminiscent of how they react to human, face-to-face interviewers. For example, Fuchs (2009) found effects from the gender of video interviewers. Female respondents were more likely to report having had a sexually transmitted disease to a female than to a male video interviewer

FIGURE 6.7. Video-recorded interviewer from Fuchs and Funke (2007). (See color insert.) Adapted with permission from Fuchs and Funke (2007).

(26 percent vs. 17 percent), but the pattern was reversed for male respondents who reported fewer instances of STDs to female than to male video interviewers (2 percent vs. 7 percent). Similarly, Krysan and Couper (2003) compared responses to race-related questions asked by live and video interviewers. The video interviewers were presented on a laptop computer rather than online. The researchers reported that black respondents gave less liberal answers to white interviewers, whether live or video-recorded, and white respondents gave more conservative responses to white than black video interviewers (see also Conrad, Schober, and Nielsen, 2011). Finally, Lind, Schober, Conrad, and Reichert (under review) reported that virtual interviewers elicited more socially desirable responses to some sensitive questions than when respondents only heard the questions.

Nonetheless, strong social reactions to video-recorded and virtual interviewers are not always observed: Fuchs and Funke (2007) measured respondents' feelings of social presence by asking several questions about their experiences answering earlier questions. Respondents reported reliably *more* social presence from a text-only than from "video-enhanced" Web questionnaire in which a video-recorded interviewer asked questions and respondents entered answers with their mouse and keyboard (see Figure 6.7).

6.4 SUMMARY

Much of the research we have reviewed suggests that there is something about using the Web that leads respondents to minimize the effort they make. The studies of Web respondents' use of definitions illustrate this point. The effort required to obtain a definition can be very low in Web surveys—as little as a mouse click or a rollover. Compared to asking an interviewer for help or clarification, it can be much easier to get help on the Web. But Web respondents are less likely to seek help than respondents in a telephone survey. The laboratory experiments reported by Conrad and his colleagues (Conrad et al., 2007) were closely modeled on the telephone interviews conducted by Schober and Conrad (1997). Yet unless Web respondents were explicitly made aware of the benefits of obtaining definitions, they requested help via a click only 23 percent of the time they were presented with complicated mappings; the figure for their telephone counterparts was 83 percent. A major challenge for Web survey designers is to motivate respondents to take advantage of interactive features that are likely to improve data quality, despite the respondents' unwillingness to invest effort.

The good news for designers is that there are techniques for reducing effort associated with interactive features that seem to increase their effectiveness. For definitions, rollovers and mixed-initiative clarification reduce effort and increase the use of definitions (e.g., Conrad et al., 2006; Conrad et al., 2007). Carrying out arithmetic for respondents in constant-sum or tally questions increased the proportion of well-formed answers and also increased their accuracy compared to designs in which respondents were required to do the math themselves (Conrad et al., 2005, 2009). And interactive grids that responsively change shading facilitate navigation and reduce missing data (Galešic et al., 2007; Couper, Tourangeau and Conrad, under review).

Not all interactive features improve data quality. Progress indicators can increase completion rates when they communicate good news but they can increase breakoffs relative to no progress indicator when they don't (Conrad et al., 2010; Yan et al., 2011). When it is not clear how progress feedback will be interpreted, presenting it on an intermittent schedule may maintain potential benefits while reducing the potential costs (Conrad, et al., 2010). Visual analog scales do not seem to improve measurement under most circumstances and may even harm data quality; they can increase breakoffs, item nonresponse, and response time (Couper et al., 2006; Funke, Reips, and Thomas, 2011).

Interactive features designed to improve data quality by preventing respondent shortcuts seem to be effective. DeRouvray and Couper (2002) demonstrated that it is possible to reduce Don't Know responses by automatically prompting respondents to provide a substantive response. Christian and her colleagues (Holland and Christian, 2009; Oudejans and Christian, 2010) increased the length of open responses by automatically prompting respondents to provide additional items. Conrad and his colleagues (Conrad et al., 2009; Conrad et al., 2011) reduced speeding and subsequent straightlining by prompting respondents when they sped. While this approach strikes us as promising, future work is required to determine whether repeated prompting may annoy respondents and introduce social presence.

The possibility of designing interactive features to maximize data quality is clearly attractive when all respondents report on the Web. However, when one or more additional modes are part of the study, the implications of this approach aren't so clear. If the design philosophy is to minimize mode effects by making the questionnaires in the different modes as similar as possible (the *unimode* approach), this would argue against the use of interactive features that cannot be implemented in the other mode(s). On the other hand, if the goal is to create the best possible questionnaire in each mode, given the capabilities of that mode (the *best practices* approach), then it is appropriate to try to improve data quality with all the tools available in Web questionnaires. We return to this issue again in Section 8.3.

/// 7 /// MEASUREMENT ERROR ON THE WEB AND IN OTHER MODES OF DATA COLLECTION

We have already touched on some of the differences between Web surveys and more traditional modes of data collection in earlier chapters. Chapter 2 examines coverage differences between Web surveys and surveys done in other modes. Chapter 3 highlights the differences in response rates between Web surveys and other types of surveys, especially mail surveys. In this chapter, we examine studies that focus on measurement differences between Web surveys and other types of surveys. The chapter presents several frameworks for looking at mode differences in measurement systematically and then reviews the findings about how the answers obtained in Web surveys may differ from those obtained through other methods of data collection.

7.1 CONCEPTUAL SCHEMES FOR UNDERSTANDING MODE EFFECTS

Mode effects refer to differences in the results of a survey depending on the method used to collect the data. Although some researchers seem to think of any mode difference as a type of measurement error, we prefer a conceptualization in which the difference between two modes reflects the net effects of differences in all of the major sources of survey error—sampling, coverage, nonresponse, and measurement error. In our view, the difference between an estimate from, say, a mail survey and a parallel estimate from a Web survey reflects two underlying differences between those methods. First, because of differences in response rates, sampling techniques, or coverage of the population, different types of people might end up completing the questions under the two modes. For example, the Web survey may overrepresent younger or more educated persons as compared to the mail survey, and these differences in the composition of the responding samples could produce differences in the distribution of answers by mode. Second, even if the same people completed the Web and mail surveys, they might still give different answers to the questions because of differences in how the mail and Web questionnaires present the questions or because of other measurement differences between the two modes. Chapters 2 and 3 have already considered differences arising from sampling, coverage, and nonresponse. In this chapter, we focus on the latter type of mode differences, those arising from measurement differences across modes.

Over the years, researchers have proposed various conceptual schemes to account for such measurement differences across different methods of data collection. Tourangeau and Smith (1996) proposed one of the first of these schemes. According to Tourangeau and Smith (see also Tourangeau, Rips, and Rasinski, 2000), the major methods of data collection differ on four major dimensions:

- Whether the questions are self-administered or administered by an interviewer;
- How the respondent is contacted (e.g., in person or by telephone);
- Whether the questionnaire is computer-assisted or presented on paper; and
- Whether the questions are conveyed to the respondent visually or aurally.

With Web surveys, the questions are self-administered and they are usually presented visually via a computer; the mode of contact with the respondents is often by email, but may also be by mail. Tourangeau and Smith argue that these objective features of the mode of data collection affect three key mediating variables—the respondents' sense of being alone or in the presence of another person as they answer the questions, the level of cognitive burden involved in answering, and the perception of the importance or legitimacy of the survey. For example, Tourangeau and Smith suggest that when respondents are contacted in person by interviewers who display photo ID badges or other legitimacy-conferring paraphernalia, respondents may see the survey as more important than they otherwise would have and they may answer differently as a result. The three mediating variables in turn affect a variety of outcomes, such as the reliability of the answers, the level of missing data, or respondents' willingness to disclose sensitive information.

Other researchers have offered alternative schemes for understanding measurement differences across modes. Groves, Fowler, Couper, Lepkowski, Singer, and Tourangeau (2009) distinguish five characteristics on which the various modes of data collection differ:

1) The degree of interviewer involvement (ranging from no involvement in mail or Web surveys to maximal involvement in face-to-face interviews, with intermediate levels of interviewer involvement with modes of data collection— such as audio computer-administered self-interviewing or interactive voice response—in which an interviewer initially contacts the respondent and then transfers them to an automated data collection system);
2) The degree of interaction with the respondent (ranging from little involvement when data are abstracted from administrative records, to intermediate levels in telephone interviews, to maximal involvement in an in-person interview conducted in the respondent's home);

3) The degree of privacy (ranging from low privacy when an interviewer and other persons are present during the interview to high privacy when the respondent completes the interview alone);

4) The channels of communication (visual, aural, or some combination of the two);

5) The use of technology (ranging from low use of technology in paper-and-pencil surveys, to intermediate levels when the survey organization provides the computers as in computer-assisted personal interviewing, to high use as in Web surveys when respondents typically provide the computer, Internet connection, browser, and so on).

This framework expands on the model provided by Tourangeau and Smith (1996) and makes it clear that some of the key characteristics on which the different modes of data collection differ are matters of degree rather than kind.

De Leeuw (1992; 2005) distinguishes three sets of factors on which the different modes of data collection vary—media-related factors, factors related to information transmission, and interviewer effects. The first of de Leeuw's factors has to do with "the social conventions and customs associated with the media utilized in survey methods" (de Leeuw, 2005, page 244). For example, in interviewer-administered surveys, because the interviewers initiated the interaction, they control the order and pacing of the questions. With paper self-administered surveys, it is the respondents who control the pace and order of the questions. And in Web surveys, the conventions and habits that apply with other interactions on the Web (such as having multiple windows open and toggling among them) may carry over to the survey setting, affecting how respondents interact with the questionnaire. The second set of de Leeuw's factors—information transmission—encompasses the channel of presentation (visual versus auditory) and the availability of different forms of potentially communicative information (such as text, nonverbal cues, and paralinguistic information, such as tone or timing) under the different channels. Features of the text (such as the use of boldfacing) in a visual survey can serve functions similar to paralinguistic cues (such as emphasis) in a survey administered orally (see Redline and Dillman, 2002). The final factor, interviewer effects, has traditionally referred to differences in the answers produced by differences in how the interviewers administer the questions or by differences in their personal characteristics, such as their race or gender. Presumably, Web surveys reduce or eliminate such effects—unless they incorporate virtual interviewers (see Chapter 6).

In their discussion of Web surveys, Couper and Bosnjak (2010) focus on five characteristics of this mode of data collection. Web surveys are self-administered, computerized, interactive, distributed, and richly visual. Couper and Bosnjak see most of these as advantages of Web surveys relative to the more traditional methods of data collection. For example, self-administration reduces data collection costs, curtails social desirability biases, and eliminates interviewer variance as a source of error. Still, as Couper and Bosnjak note, interviewers may play an important role in motivating respondents and in clarifying otherwise unclear questions. That Web surveys are distributed (that is, completed on the respondent's own computer via his or her own Internet connection) is more of a mixed blessing, since many features of the respondent's system can affect how the survey is presented. As Couper and Bosnjak (2010, page 541) put it:

> In Internet surveys,... many things can affect the look and feel of the instrument for a particular respondent. These include the browser type and version (e.g., Internet Explorer or Mozilla Firefox), the operating system (e.g., Windows, Mac, or Linux), the screen resolution, the browser security settings (e.g., whether JavaScript is active, cookies are enabled, etc.), the Internet connection method (e.g., dial-up or broadband), font size and other display settings on the browser, and so on. While the Internet is designed to work on multiple platforms and settings, these differences may change the survey experience for respondents to varying degrees, potentially affecting both nonresponse error (breakoffs) and measurement error (data quality).

Traditional modes of computer-assisted data collection use the survey organization's computers and settings and thus do not produce this level of variability across respondents.

In this chapter, we focus on two major characteristics of Web surveys that we have not covered in the earlier chapters: their use of self-administration of the questions (which eliminates interviewer involvement and offers a high level of privacy) and the low level of cognitive burden they impose (because the respondent controls the pace of the survey and can easily reread the questions on-screen). Of course, for low-education respondents who have trouble reading or who lack computer skills, the Web may increase cognitive burden.

7.2 WEB SURVEYS AS A METHOD OF SELF-ADMINISTRATION

Sensitive questions and reporting error. A major source of measurement errors in surveys is the deliberate distortion of the answers by respondents in order to save face or avoid embarrassment. Surveys often include items asking respondents about sensitive or potentially embarrassing topics, such as abortions, illicit drug use, or voting. There is ample evidence that respondents often provide inaccurate answers to questions on such topics. A study by Fu, Darroch, Henshaw, and Kolb (1998) estimates that respondents in the National Survey of Family Growth (NSFG) report only about half of all the abortions they had had. They derived this estimate of the level of underreporting by comparing the NSFG estimate of the total number of abortions performed with an estimate derived from a national survey of abortion providers (see also Tourangeau, Rasinski, Jobe, Smith, and Pratt, 1997). Similarly, Belli, Traugott, and Beckmann (2001) estimated that more than 20 percent of nonvoters claimed to have voted in the American National Election Studies (ANES);

this estimate was based on a comparison of the survey reports with voting records. Studies like these demonstrate that survey respondents consistently underreport a broad range of socially undesirable behaviors and overreport an equally broad range of socially desirable behaviors (see Tourangeau and Yan, 2007, for a recent review).

Surveys have deployed a variety of methods in an effort to improve reporting of sensitive information, including self-administration of the questions, the bogus pipeline, and the randomized response technique. The bogus pipeline refers to any device or procedure that respondents believe can detect lies. For example, in a survey that asks about smoking, respondents may be asked to provide a breath sample or a saliva sample (e.g., Bauman and Dent, 1982).[1] The randomized response technique is a method in which the respondent uses a randomizing device (such as a spinner or the toss of a coin) to determine which question he or she answers. The respondent might receive one of two statements about a sensitive topic (A: I have had an abortion; B: I have never had an abortion) with known probabilities. The respondent reports whether he or she agrees with the statement selected by the spinner or coin toss without revealing which statement it is. There is considerable evidence for the effectiveness of both the bogus pipeline (e.g., Murray, O'Connell, Schmid, and Perry, 1987) and the randomized response technique (see Lensvelt-Mulders, Hox, van der Heijden, and Maas, 2005, for a meta-analysis) for reducing social desirability bias in survey reports.

Gains from self-administration. Because of the practical difficulties involved in using the bogus pipeline and the randomized response techniques, few national studies use these methods for collecting sensitive information, but many national studies use self-administration, often in the form of audio-CASI (ACASI), in which the questions are displayed on screen while recordings of the questions are played to the respondent via earphones. For example, both the NSFG and the National Survey of Drug Use and Health (NSDUH) use ACASI to administer some of the questions. Tourangeau and Yan (2007, pp. 863–867) report strong evidence supporting the claim that self-administration increases sensitive reports, both with self-administration via paper questionnaires and self-administration via computerized methods like ACASI. A key question is whether Web surveys preserve the gains found with other methods of self-administration.

At least 14 papers have examined this issue, comparing Web administration of the items with one or more other methods of administration. Table 7.1 presents the key features of these studies. Several of the studies compare Web surveys with paper self-administration (for example, Denniston, Brener, Kann, Eaton, McManus, Kyle, Roberts, Flint, and Ross, 2010; Denscombe, 2006). Four of these studies (Chang and Krosnick, 2009; Denniston et al., 2010, and Eaton, Brener, Kann, Denniston, McManus, Kyle, Roberts, Flint, and Ross, 2010; Link and Mokdad, 2005a,b; and

---

[1] Both breath and saliva samples can be used to determine whether someone has smoked recently, making this a "true" pipeline rather than a bogus one.

TABLE 7.1. Studies on Web Surveys and Reports about Sensitive Topics

Study	Target Population	Sample Sizes (respondents), by Mode	Key Findings
Bälter et al. (2005)	Adults in a single county in Sweden	Mail: 188 Web: 295	No significant difference by mode in reports of smoking status.
Bason (2000)	Students at a university	Telephone: 161 Interactive Voice Response (IVR): 128 Mail: 204 Web: 115	No significant differences by mode in reported prevalence or frequency of drug use or binge drinking; significantly higher proportions of students report *no* alcohol use in Web and IVR
Bates and Cox (2008)	Students at a university	Paper: 73 Web: 64	No differences in reported drinking or sexual behavior by mode
Chang and Krosnick (2009)	General population	**Pre-Election** Telephone: 1,506 Web: Harris Interactive (HI): 2,306 Web: Knowledge Networks (KN): 4,933 **Post-Election** Telephone: 1,206 Web: Harris Interactive (HI): 1,028 Web: Knowledge Networks (KN): 3,416	Less social desirability bias on racial attitude item in Web surveys
Denniston et al. (2010); same study is also reported by Eaton et al., (2010)	9th and 10th grade students	In-class paper: 1,729 In-class Web (no skips): 1,735 In-class Web (skips): 1,763 Web outside of class (without skips): 559	Web administration in the classroom seen as significantly less private than paper classroom administration
Denscombe (2006)	15-year olds at one school	In-class paper: 220 In-class Web: 69	Only one item in 23 shows a significant difference by mode
Eaton et al. (2010); see Denniston et al. (2010) above	9th and 10th grade students	In-class paper: 1,729 In-class Web (no skips): 1,735 In-class Web (skips): 1,763	Significant differences between Web and paper versions of the survey in reported prevalence for seven of 74 risky behaviors; reported prevalence higher in Web for all seven

(Continued)

TABLE 7.1. *(Continued)*

Study	Target Population	Sample Sizes (respondents), by Mode	Key Findings
Knapp and Kirk (2003)	Students at a single university	Paper: 174 IVR: 121 Web: 57	No significant differences on any of 58 sensitive questions
Kreuter, Presser, and Tourangeau (2008)	Alumni at one university	Telephone: 320 IVR: 363 Web: 320	Web respondents significantly more likely to report academic problems than CATI respondents; Web respondents had lowest false negative rates for four academic problems. No differences in reporting by mode for positive academic performance.
Link and Mokdad (2005a); this is the same study reported by Link and Mokdad (2005b) below	Adults in four states	Mail: 836 Telephone: 2,072 Web: 1,143	Web respondents report significantly more days drinking and significantly more binge drinking than telephone respondents (see Table 7.2 for more detailed findings).
Link and Mokdad (2005b)	Adults in four states	Mail: 836 Telephone: 2,072 Web: 1,143	Web respondents significantly differ from telephone respondents in six of eight health conditions (reporting significantly higher rates of diabetes, high blood pressure, obesity, and binge drinking, but lower rates of smoking and STD prevention; see Table 7.2 below).
McCabe et al.(2002); this is the same study reported by McCabe (2004) and McCabe et al. (2006) below	Undergraduates at a single university	Mail: 1,412 Web: 2,194	No differences by mode in reported drinking and smoking habits.

(Continued)

TABLE 7.1. *(Continued)*

Study	Target Population	Sample Sizes (respondents), by Mode	Key Findings
McCabe (2004); this is the same study reported by McCabe et al. (2006) below	Undergraduates at a single university	Mail: 1,412 Web: 2,194	Two significant differences in reporting by mode in 32 comparisons; both men and women report greater lifetime use of cocaine via the Web.
McCabe et al. (2006)	Undergraduates at a single university	Mail: 1,412 Web: 2,194	No differences by mode in reported prevalence of consequences of drug use.

McCabe, 2004, and McCabe, Couper, Cranford, and Boyd, 2006) involve large samples and were done under realistic survey conditions, and we examine these four in more detail here.

Election surveys comparison. Chang and Krosnick (2009) compared results from two telephone surveys conducted by Ohio State University's Center for Survey Research (CSR) with results from similar surveys done over the Web with members of two major Web survey panels—the Knowledge Networks (KN) and the Harris Interactive (HI) panels. The initial round of surveys was carried out in June and July of 2000 (that is, prior to the presidential election that year) and a second round of surveys was done in November (just after the election). Respondents who completed the pre-election survey were also asked to complete the post-election survey. The response rates for the pre-election surveys were 43 percent for the CSR telephone survey and 25 percent for the KN panel; a response rate could not be calculated for the HI panel, since it is a sample of volunteers. The reinterview rates for the post-election surveys were 80 percent for respondents from the CSR telephone sample, 82 percent for the KN sample, and 45 percent for the HI sample. The comparisons across surveys clearly reflect coverage and nonresponse differences as well as measurement differences; the data from all three surveys were weighted to adjust for differences in their demographic makeup.

For our purposes, the key outcome was the answers given by white respondents to an item asking whether the federal government should give more, less, or the same amount of help to African-Americans. Chang and Krosnick argue that advocating less help is a socially undesirable response for whites. Telephone respondents were significantly less likely to select this answer (17.0 percent) than members of either Web panel (35.8 for the KN panel and 42.5 for the HI panel); these differences across the samples persisted when the data were weighted and covariates were used to adjust for differences across the samples in background characteristics.

Youth Risk Behavior Survey (YRBS) experiment. The second large-scale mode comparison study was done by Denniston and her colleagues (2010; see also Eaton et al., 2010), who examined answers to the YRBS questionnaire. Their study compared four data collection conditions: 1) a paper questionnaire administered to students in their classrooms (this is the procedure ordinarily used in the YRBS); 2) a Web survey (programmed without any skip patterns to mimic the paper version more closely) that was also administered in classrooms; 3) a Web survey *with* skip patterns administered in class; and 4) a Web survey without skip patterns completed by respondents at a location of their own choosing. The participants were 9th or 10th grade students at a convenience sample of 85 schools in 15 states. At each of the schools, four classes were selected, with one class at each school randomly assigned to each experimental condition. In most of the schools, the Web survey was administered in the school's computer lab.

The questionnaire included 77 items from the 2007 YRBS questionnaire, including 70 sensitive questions asking about "unintentional injuries and violence, tobacco use, alcohol and other drug use, sexual behaviors, weight control behaviors, and physical activity" (Eaton et al., 2010, page 141). Twelve additional questions asked about the survey itself. More than 5,000 students took part in the three in-class conditions, and more than 500 additional students completed the questionnaire on their own. The authors found little difference between the two in-class Web conditions and combined the results for these two groups. The final Web group seems to have been dropped because of the low response rate in that group (28 percent for that condition versus 90 percent or higher for the remaining three). In-school Web respondents were significantly more likely than respondents to the paper questionnaire to report seven risky behaviors (riding with a driver who'd been drinking, carrying a weapon at school, being hit by a dating partner, using marijuana on school grounds, using smokeless tobacco at school, drinking or taking drugs before having sex, and not trying to quit smoking) out of a possible 74. In addition, Denniston and colleagues (2010) report that the in-class Web survey was seen as significantly *less* private and anonymous than the paper questionnaire; those who completed the Web version of the questionnaire nonetheless reported more risky behaviors than those who completed the paper questionnaire.

Behavioral Risk Factor Surveillance System (BRFSS) experiment. The two papers by Link and Mokdad (2005a,b) report another large-scale study, this one comparing telephone, mail, and Web versions of the questionnaire used in the BRFSS. BRFSS has traditionally been conducted over the telephone but, as response rates for telephone surveys have continued to decline (Curtin, Presser, and Singer, 2005), the researchers have explored alternative methods for collecting the data. Link and Mokdad conducted two experiments in four states during the fall of 2003. The first experiment invited sample members to complete the questionnaire online; the second involved mailing a paper questionnaire to sample members. In both cases, the responses were compared to the ongoing BRFSS computer-assisted telephone interviews (CATI) done in the same states during the same months. The telephone samples were selected through RDD; only telephone numbers that were matched to an address were retained in the samples. Nonresponding cases in the mail and Internet groups were followed up by telephone (but these follow-up telephone interviews are dropped in the analyses described here). In total, more than 6,000 respondents completed the questionnaire.

Link and Mokdad (2005a,b) examine reports about a variety of health conditions and drinking behaviors, adjusting the reported prevalences within the three mode groups for state and various demographic variables. Table 7.2 shows the key results from the two papers. Relative to the telephone interviews, Web data collection elicits higher rates of reported drinking as well as higher reported prevalences of several health conditions. For the most part, these differences in reporting hold up even after demographic controls are introduced into the models.

University student experiment. McCabe and his colleagues (McCabe, 2004; McCabe, Boyd, Couper, and Crawford, and d'Arcy, 2002; McCabe, Couper,

TABLE 7.2. Prevalence Estimates, by Condition in BRFSS Experiments

	CATI	Web	Mail	Web vs. CATI
HEALTH CONDITIONS				**ADJUSTED ODDS RATIO**
Asthma	11.7	12.0	11.9	1.06
Diabetes	9.5	11.9	10.2	1.30*
High blood pressure	31.1	38.1	33.2	1.30*
BMI greater than 30	21.6	26.5	25.6	1.31*
Current smoker	22.8	16.9	17.3	0.77*
Binge drinking	14.4	12.3	21.6	1.87*
STD prevention	8.2	4.3	3.3	0.51*
Tested for HIV	38.8	30.8	32.1	0.85
DRINKING BEHAVIORS				**SIGNIFICANCE LEVEL**
Mean number of days in the last 30 had 1+ drinks	4.5	4.7	5.2	$p < .01$
Mean number of drinks per day on days with 1+ drinks	2.1	2.1	2.2	ns
Mean number of days had 5+ drinks	1.0	1.2	1.9	$p < .001$
Percent had a drink in last 30 days	55	52	60	ns

Note: Significance levels in the bottom panel of the table are not adjusted for demographic differences across mode groups. * indicates that the adjusted odds ratio differs significantly from 1.0.

Cranford, and Boyd, 2006) conducted an experiment on a sample of undergraduates at a large university, comparing mail and Web data collection. Students assigned to the mail condition were sent a letter inviting them to take part and a paper questionnaire. Those assigned to the Web condition received an email invitation to complete the survey online. McCabe and his colleagues adapted questions from the 2001 Student Life Survey, which included items about drug and alcohol use. Students reported on their lifetime and last year use of eight types of illicit drugs. McCabe (2004) controlled for demographic differences across the two samples and found that only one of the 16 comparisons was statistically significant: Both men and women reported significantly higher rates of lifetime cocaine use in the Web questionnaire than in the mail version. A follow-up study (McCabe et al., 2006) found no differences on responses to ten other sensitive questions in the questionnaire.

Maryland alumni study. One additional study, conducted by Kreuter, Presser, and Tourangeau (2008), is worth describing in detail because the researchers were able to validate the survey answers for some of the items against university records. Kreuter and her colleagues had interviewers contact alumni of the University of Maryland by telephone; after they had answered a few screening questions, respondents were asked to complete a questionnaire that included questions about their undergraduate experiences at the university. Approximately a third of the respondents were randomly assigned to complete the main questionnaire by telephone; another third was switched to an IVR system to complete the main questionnaire; and the remaining respondents were given instructions for completing the questions online. The questionnaire included items that asked about academic successes and failures during the respondent's undergraduate years, such as receiving academic honors or getting a failing grade in a course. Kreuter and her colleagues compared the survey responses to these items to the official transcripts for the alumni.

Table 7.3 presents the key results from this study. The top panel shows the rates of reporting on the nine sensitive questions from the survey for which records data were available. The bottom panel shows the false negative rates for the undesirable items (such as getting a D or an F in a course) and the false positive rates for the desirable items (e.g., having a high GPA).[2] Web respondents were significantly more likely than CATI respondents to report at least one of the undesirable items; Web respondents were also were significantly *less* likely than CATI respondents to misreport in a socially desirable direction. These mode differences seem larger for the undesirable academic outcomes than for the desirable items, but the latter may not be as sensitive as the former. The reporting differences between Web and telephone were significant for two of the four undesirable items and for a composite based on all four.

---

[2] The false negative rate is the proportion of cases with an undesirable characteristic (for example, who dropped a class) who deny it; similarly, the false positive rate is the proportion of cases without a desirable characteristic (a GPA higher than 3.5) who nonetheless falsely report that characteristic.

TABLE 7.3. Percentage Reporting and Misreporting Rates for Desirable and Undesirable Characteristics, by Condition in Maryland Alumni Survey

	CATI	IVR	Web
PERCENT REPORTING UNDESIRABLE CHARACTERISTIC			
GPA lower than 2.5	1.8	3.7	6.2
At least one D or F	42.2	44.3	50.7
Dropped a class	46.7	45.6	50.6
Received warning or placed on academic probation	10.2	13.4	13.8
DESIRABLE CHARACTERISTIC			
GPA higher than 3.5	23.8	23.8	24.2
Received honors	16.3	19.9	15.5
Ever donated to alumni fund	42.1	40.5	41.3
Donated in last year	44.2	41.9	40.5
Member of Alumni Association	24.8	21.5	23.6
FALSE NEGATIVE RATE			
GPA lower than 2.5	83.3	69.2	61.5
At least one D or F	33.0	28.3	19.9
Dropped a class	34.3	34.2	31.6
Received warning or placed on academic probation	33.3	33.3	25.0
FALSE POSITIVE RATE			
GPA higher than 3.5	7.4	1.9	6.0
Received honors	5.2	5.7	6.4
Ever donated to alumni fund	24.3	19.2	20.3
Donated in last year	25.6	25.9	23.3
Member of Alumni Association	10.7	10.1	8.1

Note: Data are from Kreuter, Presser, and Tourangeau (2008), Tables 6 and 9.

Meta-analysis results. Are there any general conclusions we can reach based on these studies about the Web as a method for collecting potentially embarrassing information? We carried out a meta-analysis of the ten mode studies summarized in Table 7.1 to determine whether there was an overall trend to the results. These studies represent the pool of studies we found that met three criteria:

- First, they reported true experiments comparing Web data collection with some other mode of data collection (with random assignment to mode of data collection) or quasi-experiments that closely approximated true experiments (e.g., Chang and Krosnick, 2009); we excluded studies in which the respondents selected the mode by which they responded.

TABLE 7.4. Mean Effect Sizes and Standard Errors for Studies, by Study and Mode Comparison

Study	Sample Sizes	Mean Effect Size	Standard Error
WEB VS. MAIL/PAPER			
Bälter et al. (2005)	Mail: 188	0.054	0.309
	Web: 295		
Bason (2000)	Mail: 204	-0.168	0.129
	Web: 115		
Bates and Cox (2008)	Mail: 73	-0.014	0.180
	Web: 64		
Eaton et al. (2010)	Mail: 1,729	0.070	0.012
	Web: 3,498		
Denscombe (2006)	Mail: 267	-0.256	0.120
	Web: 69		
Knapp and Kirk (2003)	Mail: 174	-0.077	0.119
	Web: 57		
Link and Mokdad (2005a, 2005b)	Mail: 836; 804–820	0.068	0.039
	Web: 1,143; 948–1,139		
McCabe (2002, 2004;	Mail: 1,412	0.006	0.019
McCabe et al., 2006)	Web: 2,194		
WEB VS. TELEPHONE			
Bason (2000)	Phone: 161	-0.503	0.132
	Web: 115		
Chang and Krosnick (2009)	Phone Pre-Election: 1,456	0.172	0.035
	Web Pre-Election:		
	HI: 2,313		
	KN: 4,914		
	Phone Post-Election: 1,206		
	Web Post-Election:		
	HI: 1,040		
	KN: 3,408		
Knapp and Kirk (2003)	Phone: 121	0.193	0.126
	Web: 57		
Kreuter et al. (2008)	Phone: 320	0.157	0.060
	Web: 363		
Link and Mokdad (2005a, 2005b)	Phone: 2,072; 2,066–2,070	0.026	0.031
	Web: 1,143; 948–1,139		
WEB VS. IVR			
Bason (2000)	IVR: 128	0.108	0.143
	Web: 115		
Kreuter et al. (2008)	IVR: 320	0.081	0.060
	Web: 363		

Note: Sample sizes fluctuate due to item nonresponse. The mean effect sizes are weighted averages of the log odds ratios comparing reports from Web surveys to reports obtained under other modes of data collection.

- Second, they examined responses to survey questions with clear potential for social desirability bias; we excluded studies that examined non-survey items, such as psychological measures of socially desirable responding.
- Third, the studies reported quantitative estimates (such as means or proportions) that could be converted to standard measures of effect sizes.

In total, the studies report 223 mode comparisons, 160 involving Web and paper questionnaires. Table 7.4 shows the mean effect size for each study (that is, the average log odds ratio for the estimates presented in each study) and the associated standard error for each of these study-level means. A positive effect size indicates that a higher proportion of the respondents in the Web condition reported the sensitive characteristic or behavior than those in the other mode condition. For example, the mean effect size of 0.054 from the study by Bälter and her colleagues shows that the Web respondents in that study were, on average, more likely to disclose sensitive information than the mail survey respondents. The study means are weighted averages where each effect size estimate is weighted by the inverse of its squared standard error (Lipsey and Wilson, 2001).

We analyzed the data from these 10 studies, treating the effect size estimates as clustered by study. The meta-analysis results support two main conclusions. First, relative to interviewer-administered telephone surveys, Web data collection appears to yield more reports of sensitive information (Chang and Krosnick, 2009; Kreuter, Presser, and Tourangeau, 2008; Link and Mokdad, 2005a, 2005b; but see Bason, 2000, for an apparent exception). Across the six studies comparing the two modes, the overall effect size is 0.088, but the effect does not differ significantly from zero ($t = 1.69$, df = 7), in part due to the large reversal reported by Bason. If that study is dropped, the mean effect size for telephone-Web comparisons rises to .105 (with a standard error of .052). At least one study in this group (Kreuter et al., 2008) shows that the increase in reporting represents an increase in accuracy (see the bottom two panels of Table 7.3 above). These findings are in line with prior analyses of the benefits of self-administration for eliciting potentially embarrassing information (Tourangeau and Yan, 2007).

Second, relative to paper self-administration, online administration seems to offer only a small advantage in reporting. The overall mean effect size for the Web-paper comparisons is 0.030, with a standard error of 0.023. An earlier meta-analysis by Tourangeau and Yan (2007) also found a nonsignificant advantage for computerized questionnaires (not necessarily online questionnaires) over paper questionnaires for increasing reports of sensitive information (see also Richman, Kiesler, Weisband, and Drasgow, 1999, who found that computer administration can either increase or decrease socially desirable responding depending on the type of question; with sensitive behavioral items like those used in the studies discussed here, computerization seemed to *increase* socially desirable responding).

The impact of the data collection setting. University and other school populations are attractive targets for Web surveys because Internet access is high among high school and college students and response rates for Web surveys are likely to be relatively high for these populations as well. Indeed, in McCabe's experiment with a student sample, the response rate to the Web survey was significantly higher than the response rate for the mail survey (McCabe, 2004; McCabe et al., 2006), reversing the usual trend (Lozar Manfreda, Bosnjak, Berzelak, Haas, and Vehovar, 2008; Shih and Fan, 2008; see Chapter 3). Several of the other studies summarized in Table 7.1 also use samples of students to test the effectiveness of the Web for collecting sensitive information.

One issue that naturally arises with student populations is whether to collect the data in school (for example, in a classroom or computer lab) or at home or somewhere else outside school. Researchers have argued that the school may be better than the home for collecting data on illicit drug use among adolescents (Fendrich and Johnson, 2001; Fowler and Stringfellow, 2001). Several studies have examined the effects of the data collection setting empirically. An experiment by Brener, Easton, Kann, Grunbaum, Gross, Kyle, and Ross (2006) compared computerized and paper self-administration of risk behavior questions in the classroom and outside school, typically in the respondent's home. For 30 of the 55 items the authors examined, there was a significant effect of the setting; in all cases, higher levels of risky behavior were reported in school than at home (confirming the conjecture of Fendrich and Johnson, 2001, and of Fowler and Stringfellow, 2001, that data collection in school leads to higher reports of sensitive behaviors than data collection at home). For seven of the items, computerized administration led to significantly higher levels of reporting than paper administration and for five of the 55 items the setting and mode interacted. In most cases, the computer-paper difference seemed to be larger when the students completed the questionnaire in school than when they completed it at home. Beebe and his colleagues (Beebe, Harrison, McCrae, Anderson, and Fulkerson, 1998) found little overall difference between computer and paper administration in a survey conducted in schools, but found that the computer *reduced* reporting relative to paper administration of the questions when students were seated close to each other and privacy was presumably low.

The studies by Brener and her coauthors and by Beebe and his colleagues both look at computerized administration versus paper but not at computerized administration via the Web. Bates and Cox (2008) examined both Web and paper administration of sensitive questions in three different settings—a group administration in a classroom, individual administration in a private office, and individual administration in whatever setting the respondent chose. For two of the five items, they found a significant effect for the setting (more respondents reported sensitive behaviors when they completed the questions in a setting of their own choosing than in the other settings), but this variable did not interact with the method of data collection.

Denniston and her colleagues (Denniston et al., 2010) report that Web data collection in the classroom was seen by the respondents as less confidential than paper data collection in that setting, but respondents still reported more sensitive information via the Web.

Overall, then, the school may be a better place than the home to collect sensitive information from high school students, but the setting doesn't seem to interact with the method of self-administration. For student populations, computerized self-administration, including Web administration of the questions, appears to produce higher levels of reporting of sensitive information than paper self-administration.

Humanizing the interface. Chapter 6 discussed the pros and cons of humanizing the interface in a Web survey, for example, by having "virtual" interviewers administer the questions. Here, we briefly review the findings about whether adding such humanizing touches to a Web survey may counteract some of the advantages of self-administered data collection, specifically decreased socially desirability bias and reduced interviewer effects.

Studies by Nass and his colleagues and by Kiesler and her colleagues raise the possibility that even minimal humanizing features (such as the voice used by the interface) can trigger reactions from a user like the reactions a live actor would produce (such as gender stereotyping; see, for example, Nass, Moon, and Green, 1997; Sproull, Subramini, Kiesler, Walker, and Waters, 1996). Tourangeau, Couper, and Steiger (2003) reported a series of Web experiments in which they systematically varied features of the Web interface to determine how the addition of humanizing cues affected respondents' willingness to disclose information about health behaviors, illicit drug use, and other sensitive topics. These studies examined the effects of including pictures of a male or female researcher in the Web survey, of providing tailored interactive feedback based on the respondent's answers, and of using personalized language (e.g., addressing the respondent by name). They found little evidence that respondents changed their answers to the sensitive behavioral items when the survey included such humanizing features. They did some find evidence that the pictures of the researchers affected answers to a battery of questions on sex roles; respondents gave more pro-feminist responses when the Web survey displayed pictures of a female researcher than when it displayed pictures of a male one. The effect was small but statistically significant and paralleled similar findings with live male and female interviewers (Kane and Macaulay, 1993).

More recent studies suggest that including virtual interviewers in computer-administered surveys may have bigger effects on the answers than those found by Tourangeau, Couper, and Steiger. An experiment by Krysan and Couper (2003) compared live interviewers with digitized video recordings of the same interviewers reading the questions; their experiment also systematically varied the race of the interviewers. The experiment was relatively small (with a total of 160 respondents) and most of the findings were not statistically significant. Still, among black respondents, some significant race-of-interviewer effects were found (for example, blacks reported more negative attitudes toward whites to black interviewers than to white ones). These effects tended to be similar for live and virtual interviewers and they tended to replicate Schuman and Converse's (1971) classic findings for black respondents in face-to-face interviews with live interviewers. Fuchs (2009) did a Web survey comparing two virtual interviewer conditions—with video recordings of a male and female interviewer reading the questions—with a text-only condition. (The Krysan and Couper study used a computer-administered survey on a laptop rather than an online survey.) In three of four comparisons in Fuchs's study, female respondents were significantly more likely to reveal sensitive sexual information (such as whether they had ever had a sexually transmitted disease) to the female virtual interviewer than to the male virtual interviewer; the pattern was less clear for the males, with only one of four items showing a significant sex-of-interviewer effect. Finally, two unpublished studies done by Conrad, Schober, and their colleagues (Conrad, Schober, and Nielsen, 2011, and Lind, Schober, Conrad, and Reichert, 2011) showed race-of-virtual-interviewer effects on racial attitude questions (Conrad et al., 2011) and increases in socially desirable responding on sensitive behavioral questions with virtual interviewers that showed facial movements as they administered the questions (Lind et al., 2011). With some items, the Web survey with virtual interviewers produced results that were similar to those from face-to-face interviews; with other items, the virtual interviewers produced results in between those from face-to-face interviews and those from audio-CASI interviews (Lind et al., 2011).

Taken together, the more recent results suggest that as virtual interviewers become more lifelike, their effects will resemble those of live interviewers more closely, with race- and gender-of-interviewer effects for answers to attitude questions and increases in socially desirable responding for sensitive behavioral items.

Summary. Web survey administration appears to share the virtues of earlier forms of self-administration. Our meta-analysis indicates that Web administration is, if anything, better than paper self-administration for eliciting sensitive information. An experiment by Kreuter, Presser, and Tourangeau (2008) shows that Web data collection improved reporting accuracy (at least for socially undesirable items) relative to an interviewer-administered telephone survey. Web data collection may be especially useful among student populations (at least when the data collection setting is private). Experiments in humanizing the interface in Web surveys, especially through the use of virtual interviewers, suggest that virtual interviewers may exhibit some of the same drawbacks as live ones, reducing reports of sensitive behaviors and possibly producing race- and sex-of-interviewer effects on attitude items related to race or gender. Still, as we note in Chapter 6, there may be offsetting advantages to using virtual interviewers, such as increased engagement by the respondents. For sensitive questions and questions related to race, gender, or other obvious interviewer charac-teristics, a standard interface is likely to be better than an interface that incorporates humanizing cues.

7.3 WEB SURVEYS AND COGNITIVE BURDEN

Like other methods of self-administration that rely primarily on visual presentation of the questions, Web surveys may reduce cognitive burden relative to interviewer-administered modes of data collection, particularly modes (such as telephone inter-viewing) that depend on auditory presentation. With low literacy respondents, of course, this relationship may be reversed—Web surveys may increase burden rela-tive to telephone surveys. With a Web survey, respondents can complete the ques-tions when they want to and at their own pace; in addition, they can easily reread the questions. Eye-tracking studies suggest that respondents often go back to reread the questions in Web surveys; by contrast, in telephone surveys, respondents rarely ask the interviewer to repeat the question. There are two lines of evidence that suggest that Web surveys may reduce cognitive burden relative to telephone surveys and thus produce better data.

Knowledge questions. Two studies have compared Web surveys to telephone interviews for assessing respondent knowledge. The first, by Fricker, Galešic, Tourangeau, and Yan (2005), experimented with a battery of basic science knowl-edge questions periodically used by the National Science Foundation to measure the scientific literacy of the American public (Miller, 1998). Fricker and his colleagues administered these questions to a national sample of adults selected through RDD. After the respondents completed a few screening questions, those with Internet access were randomly assigned to complete the main survey (including the science knowledge questions) either by telephone or online. Although the cases assigned to the telephone condition were much more likely to complete the survey than those assigned to the Web (almost 98 percent stayed on the telephone and completed the knowledge questions versus 52 percent of those in the Web condition), the two groups of respondents did not differ significantly in their demographic characteris-tics or educational backgrounds. The respondents who completed the survey online had higher knowledge scores than those who completed it on the telephone, getting an average of about 70 percent of the items correct versus 64 percent for the tele-phone respondents. The mode difference was larger for the open-ended items than for true-false questions, suggesting that the Web helped more with more cognitively demanding items. Fricker and his coauthors also found that the Web respondents took more time in completing the questions than the telephone respondents, with most of the difference reflecting the greater amount of time respondents spent on the open-ended questions when they answered them online.

Strabac and Aalberg (2011) report findings similar to those of Fricker and his colleagues. They administered six political knowledge questions to members of Web panels and respondents to telephone surveys in the United States and Norway. The

Gallup Organization carried out the telephone surveys in both countries; different Web panels were used as the Web arm of the study in the two countries. The study was not a true experiment, since it used existing Web panels rather than assigning sample members randomly to telephone or Web data collection. Respondents were asked to identify three political leaders (e.g., Robert Mugabe) and three international organizations (e.g., OPEC). There were significant differences in the proportion of correct answers in five of 12 unweighted comparisons, and all five favored the Web. The results were even clearer when the data were weighted to adjust the age, sex, and education distributions of the respondents. In 11 of 12 comparisons, a higher percentage of Web respondents got the right answer, and six of these differences were statistically significant.

Both of these studies made attempts to rule out the possibility that Web respondents were looking up the answers online as they completed the survey. Strabac and Aalberg (2011) gave Web respondents only 30 seconds to submit an answer to each question. Fricker and his colleagues report that the advantage for the Web respondents was greater for items that were hard to look up online (such as a question asking why a study with a control group was better than a study without one) than for those for which it was easy to look up the answers.

Scale responses. Another potential consequence of reduced cognitive burden or more thoughtful processing of the questions via the Web would be greater reliability or validity of the answers. Several studies have compared Web and paper administration of the same batteries of questions. For example, Ritter, Lorig, Laurent, and Matthews (2004) describe one experiment along these lines. Their study involved 397 respondents who completed 16 health batteries (some of them consisting of a single item) over the Internet or through the mail. A small subsample of 30 Web respondents also completed the batteries a second time. Paper administration (particularly in the form of mail questionnaires) presumably offers the same opportunities for self-pacing and rereading of the questions that the Web does. Overall, Ritter and his colleagues found no significant differences in the means for the 16 scales and no differences in the reliability of the scales (as estimated by Cronbach's alpha). These findings seem representative of the large body of studies comparing Web data collection with paper administration of the same multi-item scales.

The picture changes when the comparison is between data collection over the Web and over the telephone. Chang and Krosnick (2009) report several comparisons from their study showing that random measurement error was lower in the two Web panels than in the telephone survey; across the three samples, the reliability and predictive validity estimates for the items were lowest within the telephone sample. For example, vote choice in the 2000 presidential election was more strongly related to a set of predictors when the questions were administered online than when they were administered by telephone.

Some researchers have argued that telephone respondents are more likely than respondents to mail or Web surveys to select the most extreme answer options (e.g.,

Christian, Dillman, and Smyth, 2008; Dillman and Tarnai, 1991). By reducing this tendency to select the most extreme answer, Web administration may increase the validity of scale responses relative to telephone interviews. A meta-analysis by Ye, Fulton, and Tourangeau (2011) found that there is a systematic difference in the distribution of answers by mode, but the difference is much more marked at the positive end of the scale. Telephone respondents, they found, were more likely than mail or Web respondents to select the most extreme *positive* answer. Ye and his colleagues argue that the key variable is the presence of an interviewer rather than the visual channel of presentation. The most positive option was selected even more often by respondents interviewed face-to-face than by those interviewed over the telephone and it was selected less often in IVR interviews than in interviewer-administered telephone surveys. Most of the surveys reviewed by Ye and his coauthors collected customer satisfaction ratings.

Within Web surveys, scale reliability or validity may be affected by the method for entering the answers (for example, visual analog scales versus radio buttons) or the visual arrangement of the response options on screen (e.g., vertically or horizontally). Chapter 6 already discussed the use of slider bars and other visual analog scales and finds little evidence to recommend them. Chapter 5 examined the issues raised by the spacing and arrangement of the response options for attitude scales. At least one clear conclusion emerging from the studies reviewed there is that the appearance of the scale options ought to parallel the structure of the underlying dimension; for example, the visual midpoint of the scale should coincide with the conceptual midpoint of the dimension and the options should be evenly spaced when the scale points are intended to represent equal intervals (Tourangeau, Couper, and Conrad, 2004).

Web versus face-to-face data collection. Most of the mode comparisons involving the Web have compared Internet data collection to mail or telephone surveys (see, for example, Table 7.4). A study by Heerwegh and Loosveldt (2008) is an exception. They carried out a randomized experiment that compared a Web survey to face-to-face data collection. Heerwegh and Loosveldt report mixed results. They found less non-differentiation in the Web survey than in the face-to-face interviews, but Web respondents were more likely than those interviewed face-to-face to select DK responses and middle response options, both potential signs of survey satisficing. The Web surveys were also completed more quickly, on average, than the face-to-face interviews.

Several additional experiments have compared Web surveys with face-to-face interviews for the collection of contingent valuation (CV) data. CV studies typically present respondents with detailed information about some environmental good and then elicit the respondent's willingness to pay to protect that good. Lindhjem and Navrud (2011a) review six studies comparing face-to-face and Web CV surveys and find no consistent differences between the data collected under the two modes (see also Lindhjem and Navrud, 2011b; Marta-Pedroso, Freitas, and Domingos,

2007; and Nielsen, 2011). In general, across these studies, mean willingness to pay did not differ by mode and there was no clear evidence of reduced data quality in the Web surveys.

7.4 SUMMARY

Web surveys have several important features that may reduce measurement error relative to other methods of data collection:

1) The questions are administered by the computer rather than by an interviewer, a feature that may reduce social desirability bias in the answers and eliminate interviewer effects;
2) The primary channel for presenting the questions is visual, allowing the incorporation of photographs, video clips, etc.;
3) The survey can be interactive, providing various types of help to the respondent and routing the respondents to the appropriate questions;
4) The respondent controls the pace of the survey questions and can easily reread the questions, features that can reduce the cognitive burden of answering.

Each of these features of Web surveys can affect how easily and how accurately respondents answer the questions. Chapters 5 and 6 discussed in detail the impact of visual presentation and the interactive capabilities of Web surveys. This chapter focused on the first and fourth characteristics of Web surveys—their elimination of interviewers and their effect on cognitive burden. Of course, in addition to these four characteristics, Web surveys are automated and they offer all the usual advantages of automated data collection (e.g., the ability to tailor questions based on pre-loaded information or answers to earlier questions, automated skips and routing, edit checks that ensure the answers are within some predetermined range, randomization of the order of the questions or of the response options, and so on). These features mean that Web surveys can administer highly complex questionnaires.

The Web seems to share the advantages of earlier methods of self-administration for collecting sensitive information for respondents. The meta-analysis summarized in Table 7.4 indicates that Web surveys are at least as good as mail or other paper forms of self-administration for eliciting embarrassing admissions. The results there also suggest that Web surveys are superior to interviewer-administered telephone surveys for collecting information on illicit drug use, sexual behaviors, or other potentially sensitive topics. These advantages of Web data collection may be especially large for younger respondents and they may be undermined when the setting for completing the questions isn't private or when the interface uses virtual interviewers or incorporates other humanizing cues.

Because respondents can control the timing and pace of Web surveys, and because they can easily reread the questions, they may give more accurate answers to knowledge questions and more reliable and valid responses to batteries that assess their attitudes or other psychological traits. These advantages can be offset if the Web survey arrays the response options in misleading ways. And with populations that have difficulty reading or low computers skills, any cognitive advantages of Web survey are likely to disappear or be reversed.

/// 8 /// SUMMARY AND CONCLUSIONS

This chapter brings together the main conclusions from the earlier chapters, discussing the strengths and weaknesses of Web surveys in terms of the standard survey error concepts—sampling, coverage, nonresponse, and measurement error. This framework for classifying the sources of error in surveys results dates back at least to Deming's (1944) classic paper (see also Groves, 1989, and Lessler and Kalsbeek, 1992). Kish (1965) drew an even more basic distinction between errors that arise because the survey does not observe the entire population of interest and errors that arise during the process of observation (or measurement). The first type of error is often broken down further into sampling errors, coverage errors, and nonresponse errors, as we have done in this book. Most Web surveys are, as we have noted in Chapters 2 and 3, prone to relatively high levels of non-observation errors. This has prevented many government and academic sponsors from adopting Web surveys as a stand-alone method of data collection. The second type of errors—errors of observation—involve problems in measuring the members of the population who actually take part in the survey. As we have argued in Chapters 4, 5, 6, and 7, Web surveys offer a number of attractive measurement features and perform reasonably well in terms of observation errors in comparison with earlier methods of data collection (see, for example, the meta-analysis results from Chapter 7).

This chapter also presents a mathematical model that attempts to capture the overall impact of these several sources of error on Web survey estimates and we use this model to explore the pros and cons of combining data collected using two or more methods of data collection. Although our model focuses on combining data collected online with data collected via more traditional methods, it helps clarify the issues involved when data from *any* two modes of data collection are combined.

Finally, this chapter also summarizes the various recommendations made throughout the book (sometimes only implicitly) and concludes by discussing how Web surveys (and their error properties) are likely to evolve in the future.

8.1 NON-OBSERVATION ERRORS IN WEB SURVEYS

Sampling and coverage issues. Chapter 2 presented our major conclusions about sampling errors in Web surveys. The major problem is that there is no easy way to select probability samples either for the general population of Web users or for the household population as a whole. Web surveys that have attempted to recruit representative samples of the general population (or of the Internet population) have used some traditional sampling technique (such as area probability sampling, RDD, or address-based sampling) to select the sample and, in some cases, have then provided computers or Web access (or both) to sample members who would not otherwise be able to take part in a Web survey. This is the approach used by Knowledge Networks (Krotki and Dennis, 2001) in the United States and by the Longitudinal Internet Studies for the Social Sciences (LISS) panel in the Netherlands.

The traditional methods of data collection were typically linked with specific methods of sampling. For example, face-to-face interviewing has often been paired with area probability sampling and telephone surveys are often paired with RDD samples. There are no corresponding sampling methods for Internet surveys—that is, there is no method of sampling specifically designed for Internet surveys. As a result of these sampling difficulties, many Web surveys use self-selected samples of volunteers rather than probability samples. With opt-in Web panels, the sample may be subject to selection biases at two time points—when the recruits first decide whether to join the panel and again when panel members decide whether to complete a specific survey. Those who are *exposed* to the invitation to join a particular Web panel may already be an unrepresentative sample of Internet users; the bulk of panel members may come from just a few Web sites. For example, Chang and Krosnick (2009) report that more than 90 percent of the members of the Harris Poll Online Panel came from two Web sites. And, of course, such panels exclude those who don't have Internet access. In addition, Web panelists often belong to more than one online panel (Stenbjerre and Laugesen, 2005; Vonk, van Ossenbruggen, and Willems, 2006). As a result, a relatively high proportion of the data from Web panels may come from a relatively small number of highly active volunteers (Couper and Bosnjak, 2010, page 535).

Some panels attempt to compensate for these selection biases by making statistical adjustments to the data; for example, the data may be weighted to make the sample of respondents resemble the population with Internet access or the general population more closely. Studies evaluating such adjustments indicate that they are only partially successful (see Table 2.4).

Despite these limitations, there are some advantages to volunteer Web samples, whether the volunteers are recruited for a one-time survey or for a panel. Online recruitment can yield larger and more diverse samples than other types of non-probability samples, such as the mall intercept samples used in some market research studies or the psychology students from subject pools who populate much research in social and cognitive psychology. In addition, Web panels often collect detailed information about their members; this means that researchers can identify and target members of relatively rare subgroups. In some contexts, it may matter more whether the sample respondents are clearly members of the population of interest (whether, for example, they are part of the potential market for a given product) than whether they constitute a representative sample of that population. Because of these advantages and because of the relatively low cost of volunteer samples, they are widely used for a range of purposes. Couper (2007), for example, cites a number of health studies that used Web samples to study conditions ranging from social anxiety disorder to ulcerative colitis.

The second major problem for Web surveys of the general population is that, unless the sample members are provided with Internet access, no matter how they are selected and recruited, a sizable fraction of the population will be omitted. Even in relatively wealthy countries like the United States or the members of the European Union, Internet access is far from universal. Although the proportion of households without Internet access continues to shrink, there are still noticeable differences between those with Internet access and those without it (Tables 2.2 and 2.3; see also Bethlehem, 2010).

These drawbacks for general population samples are often *not* a problem with specific subpopulations, such as students at a given school or employees at a particular business. With such populations, a suitable frame may exist for selecting the sample and email addresses may be available as a method for contacting and recruiting them to complete the survey. Of course, nonresponse can be a major problem for Web surveys of these populations.

In general, though, Web survey samples often start out as unrepresentative, self-selected samples and, because of coverage problems, they may exclude a substantial portion of the target population. Those with Internet access are not a random subset of the population as a whole but differ systematically from those without Internet access. In the United States, the Internet population overrepresents young people and the highly educated compared to the population without Web access, and it underrepresents Blacks and Hispanics (see Table 2.2). The populations with and without Internet access may also differ in substantive ways. For example, those with Internet access seem to be healthier in many ways than those without access (see Table 2.3). This difference is likely to affect the results from Web surveys assessing the level of health in the general population or attempting to estimate the prevalence of different medical conditions. With other topics, there may be less bias from excluding the population without Internet access. Still, as we showed in Chapter 2, statistical corrections and related methods (such as sampling matching) remove only part of the bias introduced into Web surveys by these selection and coverage problems.

Nonresponse errors. In addition to the problem of starting with unrepresentative samples, Web surveys are prone to higher nonresponse rates than the more traditional methods of data collection and this may further reduce the representativeness of Web samples. As we saw in Chapter 3, two recent meta-analyses (Lozar Manfreda et al., 2008; Shih and Fan, 2008) compared nonresponse rates in Web surveys with nonresponse with other methods of data collection, and both studies agree that the difference in response rates averages roughly 11 percent, with Web surveys getting lower response rates than surveys using mail or the telephone to collect the data. The meta-analyses also show that the difference between Web survey response rates and those for other methods of data collection depends on several characteristics of the surveys. For example, the response rate difference is larger with one-time surveys (a 28 percent difference on average) than with panel surveys (a nine percent difference; see Lozar Manfreda et al., 2008). Shih and Fan (2008) find that the difference between Web and mail response rates varies by the survey population and by the number of reminders sent to sample members. The difference in response rates between Web and mail surveys is relatively small for college populations (3 percent in favor of Web surveys) but relatively large for surveys aimed at professionals (where Web response rates are 23 percent lower on average than mail response rates). The response rate advantage for mail surveys over Web surveys is larger when one or more reminders are sent to members of the sample. Multiple contacts don't raise Web response rates as much as they do with other types of surveys.

As with other methods of data collection, response rates for Web surveys (and participation rates in non-probability Web panels) seem to be dropping over time (Couper and Bosnjak, 2010). This decline in panel response rates may reflect the large number of requests that panel members receive each month. Many surveys—including both online surveys and surveys done by more traditional methods—have adopted incentives in an attempt to stem the decline in response rates, but for a variety of reasons, incentives do not seem as effective in Web surveys as in surveys using other methods of data collection (Göritz, 2006a). One problem is Web surveys typically offer the least effective type of incentives—nonmonetary incentives (such as prizes from sweepstakes) that are contingent on completion of the survey. Research has shown that with other modes of data collection monetary incentives are more effective than prizes or entries in a sweepstakes and that prepaid incentives are more effective than promised ones (Singer, 2002; Singer, van Hoewyk, and Gebler, 1999). Sending cash ahead of time may also be the most effective method for boosting response rates in Web surveys, but most Web surveys do not use this method.

In addition to the usual forms of nonresponse, Web surveys may be prone (or more prone) to some relatively novel forms. When potential respondents for a Web survey are recruited through some other method (such as by telephone), the Web survey may be susceptible to "mode switch" nonresponse (Sakshaug, Yan, and Tourangeau, 2010). Sakshaug and his coauthors examined a survey in which respondents were initially contacted by telephone. About 40 percent of those assigned to complete the questionnaire via the Web agreed to do the survey online but never actually started it. Sakshaug, Yan, and Tourangeau show that mode switch nonresponse was an important contributor to the overall error in the Web survey estimates. There is an analogous phenomenon with interactive voice response (IVR) surveys—respondents initially contacted by a live telephone interviewer sometimes agree to complete additional questions in an automated telephone interview, but hang up during the transfer to the IVR system. Web surveys can also have higher breakoff rates once respondents begin the online questionnaire than traditional forms of data collection such as telephone or face-to-face interviews. We suspect that the absence of an interviewer may make it easier for respondents to quit the survey partway through.

To summarize this discussion of nonresponse, Web surveys tend to have lower response rates than mail surveys (by 11 percent or so, on average) and they may be subject to forms of nonresponse, such as mode switch nonresponse and breakoffs, that are relatively rare or just not possible with more traditional methods of data collection. As with other types of surveys, response rates seem to be falling for Web surveys. Incentives, which are being used more often in surveys in recent years (at least in the United States), seem to have limited effectiveness in Web surveys (Göritz, 2006a), perhaps because most Web surveys use relatively ineffective types of incentive.

Overall effects. Web surveys are thus subject to all three major forms of non-observation error. If they use probability samples, estimates from Web surveys (like estimates based on any probability sample) are subject to random sampling error. Of more concern are the sampling biases that can result from the use of non-probability samples composed entirely of self-selected volunteers. Because of the absence of good sampling frames for the Internet population, and because the Internet population does not encompass the entire adult population of the United States or other countries, most Web surveys are also at risk for large coverage biases. Finally, Internet surveys get lower response rates than mail surveys and other surveys that use traditional methods of data collection. Even the best Web panels—those whose members were initially recruited from probability samples—suffer high rates of nonresponse during the multiple steps needed to contact and recruit panel members. Figure 8.1 depicts these three forms of non-observation error graphically.

What is the net effect of these three forms of error on the estimates from Web surveys? Several studies have attempted to gauge the overall effects of non-observation error on the representativeness of the sample for a given survey. Chang and Krosnick (2009) compared the demographic characteristics of respondents to a national RDD survey with those of respondents from two Web panels—the Harris Interactive panel, which consists of self-selected volunteers, and the Knowledge Networks (KN) panel, which was originally selected via RDD sampling. For this particular survey, members of the Harris Interactive panel were selected to match the demographic characteristics of the general population (and thus, that sample illustrates the limitations of sampling matching). Respondents in all three samples answered the same set of survey questions. Chang and Krosnick examined the demographic composition of the samples, using the figures from the Current Population Survey (CPS) sample as a benchmark. Prior to any statistical adjustments, the fresh RDD sample matches the CPS figures more closely than the two Web panels do; in addition, the KN sample generally comes closer to matching the CPS figures than the Harris Interactive panel does.

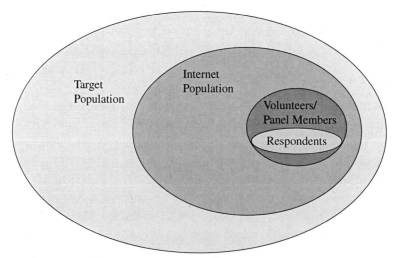

FIGURE 8.1. The largest ellipse represents the target population; the smallest ellipse, the respondents to a particular Web survey. The intermediate ellipses represent the subset of the target population with Web access and the population members who join the Web panel from which the respondents are drawn. The difference between the target and the Internet populations constitutes coverage error. The difference between the Internet population and the volunteers or panel members constitutes selection bias. The difference between the volunteers/panel members and the respondents to the survey constitutes nonresponse error. (See color insert.)

Table 8.1 shows some representative findings from the study. The top panel gives unweighted figures for the distribution of the samples by education and age; the bottom panel gives the corresponding figures after weights were applied to reduce any biases due to the non-observation errors. All three samples tend to underrepresent people with less than a high school education and to overrepresent those with a college degree or more education; these departures from the CPS figures are largest for the Harris Interactive sample and smallest for the RDD sample. Similarly, the samples underrepresent both ends of the age spectrum and overrepresent those who are between 35 and 64 years old; again, these biases are largest for the Harris Interactive sample and smallest for the RDD sample. The weights improve matters considerably, bringing the figures for all three samples into much closer alignment with the CPS figures. Tourangeau, Groves, Kennedy, and Yan (2009) report an analysis similar to the one presented by Chang and Krosnick. They compared a Web sample (drawn from two self-selected Web panels) to population figures from the American Community Survey (ACS), examining the age, sex, race, and education distribution of the Web respondents. Like the CPS, the ACS is conducted by US Census Bureau, but it has an even larger sample size. Tourangeau and his colleagues report discrepancies between the Web sample and the adult US population similar to those found by Chang and Krosnick. For example, the respondents in their study also greatly overrepresented people with a college or a more advanced degree relative to the general population.

TABLE 8.1. Composition of Samples by Education and Age, Before and After Adjustments

	Unweighted Estimates			
	RDD Sample	Knowledge Networks	Harris Interactive	CPS (March 2000)
EDUCATION				
Some high school	7.0%	6.7%	2.0%	16.9%
High school graduate	31.3	24.4	11.8	32.8
Some College	19.6	32.3	36.6	19.8
College graduate and Above	42.1	36.6	49.5	30.5
Sample size	1,504	4,925	2,306	—
AGE				
18–24	10.0%	7.8%	8.0%	13.2%
25–34	17.9	19.1	21.2	18.7
35–44	24.5	25.8	21.5	22.1
45–54	20.7	23.0	27.9	18.3
55–64	12.1	12.4	15.5	11.6
65 and older	14.9	11.9	5.8	16.1
Sample Size	1,496	4,923	2,306	—
	Weighted Estimates			
	RDD Sample	Knowledge Networks	Harris Interactive	CPS (March 2000)
EDUCATION				
Some high school	17.1%	12.3%	7.9%	16.9%
High school graduate	32.7	33.5	36.5	32.8
Some College	19.8	28.5	26.9	19.8
College graduate and above	30.3	25.6	28.8	30.5
Sample size	1,504	4,925	2,250	—
AGE				
18–24	13.5%	9.8%	6.7%	13.2%
25–34	15.3	19.1	24.4	18.7
35–44	22.7	22.8	32.3	22.1
45–54	17.8	19.8	36.6	18.3
55–64	12.4	13.4	10.4	11.6
65 and older	18.3	15.2	14.5	16.1
Sample size	1,496	4,923	2,250	—

Note: Sample sizes for a given survey fluctuate from item to item due to missing data. From Chang and Krosnick (2009).

As we noted in Chapter 2, weights are often used with Web panels to adjust the estimates. The weights are adjusted to population figures through post-stratification or raking, or they use more sophisticated methods for removing the biases;

unfortunately, substantial biases (like those found by Chang and Krosnick, 2009) often remain after the adjustments are made.

8.2 OBSERVATION ERRORS

The final form of error we address is observation, or measurement, error. Web surveys have several important features that may reduce measurement error relative to other methods of data collection:

1) The primary channel for presenting the questions is visual, allowing the incorporation of photographs, video clips, etc., to clarify the meaning of the question;
2) The survey can be interactive, providing various types of help to respondents and automatically routing them to the appropriate questions;
3) The questions are administered by the computer rather than by an interviewer, a feature that reduces social desirability bias in the answers and that offers further advantages as well;
4) The respondent controls the pace of the survey questions and can easily reread the questions, features that can reduce the cognitive burden of answering.

Each of these characteristics of Web surveys can affect how easily and how accurately respondents answer the questions.

Visual presentation. A potentially desirable feature of Web surveys is their ability to present visual information, including still images and videos, to the respondents. In some surveys, presenting the relevant visual stimuli to the respondents may be essential to the aims of the survey. Other modes of data collection also allow the presentation of visual information to respondents; for example, face-to-face interviewers often use show cards to display information visually.

As we noted in Chapter 5, images are likely to attract attention from respondents and, when they are presented alongside the questions, they can affect how respondents interpret the questions or what standards they apply in making a judgment. Couper, Tourangeau, and Kenyon (2004) present evidence from an experiment demonstrating that pictures of a target category (like shopping) can alter how respondents think about that category. A later study by Couper, Conrad, and Tourangeau (2007) also demonstrated visual context effects, this time on respondents' judgments of their health. Pictures should probably be avoided unless they are an essential part of the question (a "task" element, in the terminology of Couper et al., 2004b).

Spacing of response options and other visual cues can also influence how respondents interpret their task or the intended meaning of response scales. We (Tourangeau, Couper, and Conrad, 2004, 2007) propose that respondents apply several interpretive heuristics in assigning meaning to the response scales in Web surveys. The five heuristics are:

- Middle means typical;
- Left and top mean first;
- Near means related;
- Like (in appearance) means close (in meaning); and
- Up means good.

According to the first heuristic, the visual midpoint of a scale plays an important role in establishing the meaning of the scale points. The visual midpoint of a bipolar scale will, according to the heuristic, be taken to represent the conceptual midpoint of the dimension of judgment—that is, the neutral point or, in a probability scale, the point representing a 50–50 chance. When the underlying dimension is unipolar, respondents may assume that the visual midpoint represents the most typical value (the population median or mode). The second heuristic ("Left and top mean first") refers to the respondent's expectation that the answer options will follow some logical order. When the options are displayed horizontally, respondents expect the leftmost option to represent one extreme, the rightmost option the other, and the remaining options to proceed in conceptual order from left to right. When the options are displayed vertically, respondents expect the top and bottom options to represent the two extremes and the remaining options to proceed in order from top to bottom. The "Near means related" heuristic refers to the tendency for respondents to infer a conceptual link between two items based on their physical proximity. For example, respondents may see items in a grid as more closely related than the same items when they are displayed on separate screens (Tourangeau et al., 2004, Experiment 6). The fourth heuristic ("Like in appearance means close in meaning") refers to the tendency for respondents to gauge the conceptual similarity between two items or two response options based on their similarity in appearance. For example, when the two ends of the response scale are shades of the same hue, respondents may infer that the two extremes are closer conceptually than when the two ends of the scales are shades of different hues. This inference may lead respondents to give different answers than they otherwise would have (Tourangeau et al., 2007). The final heuristic refers to the tendency to evaluate items more favorably when they appear higher up on the screen; people associate certain physical positions with a positive evaluation and this can affect their ratings of objects (Meier and Robinson, 2004; Tourangeau, Couper, and Conrad, 2011).

Computer administration of the questions. One of the most important differences among survey modes is whether or not an interviewer asks the questions and records the answers. A substantial body of evidence shows that respondents are more willing to make potentially embarrassing revelations in surveys when an interviewer is *not* involved and, instead, the respondents fill out paper questionnaires or answer questions that the computer puts to them directly (Tourangeau and Yan, 2007). Self-administration—whether via the computer or a paper questionnaire—generally elicits more accurate answers to questions that raise social desirability concerns, such as questions about illicit drug use, alcohol consumption, and voting. Of course, a key feature of online surveys is that no interviewer is involved.

A study by Kreuter, Presser, and Tourangeau (2007) demonstrates this advantage of an Internet survey over other methods of data collection. Kreuter and her colleagues compared reporting errors under three modes of data collection—CATI, IVR, and an online survey; they were able to validate responses to some of the survey items against external records data. For all four of the socially undesirable behaviors that they examined (things like getting an unsatisfactory grade in a class or going on academic probation), the Web survey yielded the lowest rate of reporting errors, lower than both CATI (which features interviewer administration) and IVR (which does not). Some Web surveys feature "avatars" (on-screen representations of the researcher or of an interviewer) or other "humanizing" touches; to date, these features do not appear to heighten social desirability biases (Tourangeau, Couper, and Steiger, 2003, but see Conrad, Schober, and Nielsen, 2011, and Lind, Schober, Conrad and Reichert, under review). Still, such enhancements to text should probably be avoided when social desirability may be a concern. In addition, "gendered" interfaces (e.g., a Web questionnaire that displays a photograph of a female investigator) may influence responses to questions about gender-related topics (e.g., questions about women in the workplace; Tourangeau et al., 2003; see also Fuchs, 2009).

In addition to reducing social desirability biases and interviewer effects, Web surveys offer all the usual advantages of computerization and can administer very complex questionnaires.

Interactivity. A second advantage offered by Web surveys is their ability to interact with respondents in real time. This capability is a requirement for some other attractive features of computerization noted earlier; for example, Web surveys can route respondents around inapplicable items based on their answers to earlier questions, but they can do this only if the application administering the survey processes the information from the respondents as they submit it. Some researchers have advocated "static" designs for Web surveys (in which the questionnaire is embodied in a single scrollable HTML form, much like a paper questionnaire), but such designs discard much of the power that computers offer.

The interactive capabilities of Web surveys mean that Web questionnaires could, in principle, build in features that offer the respondents help and encouragement as they answer the questions. In the latter category, Web questionnaires, like other computer applications, can incorporate progress indicators to try to discourage breakoffs. We carried out a series of studies (Conrad, Couper, Tourangeau, and Peytchev, 2010) that find that, unless progress indicators provide encouraging news, they tend to *increase* rather than decrease breakoffs (see Chapter 6 for a more detailed summary of this work). Our studies compared an ordinary progress indicator with one that was designed to show rapid progress at the beginning of the questionnaire and slower progress later on; we also examined a progress indicator that displayed slow progress at the beginning of the questionnaire but more rapid progress later on. Respondents were least likely to break off part way through the questionnaire when the feedback at the beginning was the most positive. However, even the most encouraging progress indicator did not reduce the proportion of respondents breaking off relative to a version of the survey that displayed no progress indicator at all. Apparently, sometimes the best news is no news at all.

We have also done studies that examined the effectiveness of offering respondents definitions of key terms in the questions in an attempt to improve comprehension of the questions (Conrad, Couper, Tourangeau, and Peytchev, 2006; see our discussion in Section 6.2). The main lesson from these studies has been that anything that makes it more difficult for respondents to access a definition (such as requiring multiple clicks) reduces the likelihood that they will bother to do so. Respondents who merely had to move their mouse over the term to get a definition for it were more likely to seek definitions than those who had to take more onerous actions like clicking and scrolling. When respondents did consult a definition, they seemed to take it to heart and it affected how they answered the questions.

Web surveys can respond to what the respondents do, changing the appearance of an item once respondents have answered it or updating a running total of the respondents' numerical answers. A study we did with Galešic (Galešic, Tourangeau, Couper, and Conrad, 2007) examined the benefits of a responsive grid design. Grid items are often used in Web surveys to gather ratings for a series of similar items. Typically, each row of the grid presents one of the items and each column one of response options. Grid questions seem to be difficult for respondents and they produce higher levels of missing data (and higher breakoff rates) than other question formats. Our study with Galešic compared a standard grid with one that grayed out the item once respondents had rated it; the responsive grid format led to lower rates of missing data than the standard grid design. In another example of the usefulness of an interactive feature in a Web survey, DeRouvray and Couper (2002) tested an online survey that prompted respondents who skipped an item ("We would very much like to have your answer to this question. If you would like to choose one of the proposed answers, please select 'Back.'") Such prompting reduced the level of missing data. In still another example of the interactive capabilities of online surveys, we (Conrad et al., 2009) designed a survey that prompted respondents who answered a series of dietary questions unreasonably quickly; the computer displayed a message asking respondents to make sure they had given the question enough thought. These prompts reduced the respondents' tendency to rush through later items in the questionnaire.

Cognitive burden. Although images and other visual cues can have unintended consequences, the Web's reliance on visual presentation also has its advantages. One of them is that Web surveys give respondents a chance to review the questions and their answers. In a telephone interview, the interviewer reads the question and the respondent must ask to have the question repeated; in a Web survey, by contrast, the respondent can reread the question as often as he or she likes. More generally, Web surveys, like other self-administered modes of data collection, allow respondents to complete the survey at their own pace and at times that are convenient for them. These characteristics of Web surveys and other methods of self-administration—the ability to reread the question easily, to take one's time, and to complete the survey when it's convenient—may reduce the cognitive effort needed to answer the questions.

A couple of findings suggest that Web surveys *do* reduce cognitive burden compared to telephone surveys. Fricker, Galešic, Tourangeau, and Yan (2005) found that respondents to a Web survey answered a higher percentage of basic science questions correctly than their counterparts who answered the same questions in a telephone survey; the Web respondents also spent more time on these questions. The more rapid pace of the telephone interviews may have hurt performance on these questions. Chang and Krosnick (2009) found that Web respondents gave more differentiated answers to a set of attitude items than telephone respondents did; they also found that the answers from the Web respondents were more reliable and had greater concurrent and predictive validity than those from the telephone respondents. By contrast, Fricker and his colleagues (2005), found *less* differentiation in the answers of the Web respondents than in the answers of telephone respondents, perhaps because the Web survey grouped the items in a grid. So the impact of mode on cognitive burden may involve not only the mode itself but also other factors such as questionnaire design.

Summary. On the whole, then, Web surveys offer a lot of features that may reduce observation errors compared to other methods of data collection, such as telephone interviews. Web surveys offer the benefits of self-administration, automation, responsiveness, visual presentation, and reduced cognitive burden. In several experimental comparisons across modes of data collection (e.g., Chang and Krosnick, 2009; Fricker et al., 2005, Kreuter et al., 2008), Web surveys yielded both more accurate factual information and more valid attitudinal measures than telephone interviews did.

8.3 A MODEL FOR MODE EFFECTS

More and more surveys use multiple modes of data collection in an effort to reduce cost or increase response rates or both (de Leeuw, 2005). This naturally raises the questions of whether the questionnaires in the different modes should be designed to minimize any mode differences, and whether the data collected via the different methods of data collection can be combined. As an example of the type of mode difference that can occur in practice, Dillman and Christian (2005) point out that telephone surveys tend to employ rating scales that provide labels only for the endpoints, whereas mail and Web surveys are more likely to use scales that provide verbal labels for every scale point. Similarly, according to Dillman and Christian, mail and Web surveys are more likely to use check-all-that-apply formats, whereas telephone surveys elicit yes-no responses for each item.

There are two design approaches that can be adopted when a survey uses more than one mode. One approach attempts to minimize the differences across modes (the *unimode* approach); the other attempts to minimize *error* within each mode even if that means using different questions in the different modes (the *best practices* approach).

The impact of mode. To understand the relative merits of these two approaches, it is useful to apply the distinction between observation and non-observation errors in a model of the overall error in a survey estimate. We begin by exploring the error in some factual estimate from a survey. For the sake of concreteness, suppose we are trying to estimate the prevalence of a risky behavior—say, binge drinking—in the general population. Let $\hat{\theta}_A$ represent the estimate obtained from a stand-alone survey that uses a single mode of data collection, mode A:

$$(8.1) \quad \hat{\theta}_A = \mu_A + b_A + \bar{e}_A.$$

According to Equation 8.1, the estimate ($\hat{\theta}_A$) reflects three components: the mean true score among the respondents to the survey in that mode (μ_A), the systematic impact of the mode of data collection on the answers (b_A), and the average random error under that mode ($\bar{e}_A$). Together b_A and $\bar{e}_A$ represent the overall effect of observation or measurement errors on the estimate.

The non-observation errors are reflected in the difference between the mean true score for the sample respondents and the corresponding population parameter ($\mu_A - \mu$). The population mean of the true scores is also the population parameter of interest (that is, $\mu = \theta$). As we saw in Chapter 2, this difference has two components:

$$(8.2) \quad \mu_A - \mu = P_{A0}(\mu_{A1} - \mu_{A0}) + \frac{Cov(P_{A1i}, \mu_i)}{\bar{P}_{A1}}.$$

The first component ($P_{A0}[\mu_{A1} - \mu_{A0}]$) captures the impact of the complete omission of some portion of the population from a survey done in a specific mode. In a Web survey, it would be the portion with no access to the Internet. This component of the non-observation bias reflects the absence from the sample of population members whose participation propensity is zero. The second component of the bias reflects the fact that, even among those with a non-zero chance of participation, some members of the population are more likely to volunteer or to respond than others. To the extent that differences in participation propensities (the P_{A1i}'s) are related to the variable of interest (the μ_i's), there will be additional non-observation bias in the estimate; that additional error is reflected in the covariance term in Equation 8.2 ($Cov(P_{A1i}, \mu_i)/\bar{P}_{A1}$).

Combining modes. In a multimode survey, the overall estimate is a composite derived from the estimates obtained through two (or more) modes of data collection. We focus on the case where the survey uses two modes:

$$(8.3) \quad \hat{\theta}_{AB} = w\hat{\theta}_A + (1-w)\hat{\theta}_B$$
$$= w(\mu_A + b_A + \bar{e}_A) + (1-w)(\mu_B + b_B + \bar{e}_B),$$

in which $\hat{\theta}_A$ is the estimate derived from the responses to one mode (say, a telephone survey), $\hat{\theta}_B$ is the estimate from responses to the other mode (a Web survey), and w is the weight given to the cases from the first mode (often, the proportion of the responding cases from that mode).

The usual assumption is that the combination of modes improves coverage or response rates (or both) relative to a single mode alone. That is, a higher proportion of the population is able to respond to a survey offering two modes of response than is able to respond to either mode alone. In terms of the model, the proportion of the population with no chance of completing the survey via either mode A or B (P_{AB0}) is necessarily smaller than the proportion who cannot complete it by the one mode (P_{A0}) or the other (P_{B0}):

$$P_{AB0} \leq P_{A0}$$
$$\leq P_{B0}.$$

Still, this improvement in coverage *rates* doesn't guarantee that the non-observation *error* is reduced. In the same way, an increase in the response rate doesn't guarantee a reduction in non-response bias (Keeter, Kennedy, Dimock, Best, and Craighill, 2006; Keeter, Miller, Kohut, Groves, and Presser, 2000). Most researchers offer multiple modes in part to increase response rates (that is, $\bar{P}_{AB} \geq \bar{P}_A$ and $\bar{P}_{AB} \geq \bar{P}_B$ in the terms of our model), but here too the evidence is not entirely supportive. Sometimes adding a choice of modes seems to have the paradoxical effect of *reducing* response rates (Brøgger, Nystad, Cappelen, and Bakke, 2007; Griffin, Fischer, and Morgan, 2001; see Section 3.5 for a fuller discussion).

But the major worry in combining modes is the potential impact on measurement error (e.g., de Leeuw, 2005). It follows from Equation 8.3 that the total error in an estimate derived from a mixed-mode survey is:

(8.4) $\quad \hat{\theta}_{AB} - \theta = ([w\mu_A + (1-w)\mu_B] - \mu) + [w(b_A + \bar{e}_A) + (1-w)(b_B + \bar{e}_B)],$

with the first error component—the difference between the weighted sum of μ_A and μ_B and the average true score in the population (μ)—representing the effects of non-observation errors on the estimate ($\hat{\theta}_{AB}$) and the second component representing the effects of the observation errors—with b_A and b_B representing the systematic effects of the two modes and $\bar{e}_A$ and $\bar{e}_B$ representing the average random errors under the two modes. Since the expected values of $\bar{e}_A$ and $\bar{e}_B$ are zero, the expected observation error in $\hat{\theta}_{AB}$, the estimate from the mixed-mode survey, is:

(8.5) $\quad wb_A + (1-w)b_B$

Whether the quantity in expression 8.5 is larger or smaller than the measurement error in the corresponding estimate from a single-mode survey depends on several factors, including the relative magnitudes of b_A and b_B and whether the errors in the two modes are in the same or opposite directions.

Let's suppose that mode A is the traditional mode for the survey or the primary mode, the one through which most of the respondents complete the survey. The question, then, is whether $wb_A + (1-w)b_B$ is greater than, equal to, or less than b_A—that is, whether adding the second mode has increased observation error relative to a single mode, decreased it, or left it the same. If both modes have errors in the same direction (for example, respondents are likely to underreport binge drinking in all modes of data collection), then whenever $|b_B| < |b_A|$ the overall level of accuracy of the estimate will be improved by adding mode B to the mix. According to the results presented in Chapter 7, adding a Web option to a survey that relies primarily on telephone data collection will probably reduce systematic observation error, at least for sensitive behaviors. On the other hand, if the second mode of data collection has larger errors than the primary mode, adding it will increase the overall level of observation error.

The story gets a bit more complicated when the errors in the two modes are in opposite directions. In that case, the errors in the second mode can offset those in the first and the overall observation error is reduced whenever $|b_B - w_1(b_B - b_A)| < |b_A|$. In general, though, when the accuracy of an overall estimate involving some behavior or fact is at issue, the best practices approach (that is, minimizing the error in each of the modes) is likely to yield a better overall estimate than the unimode approach.

Let's consider a concrete example to illustrate the implications of this model. Suppose the traditional mode for a given survey is computer-assisted telephone interviewing and Web data collection has been added to the mix. Suppose further that a key target item asks about binge drinking ("Considering all types of alcoholic beverages, how many times during the past 30 days did you have five or more drinks on an occasion?"). We would anticipate in either mode respondents would underreport binge drinking but that the underreporting would be worse in the telephone (Link and Mokdad, 2005a). Thus, in this example, the mode effect for CATI (b_{CATI}) would be negative—say, –.15—indicating underreporting by about 15 percent. Web data collection might reduce this to 5 percent ($b_{Web} = -.05$). If we assume that 70 percent of the respondents complete the survey via CATI and 30 percent via the Web, the expression in 8.5 yields:

$$w_{CATI}b_{CATI} + (1 - w_{CATI})b_{Web} =$$
$$(.7 \times -0.15) + (.3 \times -0.05) = -0.12.$$

In this case, adding the Web reduces the expected level of underreporting from 15 percent to 12 percent. Of course, if for some reason, Web data collection led respondents to overreport binge drinking (say, $b_{Web} = +.05$), then the improvement in the overall estimate from adding in the Web would have been even greater:

$$w_{CATI}b_{CATI} + (1 - w_{CATI})b_{Web} =$$
$$(.7 \times -0.15) + (.3 \times +0.05) = -0.09.$$

Despite the improved survey estimates when errors are in opposite directions, the quality of individual responses is not necessarily improved by mixing modes, as in this scenario. Moreover, it would be a mistake for researchers to count on errors offsetting each other, as they do in this example!

Accuracy versus comparability of estimates. Still, for many studies that use mixed-modes, the key estimates are *not* overall point estimates, but comparisons of various sorts. For example, the Hospital Consumer Assessments of Healthcare Providers and Systems surveys (HCAHPS) collect data that are used to compare levels of patient satisfaction at different hospitals. The HCAHPS surveys use a total of four different modes to collect the data (mail, telephone, recruit-and-switch IVR, and mail with telephone follow-up) and there are substantial differences in the patient ratings across the modes (see Elliott, Zaslavsky, Goldstein, Lehrman, Hambarsoomians, Beckett, and Giordano, 2009). Elliott and his colleagues did a randomized experiment comparing the four modes and found that HCAHPS respondents tended to give higher ratings to the hospitals in the telephone and IVR interviews than they did in the mail questionnaires or in the mail/telephone combination. They present evidence that this difference in the ratings results from mode differences in reporting rather than differences in the types of patients who responded under the different modes.

In terms of our model, differences in average satisfaction ratings between two hospitals reflect three components—the difference in actual patient satisfaction at the two hospitals, the difference in non-observation errors (due, for example, to non-response), and the difference in the observation errors:

$$(8.6) \qquad \hat{\theta}_1 - \hat{\theta}_2 = (\mu_{1r} + b_1 + \bar{e}_1) - (\mu_{2r} + b_2 + \bar{e}_2)$$
$$= (\mu_{1r} - \mu_{2r}) + (b_1 - b_2) + (\bar{e}_1 + \bar{e}_2).$$
$$(\mu_{1r} - \mu_{2r}) = [\mu_1 + (\mu_{1r} - \mu_1)] - [\mu_2 + (\mu_{2r} - \mu_2)]$$
$$= (\mu_1 - \mu_2) + [(\mu_{1r} - \mu_1) - (\mu_{2r} - \mu_2)].$$
$$E(\hat{\theta}_1 - \hat{\theta}_2) = (\mu_{1r} - \mu_{2r}) + (b_1 - b_2)$$
$$= (\mu_1 - \mu_2) + [(\mu_{1r} - \mu_1) - (\mu_{2r} - \mu_2)] + (b_1 - b_2)$$

In the final expression, $\mu_1 - \mu_2$ represents the actual population difference in satisfaction between the two hospitals, the bracketed quantity represents the differences in nonresponse errors in the surveys for the two hospitals, and $b_1 - b_2$ represents the difference in the mode effects. Complicated though it is, Equation 8.6 only deals with the simple case of bias in an estimate of the mean. Differences across modes in the variance of the random errors can introduce bias into other types of estimates, such as regression or correlation coefficients.

An example may help make the meaning of Equation 8.6 a bit clearer. Suppose that patient satisfaction ratings are collected on a five-point scale (with five representing the highest level of satisfaction) from patients at two hospitals (hospitals A and B). Suppose that these ratings come from a mail survey for hospital A and from a Web survey for hospital B. Let's also assume that patients are actually more satisfied at hospital A than they are at B (mean population ratings of 4.2 and 3.7 respectively), but that highly satisfied patients are more likely to complete the survey than less satisfied patients (producing means among the respondents at hospital A of 4.4 and among the respondents at hospital B of 4.1, with slightly greater nonresponse bias—a difference in the biases of –.2—at hospital B). Finally, let's assume a mode difference in reporting—ratings are about .4 of a scale point lower on average on the Web than they are in a mail survey. Applying Equation 8.6, we get:

$$E(\hat{\theta}_A - \hat{\theta}_B) = (\mu_A - \mu_B) + [(\mu_{Ar} - \mu_A) - (\mu_{Br} - \mu_B)] + (b_{Mail} - b_{Web})$$
$$= (4.2 - 3.7) + [(4.4 - 4.2) - (4.1 - 3.7)] + (.2 - -0.2)$$
$$= .5 - .2 + .4 = .7$$

In the last line, .5 represents the true population difference, –.2 the difference in the nonresponse bias in the surveys for the two hospitals, and .4 the reporting difference across modes. In this case, the mode differences lead to an overestimate of the difference between the two hospitals (the estimate is .7 but the true difference is .5).

There are three ways to minimize the final term in Equation 8.6, ($b_1 - b_2$) or the difference in mode effects. First, the same mode of data collection could be used to collect satisfaction ratings from patients at both hospitals. Second, if more than one mode were used to collect the data (say, a combination of Web and mail), then the same mix of modes could be used at the different hospitals—that is, identical proportions of respondents could complete the questions in each mode (say, 40 percent Web and 60 percent mail) at both hospitals. Under both of these conditions, b_1 and b_2 should be the same for the two hospitals and the difference between them is presumably zero. Third, if neither the same mode nor same mix of modes can be used, then the unimode approach (designing the questions to minimize mode differences) could be used.

In general, then, the best practices approach to mixed-mode design is typically best when the main purpose of the survey is to make overall estimates, particularly overall estimates regarding factual matters. This is because (as we show in expression 8.5) the measurement errors across modes are basically additive when an overall estimate is made. Thus, to get the best point estimate, it is usually best to minimize the error in each mode. By contrast, the unimode approach may be more suitable when comparisons of ratings are the survey's main objective. This is because, with comparisons, it is differences in the magnitudes of the errors by mode that bias the comparison (see Equation 8.6). To get the least biased comparisons, it is often best to equalize the errors in each mode. When the absolute levels of the estimates are not important (for example, when the most variables in the survey are opinion items on arbitrary rating scales), comparability across modes is likely to be a crucial consideration and the unimode approach is likely to make more sense. This conclusion is based only on bias considerations. When there are large differences in *variances* by mode, this may outweigh bias considerations and push researchers in the direction of reducing variance in each mode—that is, push them to adopt the best practices approach.

8.4 RECOMMENDATIONS FOR WEB SURVEYS

Throughout this book, we have discussed design features that can affect the estimates from Web surveys for better or worse. We have avoided making explicit recommendations on most of these issues because we believe that practitioners are best served if they understand the principles and findings on which such recommendations might be based rather than by providing specific guidelines about what they should do. Every survey is different and no guideline will apply equally well to all of them. Nonetheless, several recommendations can be gleaned from our discussion. In this section, we make these recommendations explicit and present them in a single place.

Reducing non-observation error. Although it is a virtual certainty that Internet access will continue to grow, for the foreseeable future Web surveys are likely to have serious limitations in their ability to support inferences to the general population. Here are our recommendations for minimizing those limitations.

1) If the goal of the survey is to generalize to a known population, start with a probability sample. Even when they have low response rates, probability samples seem to represent the population from which they were drawn more closely than self-selected samples do (see, for example, Table 8.1 above, adapted from Chang and Krosnick, 2009).

2) Calibrating Web survey results to those of a parallel telephone survey can leave substantial bias in the Web estimates and increase their variances (Bethlehem, 2010; Lee and Valliant, 2009); where possible, avoid this method for correcting for non-observation biases (see our discussion in Section 2.3).

3) Still, it helps to use *some* method of weighting or adjustment to correct for the deficiencies of Web samples; the exact weighting method is probably less important than incorporating covariates that are strongly related to the key survey variables (see Table 2.4 and Equation 2.4 in Chapter 2).

4) Try to minimize nonresponse bias by taking steps to increase response propensities or to equalize them across different subgroups. Advance notification in some mode other than email seems to increase Web response rates. This can be followed by an email invitation with a link to the URL for the survey (see our discussion in Section 3.5).

5) Use prepaid cash incentives if possible; if a sweepstakes incentive is used, inform sample members of the outcome immediately (Tuten, Galešic, and Bosnjak, 2004). Incentives increase the proportion of sample members who start the survey and also reduce breakoffs (see Section 3.5 above).

6) Unpleasant surprises—unexpectedly slow progress, a longer survey than was promised, harder-than-expected items (such as complicated grids or text boxes requiring lengthy answers)—lead to breakoffs (see the discussion in Sections 3.6 and 6.2). Try to minimize such surprises.

7) Probing for missing answers can reduce item nonresponse, apparently without much effect on the breakoff rate. If some item is critical for the survey, include follow-up probes to reduce the level of missing data (see Section 6.2 above).

Reducing observation error. We group our recommendations for minimizing observation (or measurement) errors into four categories—(1) basic design issues, (2) visual aspects of survey design, (3) interactive features, and (4) self-administration and cognitive burden. Again, earlier sections of the book present the theoretical or empirical basis for these recommendations.

Basic Design Issues:

1) A paging design is generally preferable to a scrolling design and allows the survey to use the interactive capabilities of the Web (see Section 4.3).
2) Use a white or light color background (such as light blue) for the Web survey; avoid background graphics (Section 4.4).
3) Grids can encourage breakoffs, missing data, and non-differentiation. They should be used sparingly and their design should be as simple as possible. Avoid multiple contingent questions within a single grid. Shading every other row or graying out completed items can reduce missing data (Sections 4.7 and 6.2)
4) Follow standard conventions throughout the survey. For example, use boldface print for question text, regular type for response options, and capitalization or italics for emphasis (Section 4.4).
5) Make sure the input tool matches the intended function (e.g., use radio buttons when a single answer is needed; Section 4.6).
6) The top left section of a Web page is the most visually prominent (Section 5.3); put the most important information there.
7) Left-justify the questions and number them if the survey presents multiple questions on a page; numbering makes it easier for respondents to see how many questions there are (Section 4.4).
8) Put the input field for a response option to the left of the corresponding label (Section 4.4); where possible, present all the response options in a single column (or a single row). Avoid multi-column arrangements of response categories; these can confuse respondents and lead them to select multiple answers.
9) Include a "Next" and a "Previous" button on the bottom of each screen; if possible, make the "Previous" button somewhat less visually prominent than the "Next" button (Section 4.5).

Visual Aspects:

1) Respondents notice images. Because they are powerful contextual stimuli, they should be chosen carefully (or avoided; see our discussion in Section 5.2).
2) Images are necessarily concrete. They can narrow the interpretation of the category of interest (Section 5.2). This is another reason for choosing them carefully or using verbal examples instead.
3) The visual cues should be consistent with the intended use of a rating scale. If the scale points are supposed to be equally spaced conceptually, make sure they

are equally spaced visually and appear this way across browsers and devices. The middle option should be the neutral point, 50/50, etc.; the conceptual and visual midpoint of the scale should coincide (Section 5.1).

4) Avoid displaying non-substantive options (Don't Know or No Opinion), but, if they are needed, separate them from the substantive options visually (Section 5.1).

5) Don't use colors, numbers, or other features that can lead to unwanted inferences (Section 5.1). If numbers are necessary, use the counting numbers (from 1 to n).

6) Provide verbal labels for every scale point (Section 5.1).

Interactive Features:

1) Offer definitions for technical terms and make it easy for respondents to access them. The best approaches may be to display definitions automatically when respondents seem to be struggling (for example, when they take a long time to answer) or just to display the definitions with the questions (Section 6.2).

2) Asking unreasonably fast respondents to take more time can help slow them down, but appears to affect only some of these "speeders." This approach also seems to reduce satisficing behavior on later items (Section 6.2).

3) Progress indicators can reduce breakoffs but only when the news they give is encouraging; often, no progress indicator at all reduces breakoffs relative to any form of progress indicator (Section 6.3).

4) Tallies and other interactive devices can help respondents cope with otherwise demanding questions. Use the computer to perform tasks that computers do better than people (Section 6.4).

5) It may be possible to engage respondents with humanized interfaces, but this may also foster social desirability bias and race and gender of (virtual) interviewer effects. It is not clear whether the gains from such interfaces outweigh the costs (Section 6.4).

Self-Administration and Cognitive Burden:

1) Web surveys seem to be a good vehicle for collecting potentially sensitive information. This advantage of Web data collection may be undermined if the setting isn't private (for example, if data collection takes place in a school computer lab) or if a humanlike interface is used (Section 7.2).

2) Web surveys are also a good mode of data collection for assessing respondent knowledge and administering standardized psychological batteries. When assessing respondent knowledge, it is important to take steps to prevent respondents from looking up the answers online (see Section 7.3).

As with all such guidelines, it is more important to understand the principles underlying the recommendations than simply to follow them slavishly. Every survey has its wrinkles and complexities and there will be times when it makes sense to ignore these recommendations. Still, we believe there is good evidence, reviewed in the earlier chapters, that supports each of these guidelines.

8.5 THE FUTURE OF WEB SURVEYS

A major issue for Web surveys is lack of universal access to the Internet. A key limiting factor on the appeal of Web surveys for many survey researchers is the presence of substantial noncoverage among the populations (such as the general household population) that are the target populations for many surveys. However, both the Internet and the meaning of the Internet access are undergoing rapid changes. Why people use the Internet and how they get online are evolving rapidly.

Consider how we use the Internet. A recent report from the Pew Internet & American Life Project (Purcell, 2011) notes that, although searching for information online and sending and receiving email remain the top uses of the Internet (with more than 90 percent of Internet users reporting these activities), social networking has grown explosively since 2004, the year Facebook came online. According to the Pew surveys, 65 percent of the Internet population now uses social network sites. Although estimates vary, approximately 40 percent of the adult US population have a Facebook account (at the time of this writing). E-commerce, blogging, downloading music and videos, taking part in interactive virtual worlds, and other forms of online entertainment are supplanting (or catching up to) email and information search as the major uses of the Internet. It is not clear how these changes in the way people use the Internet will affect their willingness to do surveys online or how they answer the questions.

At the same time, methods for accessing the Web have expanded in the last decade or so, with many (perhaps most) users getting online via their cell phones or tablet computers. Another Pew study finds that "Nearly half of all American adults (47%) report that they get at least some local news and information on their cellphone or tablet computer" (Purcell, Rainie, Rosenstiel, and Mitchell, 2011). This is just one illustrative manifestation of the sea change in how people access the Internet. The new forms of Internet access and the new uses of the Internet are likely to alter the coverage of Web surveys and to change the character of the digital divide.

To our knowledge, virtually all of the research on Web surveys is based on surveys accessed through browsers on laptop or desktop computers. As more and more Web surveys are completed on mobile devices, including telephones and tablets, many of the conclusions presented here will probably need to be modified and extended. Just to cite some likely differences, respondents completing a Web survey on a smart phone may well be more distracted than those completing the survey on a desktop computer because of incoming text messages or a noisy external environment; as a result, the effort involved may be greater rather than less than is required to complete a traditional telephone interview (see our discussion in Chapter 7). Some issues, such as the position of information on the screen, are likely to assume even greater importance as respondents complete Web surveys on devices with more limited visual real estate. The Internet is still changing rapidly and only time can tell how its future development will affect Web surveys.

REFERENCES

AAPOR (2010). *AAPOR report on online panels*. Deerfield, IL: American Association for Public Opinion Research.

AAPOR (2011). *Standard definitions: Final dispositions of case codes and outcome rates for surveys* (7th ed.). Deerfield, IL: American Association for Public Opinion Research.

Albaum, G., Roster, C. A., Wiley, J., Rossiter, J., & Smith, S. M. (2010). Designing Web surveys in marketing research: Does use of forced answering affect completion rates? *Journal of Marketing Theory and Practice*, *18*, 285–293.

Alexander, G. L., Divine, G. W., Couper, M. P., McClure, J. B., Stopponi, M. A., Fortman, K. K., Tolsma, D. D., Strecher, V. J., & Johnson, C. C. (2008). Effect of incentives and mailing features on recruitment for an online health program. *American Journal of Preventive Medicine*, *34*, 382–388.

Alvarez, R. M., Sherman, R. P., & VanBeselaere, C. (2003). Subject acquisition for Web-based surveys. *Political Analysis*, *11*, 23–43.

Atrostic, B. K., Bates, N., Burt, G., & Silberstein, A. (2001). Nonresponse in U.S. government household surveys: Consistent measures, recent trends, and new insights. *Journal of Official Statistics*, *17*, 209–226.

Baker, R. P., & Couper, M. P. (2007). The impact of screen size and background color on response in Web surveys. Paper presented at the General Online Research Conference (GOR'07), Leipzig, March.

Bälter, K. A., Bälter, O., Fondell, E., & Lagaross, Y. T. (2005). Web-based and mailed questionnaires: A comparison of response rates and compliance. *Epidemiology*, *16*, 577–579.

Bandilla, W., Blohm, M., Kaczmirek, L., & Neubarth, W. (2007). Differences between respondents and nonrespondents in an Internet survey recruited from a face-to-face survey. Paper presented at the European Survey Research Association conference, Prague, June.

Bason, J. J. (2000). Comparison of telephone, mail, Web, and IVR surveys of drugs and alcohol use among University of Georgia students. Paper presented at the 55th Annual Conference of the American Association for Public Opinion Research, Portland, OR, May.

Bates, N. (2001). Internet versus mail as a data collection methodology from a high-coverage population. Paper presented at the 56th Annual Conference of the American Association for Public Opinion Research, Montreal, Quebec, May.

Bates, S. C., & Cox, J. M. (2008). The impact of computer versus paper-pencil survey, and individual versus group administration, on self-reports of sensitive behaviors. *Computers in Human Behavior*, *24*, 903–916.

Bauman, K., & Dent, C. W. (1982). Influence of an objective measure on self-reports of behavior. *Journal of Applied Psychology*, *67*, 623–628.

Beebe, T. J., Harrison, P. A., McRae, J. A., Anderson, R. E., & Fulkerson, J. A. (1998). An evaluation of computer-assisted self-interviews in a school setting. *Public Opinion Quarterly*, *62*, 623–632.

Bell, D. S., Mangione, C. M., & Kahn, C. E. (2001). Randomized testing of alternative survey formats using anonymous volunteers on the World Wide Web. *Journal of the American Medical Informatics Association, 8*, 616–620.

Belli, R. F., Traugott, M. W., & Beckmann, M. N. (2001). What leads to voting overreports? Contrasts of overreporters to validated voters and admitted nonvoters in the American National Election Studies. *Journal of Official Statistics, 17*, 479–498.

Belson, W. A. (1981). *The design and understanding of survey questions*. Aldershot: Gower.

Benway, J. P. (1998). Banner blindness: The irony of attention grabbing on the World Wide Web. In *Proceedings of the Human Factors and Ergonomics Society 42nd Annual Meeting*, pp. 463–467.

Benway, J. P. & Lane, D. M. (1998). Banner blindness: Web searchers often miss 'obvious' links. *ITG Newsletter, 1* (3). http://www.internettg.org/newsletter/dec98/banner_blindness.html

Berrens, R. P., Bohara, A. K., Jenkins-Smith, H., Silva, C., & Weimer, D. L. (2003). The advent of Internet surveys for political research: A comparison of telephone and Internet surveys. *Political Analysis, 11*, 1–22.

Bethlehem, J. G. (2002). Weighting nonresponse adjustments based on auxiliary information. In R. M. Groves, D. Dillman, J. L. Eltinge, & R. J. A. Little (Eds.), *Survey Nonresponse* (pp. 275– 288). New York: John Wiley.

Bethlehem, J. (2010). Selection bias in Web surveys. *International Statistical Review, 78*, 161–188.

Birnholtz, J. P., Horn, D. B., Finholt, T. A., & Bae, S. J. (2004). The effects of cash, electronic, and paper gift certificates as respondent incentives for a Web-based survey of technologically sophisticated respondents. *Social Science Computer Review, 22*, 355–362.

Boltz, M. G. (1993). Time estimation and expectancies. *Memory and Cognition, 21*, 853–863.

Bosnjak, M., Neubarth, W., Couper, M. P., Bandilla, W., & Kaczmirek, L. (2008). Prenotification in Web-based access panel surveys: The influence of mobile text messaging versus e-mail on response rates and sample composition. *Social Science Computer Review, 26*, 213–223.

Bosnjak, M., & Tuten, T. L. (2002). Prepaid and promised incentives in Web surveys – an experiment. *Social Science Computer Review, 21*, 208–217.

Brener, N. D., Eaton, D. K., Kann, L., Grunbaum, J. A., Gross, L. A., Kyle, T. M., & Ross, J. G. (2006). The association of survey setting and mode with self-reported risk behavior among high schools students. *Public Opinion Quarterly, 70*, 354–374.

Brennan, M. (2005). The effect of a simultaneous mixed-mode (mail and Web) survey on respondent characteristics and survey responses. Paper presented at the ANZMAC 2005 Conference.

Brick, J. M., Brick, P. D., Dipko, S., Presser, S., Tucker, C., & Yuan, Y. (2007). Cell phone survey feasibility in the U.S.: Sampling and calling cell numbers versus landline numbers. *Public Opinion Quarterly, 71*, 23–39.

Brick, J. M., Waksberg, J., Kulp, D., & Starer, A. (1995). Bias in list-assisted telephone surveys. *Public Opinion Quarterly, 59*, 218–235.

Brøgger, J., Nystad, W., Cappelen, I., & Bakke, P. (2007). No increase in response rate by adding a Web response option to a postal population survey: A randomized trial. *Journal of Medical Internet Research, 9*, e40.

Brunner, L. J. (1979) Smiles can be backchannels. *Journal of Personality and Social Psychology, 37*, 728–734.

Burris, J., Chen, J., Graf, I., Johnson, T., & Owens, L. (2001). An experiment in Web survey design. Paper presented at the 56th Annual Conference of the American Association for Public Opinion Research, Montreal, Quebec, May.

Callegaro, M., & DiSogra, C. (2008). Computing response metrics for online panels. *Public Opinion Quarterly, 72*, 1008–1032.

Callegaro, M., Shand-Lubbers, J., & Dennis, J. M. (2009). Presentation of a single item versus a grid: Effects on the Vitality and Mental Health Subscales of the SF-36v2 health survey. Paper presented at the 64th Annual Conference of the American Association for Public Opinion Research, Hollywood, FL, May.

Callegaro, M., Villar, A., & Yang, Y. (2011). A meta-analysis of experiments manipulating progress indicators in Web surveys. Paper presented at the 66th Annual Conference of the American Association for Public Opinion Research, Phoenix, AZ, May.

Cantor, D., Brick, P. D., Han, D., & Aponte, M. (2010). Incorporating a Web option in a two-phase mail survey. Paper presented at the 65th Annual Conference of the American Association for Public Opinion Research, Chicago, May.

Carbonell, J. (1983). Derivational analogy in problem solving and knowledge acquisition. In R.S. Michalski (Ed.), *Proceedings of the International Machine Learning Workshop* (pp. 12–18). Urbana, IL: Department of Computer Science, University of Illinois at Urbana-Champaign.

Casady, R. J., & Lepkowski, J. M. (1993). Stratified telephone survey designs. *Survey Methodology, 19*, 103–113.

Catania, J. A., Binson, D., Canchola, J., Pollack, L. M., Hauck, W., & Coates, T. J. (1996). Effects of interviewer gender, interviewer choice, and item wording on responses to questions concerning sexual behavior. *Public Opinion Quarterly, 60*, 345–375.

Chang, L., & Krosnick, J. A. (2009). National surveys via RDD telephone interviewing versus the Internet: Comparing sample representativeness and response quality. *Public Opinion Quarterly, 73*, 641–678.

Childers, T. L., & Jass, J. (2002). All dressed up with something to say: Effects of typeface semantic associations on brand perceptions and consumer memory. *Journal of Consumer Psychology, 12*, 93–106.

Christian, L. M., & Dillman, D. A. (2004). The influence of graphical and symbolic language manipulations on responses to self-administered questions. *Public Opinion Quarterly, 68*, 57–80.

Christian, L. M., Dillman D. A., & Smyth J. D. (2007). Helping respondents get it right the first time: The influence of words, symbols, and graphics in Web surveys. *Public Opinion Quarterly, 71*, 113–125.

Christian, L. M., Dillman D. A., & Smyth J. D. (2008). The effects of mode and format on answers to scalar questions in telephone and Web surveys. In J. M. Lepkowski, C. Tucker, J. M. Brick, E. D. de Leeuw, L. Japec, P. J. Lavrakas, M. W. Link, & R. L. Sangster (Eds.), *Advances in telephone survey methodology* (pp. 250–275). New York: John Wiley.

Christian, L. M., Parsons, N. L., & Dillman, D. A. (2009). Designing scalar questions for Web surveys. *Sociological Methods and Research, 37*, 393–425.

Church, A. H. (1993). Estimating the effect of incentives on mail survey response rates: A meta-analysis. *Public Opinion Quarterly, 57*, 62–79.

Clark, H. H., & Schaefer, E. F. (1989). Contributing to discourse. *Cognitive Science, 13*, 259–294.

Clark, H. H., & Schober, M. F. (1991). Asking questions and influencing answers. In J. M. Tanur (Ed.), *Questions about questions: Inquiries into the cognitive bases of surveys* (pp. 15–48). New York: Russell Sage Foundation.

Clark, R. L., & Nyiri, Z. (2001). Web survey design: Comparing a multi-screen to a single screen survey. Paper presented at the 56th Annual Conference of American Association for Public Opinion Research, Montreal, Quebec, May.

Conrad, F. G., Couper, M. P., Tourangeau, R., Galešic, M., & Yan, T. (2009). Interactive feedback can improve the quality of responses in Web surveys. Paper presented at the conference of the European Survey Research Association. Warsaw, Poland. July.

Conrad, F. G., Couper, M. P., Tourangeau, R., & Peytchev, A. (2005). Effectiveness of progress indicators in Web surveys: First impressions matter. Proceedings of *SIGCHI 2005: Human Factors in Computing Systems* Portland, OR.

Conrad, F. G., Couper, M. P., Tourangeau, R., & Peytchev, A. (2006). Use and non-use of clarification features in Web surveys. *Journal of Official Statistics, 22*, 245–269.

Conrad, F. G., Couper, M. P., Tourangeau, R., & Peytchev, A. (2010). Impact of progress indicators on task completion. *Interacting with Computers, 22*, 417–427.

Conrad, F. G., & Schober, M. F. (2000). Clarifying question meaning in a household telephone survey. *Public Opinion Quarterly, 64,* 1–28.

Conrad, F. G., Schober, M. F., & Coiner, T. (2007). Bringing features of human dialogue to Web surveys. *Applied Cognitive Psychology, 21,* 165–188.

Conrad, F. G., Schober, M. F., Jans, M., Orlowski, R., Nielsen, D., & Levenstein, R. (2008). Virtual interviews on mundane, non-sensitive topics: Dialog capability affects response accuracy more than visual realism does. Paper presented at 63rd Annual Conference of the American Association for Public Opinion Research, New Orleans, LA.

Conrad, F. G., Schober, M. F., & Nielsen, D. (2011). Race of virtual interviewer effects. Paper presented at the 66th Annual Conference of the American Association for Public Opinion Research, Phoenix, AZ, May.

Conrad, F. G., Tourangeau, R., Couper, M. P., & Kennedy, C. (2009). Interactive interventions in Web surveys increase respondent conscientiousness. Paper presented at the 64th Conference of the American Association for Public Opinion Research, Hollywood, FL, May.

Conrad, F., Tourangeau. R., Couper, M. P., & Zhang, C. (2011). Interactive interventions in Web surveys can increase response accuracy. Paper presented at the Annual Conference of the American Association for Public Opinion Research, Phoenix, AZ.

Conrad, F. G., Tourangeau, R., Couper. M. P., & Zhang, C. (In preparation). Interactive intervention to reduce satisficing in Web surveys.

Cooley, P. C., Miller, H. G., Gribble, J. N., & Turner, C. F. (2000). Automating telephone surveys: Using T-ACASI to obtain data on sensitive topics. *Computers and Human Behavior, 16,* 1–11.

Couper, M. P. (2000). Web surveys: A review of issues and approaches. *Public Opinion Quarterly, 64,* 464–494.

Couper, M. P. (2007). Issues of representation in eHealth research (with a focus on Web surveys). *American Journal of Preventive Medicine, 32,* S83–S89.

Couper, M. P. (2008a). *Designing effective Web surveys.* New York: Cambridge University Press.

Couper, M. P. (2008b). Technology and the survey interview/questionnaire. In M. F. Schober and F. G. Conrad (Eds.), *Envisioning the survey interview of the future* (pp. 58–76). New York: John Wiley.

Couper, M. P., Baker, R. P., & Mechling, J. (2011). Placement of navigation buttons in Web surveys. *Survey Practice,* February, http://surveypractice.org/2011/02/14/navigation_buttons/

Couper, M. P., & Bosnjak, M. (2010). Internet surveys. In P. V. Marsden & J. D. Wright (Eds.). *The handbook of survey research* (2nd ed., pp. 527–556). Bingley, UK: Emerald.

Couper, M. P., Conrad, F. G., & Tourangeau, R. (2007). Visual context effects in Web surveys. *Public Opinion Quarterly, 71,* 91–112.

Couper, M. P., Kapteyn, A., Schonlau, M., & Winter, J. (2007). Noncoverage and nonresponse in an Internet survey. *Social Science Research, 36,* 131–148.

Couper, M. P., Kennedy, C., Conrad, F. G., & Tourangeau, R. (2011). Designing input fields for non-narrative open-ended responses in Web surveys. *Journal of Official Statistics, 27,* 65–85.

Couper, M. P., Tourangeau, R., & Conrad, F. G. (2009). Improving the design of complex grid questions. Paper presented at the Internet Survey Methodology Workshop, Bergamo, Italy.

Couper, M. P., Tourangeau, R., Conrad, F. G., & Zhang, C. (In press). The design of grids in Web surveys. *Social Science Computer Review.*

Couper, M. P., Tourangeau, R., Conrad, F. G., & Crawford, S. (2004). What they see is what we get: Response options for Web surveys. *Social Science Computer Review, 22,* 111–127.

Couper, M. P., Tourangeau, R., Conrad, F. G., & Singer, E. (2006). Evaluating the effectiveness of visual analog scales: A Web experiment. *Social Science Computer Review, 24,* 227–245.

Couper, M. P., Tourangeau, R., & Kenyon, K. (2004). Picture this! Exploring visual effects in Web surveys. *Public Opinion Quarterly, 68,* 255–266.

Couper, M. P., Traugott, M., & Lamias, M. (2001). Web survey design and administration. *Public Opinion Quarterly, 65,* 230–253.

Cox, S., Parmer, R., Tourkin, S., Warner, T., Lyter, D. M., & Rowland, R (2007). *Documentation for the 2004–05 Teacher Follow-up Survey*. Washington, DC: National Center for Education Statistics, NCES 2007–349.

Crawford, S., Couper, M. P., & Lamias, M. (2001). Web surveys: Perception of burden. *Social Science Computer Review, 19*, 146–162.

Crawford, S. D., McCabe, S. E., Saltz, B., Boyd, C. J., Freisthler, B., & Paschall, M. J. (2004). Gaining respondent cooperation in college Web-based alcohol surveys: Findings from experiments at two universities. Paper presented at the 59th Annual Conference of the American Association for Public Opinion Research, Phoenix, AZ, May.

Curtin, R., Presser, S., & Singer, E. (2005). Changes in telephone survey nonresponse over the past quarter century. *Public Opinion Quarterly, 69*, 87–98.

de Leeuw, E. D. (2005). To mix or not to mix data collection modes in surveys. *Journal of Official Statistics, 21*, 233–255.

de Leeuw, E. D., & de Heer, W. (2002). Trends in household survey nonresponse: A longitudinal and international comparison. In R. M. Groves, D. Dillman, J. L. Eltinge, & R. J. A. Little (Eds.), *Survey Nonresponse* (pp. 41–54). New York: John Wiley.

Delavande, A., & Rohwedder, S. (2008). Eliciting subjective probabilities in Internet surveys. *Public Opinion Quarterly, 72*, 866–891.

Deming, W. E. (1944). On errors in surveys. *American Sociological Review, 9*, 359–369.

Denniston, M. M., Brener, N. D., Kann, L., Eaton, D. K., McManus, T., Kyle, T. M., Roberts, A. M., Flint, K. H., & Ross, J. G. (2010). Comparison of paper-and-pencil versus Web administration of the Youth Risk Behavior Survey (YRBS): Participation, data quality, and perceived privacy and anonymity. *Computers in Human Behavior, 26*, 1054–1060.

Denscombe, M. (2006). Web-based questionnaires and the mode effect: An evaluation based on completion rates and data contents of near-identical questionnaires delivered in different modes. *Social Science Computer Review, 24*, 246–254.

Denscombe, M. (2009). Item non-response rates: A comparison of online and paper questionnaires. *International Journal of Social Research Methodology, 12*, 281–291.

DeRouvray, C., & Couper, M. P. (2002). Designing a strategy for reducing no opinion responses in Web-based surveys. *Social Science Computer Review, 20*, 3–9.

Dever, J. A., Rafferty, A., & Valliant, R. (2008). Internet surveys: Can statistical adjustments eliminate coverage bias? *Survey Research Methods, 2*, 47–62.

Dillman, D. A. (2000). *Mail and Internet surveys: The tailored design method*. New York: John Wiley.

Dillman, D.A. (2007). *Mail and internet surveys: The tailored design method* (2nd ed.). New York: John Wiley.

Dillman, D. A., & Christian, L. M. (2005). Survey mode as a source of instability in responses across surveys. *Field Methods, 17*, 30–52.

Dillman, D. A., Sinclair, M. D., & Clark, J. R. (2003). Effects of questionnaire length, respondent-friendly design, and a difficult question on response rates for occupant-addressed census mail surveys. *Public Opinion Quarterly, 57*, 289–304.

Dillman, D. A., Smyth, J. D., & Christian, L. M. (2009). *Internet, mail, and mixed-mode surveys: The tailored design method*. New York: John Wiley.

Dillman, D. A., & Tarnai, J. (1991). Mode effects of cognitively designed recall questions: A comparison of answers to telephone and mail surveys. In P. P. Biemer, R. M. Groves, L. E. Lyberg, N. A. Mathiowetz, & S. Sudman (Eds.), *Measurement errors in surveys* (pp. 73–93). New York: John Wiley.

DiSogra, C., Callegaro, M., & Hendarwan, E. (2009). Recruiting probability-based Web panel members using an address-based sample frame: Results from a pilot study conducted by Knowledge Networks. In *Proceedings of the Joint Statistical Meetings, Survey Research Method Section*, (pp. 5270–5283).

Duncan, S., & Fiske, D. W. (1977). *Face-to-face interaction*. Hillsdale, NJ: Erlbaum.

Eaton, D. K., Brener, N. D., Kann, L., Denniston, M. M., McManus, T., Kyle, T. M., Roberts, A. M., Flint, K. H., & Ross, J. G. (2010). Comparison of paper-and-pencil versus Web administration of the Youth Risk Behavior Survey (YRBS): Risk behavior prevalence estimates. *Evaluation Review, 34*, 137–153.

Ehlen, J., & Ehlen, P. (2007). Cellular-only substitution in the United States as lifestyle adoption: Implications for telephone survey coverage. *Public Opinion Quarterly, 71*, 717–733.

Elliott, M. N., Zaslavsky, A. M., Goldstein, E., Lehrman, W., Hambarsoomians, K., Beckett, M. K., & Giordano, L. (2009). Effects of survey mode, patient mix, and nonresponse on CAHPS® Hospital Survey scores. *Health Services Research, 44*, 501–518.

Fendrich, M., & Johnson, T. P. (2001). Examining prevalence differences in three national surveys of youth: Impact of consent procedures, mode, and editing rules. *Journal of Drug Issues, 31*, 615–642.

Flemming, G., & Sonner, M. (1999). Can Internet polling work? Strategies for conducting public opinion surveys online. Paper presented at the 54th Annual Conference of the American Association of Public Opinion Research, St. Petersburg Beach, Florida, May.

Fowler, F. J., & Stringfellow, V. L. (2001). Learning from experience: Estimating teen use of alcohol, cigarettes, and marijuana from three survey protocols. *Journal of Drug Issues, 31*, 643–664.

Fricker, S., Galešic, M., Tourangeau, R., & Yan, T. (2005). An experimental comparison of Web and telephone surveys. *Public Opinion Quarterly, 69*, 370–392.

Fu, H., Darroch, J. E., Henshaw, S. K., & Kolb, E. (1998). Measuring the extent of abortion underreporting in the 1995 National Survey of Family Growth. *Family Planning Perspectives, 30*, 128–133 & 138.

Fuchs, M. (2009). Gender-of-interviewer effects in a video-enhanced Web survey: Results from a randomized field experiment. *Social Psychology, 40*, 37–42.

Fuchs, M. (2009). Asking for numbers and quantities: Visual design effects in paper and pencil surveys. *International Journal of Public Opinion Research, 21*, 65–84.

Fuchs, M., & Funke, F. (2007). Video Web survey—Results of an experimental comparison with a text-based Web survey. In M. Trotman (Ed.), *Challenges of a changing world. Proceedings of the Fifth International Conference of the Association for Survey Computing* (pp. 63–80). Berkeley: Association for Survey Computing.

Funke, F., Reips, U.-D., & Thomas, R. K. (2011). Sliders for the smart: Type of rating scale on the Web interacts with educational level. *Social Science Computer Review, 29*, 221–231.

Galešic, M. (2006). Dropouts on the Web: Effects of interest and burden experienced during an online survey. *Journal of Official Statistics, 22*, 313–328.

Galešic, M., Tourangeau, R., Couper, M. P., & Conrad, F. G. (2007). Using change to improve navigation in grid questions. Paper presented at the General Online Research Conference (GOR'07). Leipzig, March.

Galešic, M., Tourangeau, R., Couper, M. P., & Conrad, F. G. (2009). Eye-tracking data: New insights on response order effects and other cognitive shortcuts in survey responding. *Public Opinion Quarterly, 72*, 892–913.

Gentry, R., & Good, C. (2008). Offering respondents a choice of survey mode: Use patterns of an Internet response option in a mail survey. Paper presented at the 63rd Annual Conference of the American Association for Public Opinion Research, New Orleans, May.

Gibson, J. J. (1979). *The ecological approach to visual perception*. New York: Harper and Row.

Goodwin, C. (1981). *Conversational organization: Interaction between speakers and hearers*. New York: Academic Press.

Göritz, A. S. (2006a). Incentives in Web studies: Methodological issues and a review. *International Journal of Internet Science, 1*, 58–70.

Göritz, A. S. (2006b). Cash lotteries as incentives in online panels. *Social Science Computer Review, 24*, 445–459.

Göritz, A. S. (2010). Using lotteries, loyalty points, and other incentives to increase participant response and completion. In S.D. Gosling & J.A. Johnson (Eds.), *Advanced methods for behavioral research on the Internet* (pp. 219–233). Washington, DC: American Psychological Association.

Gray, W. D. & Fu, W. (2004). Soft constraints in interactive behavior: The case of ignoring perfect knowledge in-the-world for imperfect knowledge in-the-head. *Cognitive Science, 28*, 359–382.

Griffin, D. H., Fischer, D. P., & Morgan, M. T. (2001). Testing an Internet response option for the American Community Survey. Paper presented at the 56th Annual Conference of the American Association for Public Opinion Research, Montreal, Quebec, May.

Groves, R. M. (1989). *Survey costs and survey errors.* New York: John Wiley.

Groves, R. M. (2006). Nonresponse rates and nonresponse error in household surveys. *Public Opinion Quarterly, 70*, 646–675.

Groves, R. M., & Couper, M. P. (1998). *Nonresponse in household interview surveys.* New York: John Wiley.

Groves, R. M., Couper, M. P., Presser, S., Singer, E., Tourangeau, R., Acosta, G. P., & Nelson, L. (2006). Experiments in producing nonresponse bias. *Public Opinion Quarterly, 70*, 720–736.

Groves, R. M., Fowler, F. J., Couper, M. P., Lepkowski, J. M., Singer, E., & Tourangeau, R. (2009). *Survey methodology* (2nd ed.). New York: John Wiley.

Groves, R. M., & Lyberg, L. (2010). Total survey error: Past, present, and future. *Public Opinion Quarterly, 74*, 849–879.

Groves, R. M., & Peytcheva, E. (2008). The impact of nonresponse rates on nonresponse bias: A meta-analysis. *Public Opinion Quarterly, 72*, 167–189.

Guéguen, N. & Jacob, C. (2002). Solicitations by e-Mail and solicitor's status: A field study of social influence on the Web. *CyberPsychology and Behavior, 5*, 377–383.

Hammen, K. (2010). The impact of visual and functional design elements in online survey research. Paper presented at the General Online Research conference, Pforzheim, Germany, May.

Harmon, M. A., Westin, E. C., & Levin, K. Y. (2005). Does type of pre-notification affect Web survey response rates? Paper presented at the 60th Annual Conference of the American Association for Public Opinion Research, Miami Beach, May.

Hays, R. D., Bode, R., Rothrock, N., Riley, W., Cella, D., & Gershon, R. (2010). The impact of next and back buttons on time to complete and measurement reliability in computer-based surveys. *Quality of Life Research, 19*, 1181–1184.

Healey, B. (2007). Drop downs and scroll mice: The effect of response option format and input mechanism employed on data quality in Web surveys. *Social Science Computer Review, 25*, 111–128.

Healey, B., Macpherson, T., & Kuijten, B. (2005). An empirical evaluation of three Web survey design principles. *Marketing Bulletin, 16*, Research note 2.

Heerwegh, D. (2003). Explaining response latencies and changing answers using client-side paradata from a Web survey. *Social Science Computer Review, 21*, 360–373.

Heerwegh, D. (2005). Effects of personal salutations in e-mail invitations to participate in a Web survey. *Public Opinion Quarterly, 69*, 588–598.

Heerwegh, D., & Loosveldt, G. (2002). An evaluation of the effect of response formats on data quality in Web surveys. *Social Science Computer Review, 20*, 471–484.

Heerwegh, D., & Loosveldt, G. (2006). An experimental study on the effects of personalization, survey length statements, progress indicators, and survey sponsor logos in Web surveys. *Journal of Official Statistics, 22*, 191–210.

Heerwegh, D., & Loosveldt, G. (2008). Face-to-face versus Web surveying in a high-Internet-coverage population. *Public Opinion Quarterly, 72*, 836–846.

Heerwegh, D., Vanhove, T., Matthijs, K., & Loosveldt, G. (2005). The effect of personalization on response rates and data quality in Web surveys. *International Journal of Social Science Methodology, 8*, 85–99.

Heinberg, A., Hung, A., Kapteyn, A., Lusardi, A., & Yoong, J. (2010). *Five steps to planning success.* Report to the Social Security Administration. Santa Monica, CA: Rand Corporation

Heuer, R., Kuhr, B., Fahimi, M., Curtin, T. R., Hinsdale, M., Carley-Baxter, L., & Green, P. (2006). *National Study of Postsecondary Faculty (NSOPF:04) methodology report (NCES 2006–179).* U.S. Department of Education. Washington, DC: National Center for Education Statistics.

Holbrook, A. L., Krosnick, J. A., Moore, D., & Tourangeau, R. (2007). Response order effects in dichotomous categorical questions presented orally: The impact of question and respondent attributes. *Public Opinion Quarterly, 71,* 325–348.

Holland, J. L., & Christian, L. M. (2009). The influence of topic interest and interactive probing on responses to open-ended questions in Web surveys. *Social Science Computer Review, 27,* 196–212.

Holmberg, A., Lorenc, B., & Werner, P. (2010). Contact strategies to improve participation via the Web in a mixed-mode mail and Web survey. *Journal of Official Statistics, 26,* 465–480.

International Organization for Standardization (2009). *ISO 26362:2009 Access panels in market, opinion, and social research—Vocabulary and service requirements.* Geneva: ISO.

International Telecommunication Union (2007). *Yearbook of statistics.* Geneva, Switzerland: ITU.

Israel, G. (2009). Obtaining responses by mail or Web: Response rates and data consequences. *Survey Practice*, June 2009.

Iyengar, S. S., & Lepper, M. (2000). When choice is demotivating: Can one desire too much of a good thing? *Journal of Personality and Social Psychology, 76,* 995–1006.

Jenkins, C. R., & Dillman, D. A. (1997). Towards a theory of self-administered questionnaire design. In L. Lyberg, P. Biemer, M. Collins, E. de Leeuw, C. Dippo, N. Schwarz, & D. Trewin (Eds.), *Survey measurement and process quality* (pp. 165–196). New York: John Wiley.

Joinson, A. N., & Reips, U.-D. (2007). Personalized salutation, power of sender and response rates to Web-based surveys. *Computers in Human Behavior, 23,* 1372–1383.

Joinson, A. N., Woodley, A., & Reips, U. -D. (2007). Personalization, authentication and self-disclosure in self-administered Internet surveys. *Computers in Human Behavior, 23,* 275–285.

Kaczmirek, L. (2009). *Human-survey interaction: Usability and nonresponse in online surveys.* Cologne: Herbert von Halem Verlag.

Kaczmirek, L. (2011). Attention and usability in Internet surveys: Effects of visual feedback in grid questions. In M. Das, P. Ester, & L. Kaczmirek (Eds.), *Social research and the Internet* (pp. 191–214). New York: Taylor and Francis.

Kalton, G., & Flores-Cervantes, I. (2003). Weighting methods. *Journal of Official Statistics, 19,* 81–97.

Kane, E. W., & Macaulay, L. J. (1993). Interviewer gender and gender attitudes. *Public Opinion Quarterly, 57,* 1–28.

Kaplowitz, M. D., Hadlock, T. D., & Levine, R. (2004). A comparison of Web and mail survey response rates. *Public Opinion Quarterly, 68,* 94–101.

Kaplowitz, M. D., Lupi, F., Couper, M. P., & Thorp, L. (2012). The effect of invitation design on Web survey response rates. *Social Science Computer Review, 30,* 339–349.

Keeter S., Kennedy, C., Dimock, M., Best, J., & Craighill, P. (2006). Gauging the impact of growing nonresponse on estimates from a national RDD telephone survey. *Public Opinion Quarterly, 70,* 259–279.

Keeter S., Miller, C., Kohut, A., Groves, R. M., & Presser, S. (2000). Consequences of reducing nonresponse in a large national telephone survey. *Public Opinion Quarterly, 64,* 125–148.

Kent, R., & Brandal, H. (2003). Improving email response in a permission marketing context. *International Journal of Market Research, 45,* 489–506.

Kish, L. (1965). *Survey sampling.* New York: John Wiley.

Knapp, H., & Kirk, S. A. (2003). Using pencil and paper, Internet and Touch-Tone phones for self-administered surveys: Does methodology matter? *Computers in Human Behavior, 19,* 117–134.

Kreuter, F., Presser, S. & Tourangeau, R. (2008). Social desirability bias in CATI, IVR and Web surveys: The effects of mode and question sensitivity. *Public Opinion Quarterly, 72,* 847–865.

Krosnick, J. (1991). Response strategies for coping with the cognitive demands of attitude measures in surveys. *Applied Cognitive Psychology, 5,* 213–236.

Krosnick, J. A. (1999). Survey research. *Annual Review of Psychology, 50,* 537–567.

Krosnick, J. A., & Alwin, D. (1987). An evaluation of a cognitive theory of response order effects in survey measurement. *Public Opinion Quarterly, 51,* 201–219.

Krosnick, J. A., Ackermann, A., Malka, A., Yeager, D., Sakshaug, J., Tourangeau, R., DeBell, M., & Turakhia, C. (2009). Creating the face-to-face recruited Internet survey platform (FFRISP). Paper presented at the Third Annual Workshop on Measurement and Experimentation with Internet Panels, Santpoort, The Netherlands, August.

Krotki, K., & Dennis, J. M. (2001). Probability-based survey research on the Internet. In *Proceedings of the 53rd Conference of the International Statistical Institute,* Seoul, Korea, August.

Krysan, M. & Couper, M. P. (2003). Race in the live and the virtual interview: Racial deference, social desirability, and activation effects in attitude surveys. *Social Psychology Quarterly, 66,* 364–383.

Kwak, N., & Radler, B. T. (2002). A Comparison between mail and Web surveys: Response pattern, respondent profile, and data quality. *Journal of Official Statistics, 18,* 257–273.

Lebrasseur, D., Morin, J. -P., Rodrigue, J. -F., & Taylor, J. (2010). Evaluation of the innovations implemented in the 2009 Canadian census test. *Proceedings of the American Statistical Association Survey Research Methods Section,* pp. 4089–4097.

Lee, S. (2006a). An evaluation of nonresponse and coverage errors in a prerecruited probability Web panel survey. *Social Science Computer Review, 24,* 460–475.

Lee, S. (2006b). Propensity score adjustment as a weighting scheme for volunteer panel Web surveys. *Journal of Official Statistics, 22,* 329–349.

Lee, S., & Valliant, R. (2008). Weighting telephone samples using propensity scores. In J. M. Lepkowski, C. Tucker, J. M. Brick, E. D. de Leeuw, L. Japec, P. J. Lavrakas, M. W. Link, & R. L. Sangster (Eds.), *Advances in telephone survey methodology* (pp. 170–183). New York, NJ: John Wiley.

Lee, S., & Valliant, R. (2009). Estimation for volunteer panel Web surveys using propensity score adjustment and calibration adjustment. *Sociological Methods and Research, 37,* 319–343.

Lenhart, A., Horrigan, J., Rainie, L., Allen, K., Boyce, A., Madden, M., & O'Grady, E. (2003). *The ever-shifting Internet population: A new look at Internet access and the digital divide.* Washington, D. C.: The Pew Internet and American Life Project.

Lensvelt-Mulders, G. J. L. M., Hox, J., van der Heijden, P. G. M, & Maas, C. J. M. (2005). Meta-analysis of randomized response research. *Sociological Methods and Research, 33,* 319–348.

Lepkowski, J. M. (1988). Telephone sampling methods in the United States. In R. M. Groves, P. Biemer, L. Lyberg L, J. Massey, W. Nicholls W, & J. Waksberg (Eds.), *Telephone survey methodology.* New York: John Wiley.

Lesser, V. M., Newton, L., & Yang, D. (2010). Does providing a choice of survey modes influence response? Paper presented at the 65th Annual Conference of the American Association for Public Opinion Research, Chicago, May.

Lessler, J. T., & Kalsbeek, W. D. (1992). *Nonsampling error in surveys.* New York: John Wiley.

Lind, L. H., Schober, M. F., Conrad, F. G., & Reichert, H. (under review). Why do survey respondents disclose more when computers ask the questions?

Link, M. W., & Mokdad, A. H. (2005a). Effects of survey mode on self-reports of adult alcohol consumption: A comparison of mail, Web, and telephone approaches. *Journal of Studies on Alcohol, 66,* 239–245.

Link, M. W., & Mokdad, A. H. (2005b). Alternative modes for health surveillance surveys: An experiment with Web, mail, and telephone. *Epidemiology, 16,* 701–709.

Lindhjem, H., & Navrud, S. (2011a). Using Internet in stated preference surveys: A review and comparison of survey modes. *International Review of Environmental and Resource Economics*, *5*, 309–351.

Lindhjem, H., & Navrud, S. (2011b). Are Internet surveys an alternative to face-to-face interviews in contingent valuation? *Ecological Economics*, *70*, 1628–1637.

Lipsey, M. W., & Wilson, D. B. (2001). *Practical meta-analysis*. Thousand Oaks, CA: Sage Publications.

Little, R. J., & Rubin, D. B. (2002). *Statistical analysis with missing data* (2nd ed.). New York: John Wiley.

Little, R. J., & Vartivarian, S. L. (2004). Does weighting for nonresponse increase the variance of survey means? (April 2004). *The University of Michigan Department of Biostatistics Working Paper Series*. Working Paper 35.

Lozar Manfreda, K., Bosnjak, M., Berzelak, J., Haas, I., & Vehovar, V. (2008). Web surveys versus other survey modes: A meta-analysis comparing response rates. *International Journal of Market Research*, *50*, 79–104.

Lynch, P. J., & Horton, S. (2001). *Web style guide: Basic design principles for creating Web sites* (2nd ed.). New Haven: Yale University Press.

MacElroy, B. (2000). Measuring response rates in online surveys. Modalis Research Technologies, unpublished paper, www.modalis.com.

Marta-Pedroso, C., Freitas, H., & Domingos, T. (2007). Testing for the survey mode effect on contingent valuation data quality: A case study of Web based versus in-person interviews. *Ecological Economics*, *62*, 388–398.

Matzat, U., Snijders, C., & van der Horst, W. (2009). Effects of different types of progress indicators on drop-out rates in Web surveys. *Social Psychology*, *40*, 43–52.

McCabe, S. E. (2004). Comparison of Web and mail surveys in collecting illicit drug use data: A randomized experiment. *Journal of Drug Education*, *34*, 61–72.

McCabe, S. E., Boyd, C. J., Couper, M. P., Crawford, S., & D'Arcy H. (2002). Mode effects for collecting alcohol and other drug use data: Web and U.S. mail. *Journal of Studies on Alcohol*, *63*, 755–761.

McCabe, S. E., Couper, M. P., Cranford, J. A., & Boyd, C. J. (2006). Comparison of Web and mail surveys for studying secondary consequences associated with substance abuse: Evidence for minimal mode effects. *Addictive Behaviors*, *31*, 162–168.

McCarthy, M. S., & Mothersbaugh, D. L. (2002). Effects of typographic factors in advertising-based persuasion: A general model and initial empirical tests. *Psychology and Marketing*, *19*, 663–691.

Meier, B. P., & Robinson, M. D. (2004). Why the sunny side is up: Associations between affect and vertical position. *Psychological Science*, *15*, 243–247.

Millar, M. M., & Dillman, D. A. (2011). Improving response to Web and mixed-mode surveys. *Public Opinion Quarterly*, *75*, 249–269.

Miller, J. (2006). Online marketing research. In R. Grover & M. Vriens (Eds.), *The handbook of marketing research* (pp. 110–131). Thousand Oaks, CA: Sage.

Miller, J. D. (1998). The measurement of civic scientific literacy. *Public Understanding of Science*, *7*, 203–223.

Muñoz-Leiva, F., Sánchez-Fernández, J., Montoro-Ríos, F., & Ibáñez-Zapata, J. A. (2010). Improving the response rate and quality in Web-based surveys through the personalization and frequency of reminder mailings. *Quality and Quantity*, *44*, 1037–1052.

Murray, D., O'Connell, C., Schmid, L., & Perry, C. (1987). The validity of smoking self-reports by adolescents: A reexamination of the bogus pipeline procedure. *Addictive Behaviors*, *12*, 7–15.

Nass, C., Moon, Y., & Green, N. (1997). Are machines gender neutral? Gender-stereotypic responses to computers with voices. *Journal of Applied Social Psychology*, *27*, 864–876.

Nielsen, J. (2000). *Designing Web usability*. Berkeley, CA: New Riders.

Nielsen, J. (2005). Guidelines for visualizing links. http://www.useit.com/alertbox/20040510.html

Nielsen, J. (2006). F-shaped pattern for reading Web content. Alert Box, April 17, 2006. Available at http://www.useit.com/alertbox/reading_pattern.html

Nielsen, J., & Loranger, H. (2006). *Prioritizing Web usability*. Berkeley, CA: New Riders.

Nielsen, J., & Pernice, K. (2010). *Eyetracking Web usability*. Berkeley, CA: New Riders.

Nielsen, J. S. (2011). Use of the Internet for willingness-to-pay surveys: A comparison of face-to-face and Web-based inteviews. *Resource and Energy Economics*, *33*, 119–129.

Norman, D. A. (1988). *The design of everyday things*. New York: Doubleday.

Norman, K. L., Friedman, Z., Norman, K., & Stevenson, R. (2001). Navigational issues in the design of online self-administered questionnaires. *Behaviour and Information Technology*, *20*, 37–45.

Norris, P. (2001). *Digital divide: Civic engagement, information poverty, and the Internet worldwide*. Cambridge: Cambridge University Press.

Novemsky, N., Dhar, R., Schwarz, N., & Simonson, I. (2007). Preference fluency in choice. *Journal of Marketing Research*, *44*, 347–356.

Nyiri, Z., & Clark, R. L. (2003). Web survey design: Comparing static and dynamic survey instruments. Paper presented at the 58th Annual Conference of the American Association for Public Opinion Research, Nashville, May.

O'Muircheartaigh, C., Gaskell, G., & Wright, D. B. (1995). Weighing anchors: Verbal and numeric labels for response scales. *Journal of Official Statistics*, *11*, 295–307.

Oudejans, M., & Christian, L. M. (2010). Using interactive features to motivate and probe responses to open-ended questions. In M. Das, P. Ester, & L. Kaczmirek, L. (Eds.), *Social research and the Internet: Advances in applied methods and research strategies* (pp. 215–244). New York: Routledge.

Oviatt, S. & Adams, V. (2000). Designing and evaluating conversational interfaces with animated characters. In J. Cassell, J. Sullivan, S. Prevost, & E. Churchill (Eds.), *Embodied conversational agents* (pp. 319–346). Cambridge, MA: MIT Press.

Pagendarm, M., & Schaumburg, H. (2001). Why are users banner-blind? The impact of navigation style on the perception of Web banners. *Journal of Digital Information*, *2*. http://journals.tdl.org/jodi/index.php/jodi/article/viewArticle/36/38

Page-Thomas, K. (2006). Measuring task-specific perceptions of the World Wide Web. *Behaviour and Information Technology*, *25*, 469–477.

Pearson, J., & Levine, R. A. (2003), Salutations and response rates to online surveys. Paper presented at the Association for Survey Computing Fourth International Conference on the Impact of Technology on the Survey Process, Warwick, England, September.

Peytchev, A. (2005). How questionnaire layout induces measurement error. Paper presented at the 60th Annual Conference of the American Association for Public Opinion Research, Miami Beach, FL, May.

Peytchev, A. (2009). Survey breakoff. *Public Opinion Quarterly*, *73*, 74–97.

Peytchev, A., Conrad, F. G., Couper, M. P., & Tourangeau, R. (2010). Increasing respondents' use of definitions in Web surveys. *Journal of Official Statistics*, *26*, 633–650.

Peytchev, A. Couper, M. P., McCabe, S. E., & Crawford, S. D. (2006). Web survey design: Paging versus scrolling. *Public Opinion Quarterly*, *70*, 596–607.

Pope, D., & Baker, R. (2005). Experiments in color for Web-based surveys. Paper presented at the FedCASIC Workshops, Washington, D.C., March.

Porter, S. R., & Whitcomb, M. E. (2005). E-mail subject lines and their effect on Web survey viewing and response. *Social Science Computer Review*, *23*, 380–387.

Purcell, K. (2011). Search and email still top the list of most popular online activities. http://www.pewinternet.org/~/media/files/reports/2011/pip_search-and-email.pdf

Purcell, K., Rainey, L., Rosenstiel, T., & Mitchell, A. (2011). How mobile devices are changing community information environment. http://www.pewinternet.com/~/media/Files/Reports/2011/PIP-Local%20mobile%20survey.pdf

Reber, R., & Schwarz, N. (1999). Effects of perceptual fluency on judgments of truth. *Consciousness and Cognition, 8*, 338–342.

Redline, C. D., & Dillman, D. A. (2002). The influence of alternative visual designs on respondents' performance with branching instructions in self-administered questionnaires. In R. M. Groves, D. A. Dillman, J. L. Eltinge, & R. J. A. Little (Eds.), *Survey nonresponse* (pp. 179–193). New York: John Wiley.

Redline, C. D., Dillman, D. A., Dajani, A. N., & Scaggs, M. A. (2003). Improving navigational performance in U.S. Census 2000 by altering the visually administered languages of branching instructions. *Journal of Official Statistics, 19*, 403–419.

Redline, C. D., Tourangeau, R., Couper, M. P., & Conrad, F. G. (2009). Formatting long lists of response options in demographic questions. Paper presented at the Annual Federal Conference on Survey Methodology.

Richman, W. L., Kiesler, S., Weisband, S., & Drasgow, F. (1999). A meta-analytic study of social desirability distortions in computer-adminstered questionnaires, traditional questionnaires, and interviews. *Journal of Applied Psychology, 84*, 754–775.

Ritter, P., Lorig, K., Laurent, D., & Matthews, K. (2004). Internet versus mailed questionnaires: A randomized comparison. *Journal of Medical Internet Research, 6*, e29.

Rivers, D. (2006). Web surveys for health measurement. Paper presented at Building Tomorrow's Patient-Reported Outcome Measures: The Inaugural PROMIS Conference, Gaithersburg, MD, September.

Rivers, D., & Bailey, D. (2009). Inference from matched samples in the 2008 U.S. national elections. Paper presented at the 64th Annual Conference of the American Association for Public Opinion Research, Hollywood, FL, May.

Rookey, B. D., Hanway, S., & Dillman, D. A. (2008). Does a probability-based household panel benefit from assignment to postal response as an alternative to Internet-only? *Public Opinion Quarterly, 72*, 962–984.

Rosenbaum, P. R., & Rubin, D. B. (1984). Reducing bias in observational studies using subclassification on the propensity score. *Journal of the American Statistical Association, 79*, 516–524.

Sakshaug, J., Tourangeau, R., Krosnick, J. A., Ackermann, A., Malka, A., DeBell, M., & Turakhia, C. (2009). Dispositions and outcome rates in the 'Face-to-Face Recruited Internet Survey Platform' (the FFRISP). Paper presented at the 64th Annual Conference of the American Association for Public Opinion Research, Hollywood, FL, May.

Sakshaug, J., Yan, T., & Tourangeau, R. (2010). Nonresponse error, measurement error, and mode of data collection: Tradeoffs in a multi-mode survey. *Public Opinion Quarterly, 74*, 907–933.

Schegloff, E. A. (1982). Discourse as an interactional achievement: Some uses of "uh huh" and other things that come between sentences. In D. Tannen (Ed.), *Georgetown University Roundtable on Languages and Linguistics 1981; Analyzing discourse: Text and talk* (pp. 71–93). Washington, DC: Georgetown University Press.

Scherpenzeel, A., & Das, M. (2011). "True" longitudinal and probability-based Internet panels: Evidence from the Netherlands. In M. Das, P. Ester, & L. Kaczmirek (Eds.). *Social research and the Internet* (pp. 77–104). New York: Taylor and Francis.

Schneider, S. J., Cantor, D., Malakhoff, L., Arieira, C., Segal, P., Nguyen, K.-L., & Tancreto, J. G. (2005). Telephone, Internet, and paper data collection modes for the Census 2000 short form. *Journal of Official Statistics, 21*, 89–101.

Schober, M. F., & Conrad, F. G. (1997). Does conversational interviewing reduce survey measurement error? *Public Opinion Quarterly, 61*, 576–602.

Schober, M. F., Conrad, F. G., & Fricker, S. S. (2004). Misunderstanding standardized language in research interviews. *Applied Cognitive Psychology, 18*, 169–188.

Schonlau, M., van Soest, A., & Kapteyn, A. (2007). Are 'Webographic' or attitudinal questions useful for adjusting estimates from Web surveys using propensity scoring? *Survey Research Methods, 1*, 155–163.

Schonlau, M., van Soest, A., Kapteyn, A., & Couper, M. P. (2009). Selection bias in Web surveys and the use of propensity scores. *Sociological Methods and Research, 37*, 291–318.

Schonlau, M., Zapert, K., Simon, L. P., Sanstad, K. H., Marcus, S. M., Adams, J., Spranca, M., Kan, H., Turner, R., & Berry, S. H. (2004). A comparison between responses from a propensity-weighted Web survey and an identical RDD survey. *Social Science Computer Review, 22*, 128–138.

Schriver, K. A. (1997). *Dynamics of document design.* New York: John Wiley.

Schuman, H., & Presser, S. (1981). *Questions and answers in attitude surveys.* New York: Academic Press.

Schwartz, B. (2000). *The paradox of choice: Why more is less.* New York: Harper Collins.

Schwarz, N. (1996). *Cognition and communication: Judgmental biases, research methods, and the logic of conversation.* Mahwah, NJ: Lawrence Erlbaum.

Schwarz, N., Grayson, C. E., & Knäuper, B. (1998). Formal features of rating scales and the interpretation of question meaning. *International Journal of Public Opinion Research, 10*, 177–183.

Schwarz, N., & Hippler, H. -J. (1987). What response scales may tell your respondents: Information functions of response alternatives In H. -J. Hippler, N. Schwarz, & S. Sudman (Eds.), *Social information processing and survey methodology* (pp. 163–178). New York: Springer-Verlag.

Schwarz, N., Knäuper, B., Hippler, H. -J., Noelle-Neumann, E., & Clark, F. (1991). Rating scales: Numeric values may change the meaning of scale labels. *Public Opinion Quarterly, 55*, 618–630.

Scott, J., & Barrett, D. (1996). *1995 National Census Test: Image optimization test final report.* Washington, D.C.: U.S. Census Bureau, unpublished report.

Shih, T. -H., & Fan, X. (2008). Comparing response rates from Web and mail surveys: A meta-analysis. *Field Methods, 20*, 249–271.

Short, J., Williams, E., & Christie, B. (1976). *The social psychology of telecommunications.* London: John Wiley.

Simon, H. A. (1956). Rational choice and the structure of the environment. *Psychological Review, 63*, 129–138.

Singer, E. (2002). The use of incentives to reduce nonresponse in household surveys. In R. M. Groves, D. Dillman, J. L. Eltinge, & R. J. A. Little (Eds.), *Survey nonresponse* (pp. 163–177). New York: John Wiley.

Singer, E., Van Hoewyk, J., & Gebler, N. (1999). The effect of incentives on response rates in interviewer-mediated surveys. *Journal of Official Statistics, 15*, 217–230.

Singer, E., Van Hoewyk, J., & Maher, M. P. (2000). Experiments with incentives in telephone surveys. *Public Opinion Quarterly, 64*, 171–188.

Smith, R. M., & Kiniorski, K. (2003). Participation in online surveys: Results from a series of experiments. Paper presented at the 58th Annual Conference of the American Association for Public Opinion Research, Nashville, TN, May.

Smith, T. W. (1995). Little things matter: A sampler of how differences in questionnaire format can affect survey responses. In *Proceedings of the American Statistical Association, Survey Research Methods Section* (pp. 1046–1051). Alexandria, VA: American Statistical Association.

Smith, T. W. (2003). An experimental comparison of Knowledge Networks and the GSS. *International Journal of Public Opinion Research, 15*, 167–179.

Smyth, J. D., Dillman, D. A., Christian, L. M., & McBride, M. (2009). Open-ended questions in Web surveys: Can increasing the size of answer boxes and providing verbal instructions improve response quality. *Public Opinion Quarterly, 73*, 325–337.

Smyth, J. D., Dillman, D. A., Christian, L. M., & O'Neill, A. C. (2010). Using the Internet to survey small towns and communities: Limitations and possibilities in the early 21st century. *American Behavioral Scientist, 53* (9): 1423–1448.

Song, H., & Schwarz, N. (2008a). If it's hard to read, it's hard to do: Processing fluency effort prediction and motivation. *Psychological Science, 19*, 986–988.

Song, H., & Schwarz, N. (2008b). Fluency and the detection of misleading questions: Low process-ing fluency attenuates the Moses illusion. *Social Cognition, 26,* 791–799.

Spiekermann, E., & Ginger, E. M. (2003). *Stop stealing sheep and find out how type works* (2nd ed.). Berkeley, CA: Adobe Press.

Sproull, L., Subramani, R., Kiesler, S., Walker, J. H., & Waters, K. (1996). When the interface is a face. *Human-Computer Interaction, 11,* 97–124.

Stenbjerre, M., & Laugesen, J. M. (2005). Conducting representative online research: A summary of five years of learnings. Paper presented at ESOMAR Worldwide Panel Research Conference, Budapest, April 17–19.

Stern, M. J. (2008). The use of client-side paradata in analyzing the effects of visual layout on chang-ing responses in Web surveys. *Field Methods, 20,* 377–398.

Strabac, Z., & Aalberg, T. (2011). Measuring political knowledge in telephone and Web surveys: A cross-national comparison. *Social Science Computer Review, 29,* 175–192.

Sudman, S., Bradburn, N., & Schwarz, N. (1996). *Thinking about answers: The application of cogni-tive processes to survey methodology.* San Francisco: Jossey-Bass.

Suessbrick, A, Schober, M. F., & Conrad, F. G. (2000). Different respondents interpret ordi-nary questions quite differently. In *Proceedings of the American Statistical Association, Survey Research Methods Section* (pp. 907–912). Alexandria, VA: American Statistical Association.

Szoc, R. Z., Thomas, R. K., & Barlas, F. M. (2010). Making it all add up: A comparison of con-stant sum tasks on self-reported behavior. Paper presented at the 65th Annual Conference of the American Association for Public Opinion Research, Chicago, IL.

Taylor, H., Bremer, J., Overmeyer, C., Siegel, J. W., & Terhanian, G. (2001). The record of Internet-based opinion polls in predicting the results of 72 races in the November 2007 US elec-tions. *International Journal of Market Research, 43,* 127–135.

Thomas, R. (2010). Visual effects: A comparison of visual analog scales in models predicting behav-ior. Paper presented at the 65th Annual Conference of the American Association for Public Opinion Research, Chicago, IL.

Thornberry, O., & Massey, J. (1988). Trends in United States telephone coverage across time and subgroups. In. R. Groves, P. Biemer, L. Lyberg, J. Massey, W. Nicholls, & J. Waksberg (Eds.), *Telephone Survey Methodology* (pp. 41–54). New York: John Wiley.

Toepoel, V., Das, M., & van Soest, A. (2008). Effects of design in Web surveys: Comparing trained and fresh respondents. *Public Opinion Quarterly, 72,* 985–1007.

Toepoel, V., Das, M., & van Soest, A. (2009a). Design of Web questionnaires: The effect of layout in rating scales. *Journal of Official Statistics, 25,* 509–528.

Toepoel, V., Das, M., & van Soest, A. (2009b). Design of Web questionnaires: The effects of the number of items per screen. *Field Methods, 21,* 200–213.

Toepoel, V., Das, M., & van Soest, A. (2009c). Relating question type to panel conditioning: Comparing trained and fresh respondents. *Survey Research Methods, 3,* 73–80.

Toepoel, V., & Dillman, D. A. (2008). *Words, numbers, and visual heuristics in Web survey: Is there a hierarchy of importance?* Unpublished paper. Tilburg University.

Tourangeau, R. (2007). Incentives, falling response rates, and the respondent-researcher relation-ship. *Proceedings of the Ninth Conference on Health Survey Research Methods* (pp. 244–253). Hyattsville, MD: National Center for Health Statistics.

Tourangeau, R., Conrad, F., Arens, Z., Fricker, S., Lee, S., & Smith, E. (2006). Everyday concepts and clas-sification errors: Judgments of disability and residence. *Journal of Official Statistics, 22,* 385–418.

Tourangeau, R., Conrad, F. G., Couper, M. P., & Ye, C. (2011). The effects of providing examples in survey questions. Unpublished manuscript,

Tourangeau, R., Couper, M. P., & Conrad, F. G. (2004). Spacing, position, and order: Interpretive heuristics for visual features of survey questions. *Public Opinion Quarterly, 68,* 368–393.

Tourangeau, R., Couper, M. P., & Conrad, F. G. (2007). Color, labels and interpretive heuristics for response scales. *Public Opinion Quarterly, 71,* 91–112.

Tourangeau, R., Couper, M. P., & Conrad, F. G (in press). Up means good: The impact of screen position on evaluative ratings in Web surveys. *Public Opinion Quarterly.*

Tourangeau, R., Couper, M. P., & Galešic, M. (2005). Use of eye-tracking for studying survey response processes. Paper presented at the ESF Workshop, Dubrovik, Croatia. September.

Tourangeau, R., Couper, M. P., & Steiger, D. M. (2003). Humanizing self-administered surveys: Experiments on social presence in Web and IVR surveys. *Computers in Human Behavior, 19,* 1–24.

Tourangeau, R., Groves, R. M., Kennedy, C., & Yan, T. (2009). The presentation of a Web survey, nonresponse, and measurement error among members of Web panel. *Journal of Official Statistics, 25,* 299–321.

Tourangeau, R., Groves, R. M., & Redline, C. D. (2010). Sensitive topics and reluctant respondents: Demonstrating a link between nonresponse bias and measurement error. *Public Opinion Quarterly, 74,* 413–432.

Tourangeau, R., & Rasinski, K. A. (1988). Cognitive processes underlying context effects in attitude measurement. *Psychological Bulletin, 103,* 299–314.

Tourangeau, R., Rasinski, K., Jobe, J., Smith, T., & Pratt, W. (1997). Sources of error in a survey of sexual behavior. *Journal of Official Statistics, 13,* 341–365.

Tourangeau, R., Rips, L. J., & Rasinski, K.. (2000). *The psychology of survey response.* New York: Cambridge University Press.

Tourangeau, R., & Smith, T. W. (1996). Asking sensitive questions: The impact of data collection mode, question format, and question context. *Public Opinion Quarterly, 60,* 275–304.

Tourangeau, R., Steiger, D. M., & Wilson, D. (2002). Self-administered questions by telephone: Evaluating interactive voice response. *Public Opinion Quarterly, 66,* 265–278.

Tourangeau, R., & Yan, T. (2007). Sensitive questions in surveys. *Psychological Bulletin, 133,* 859–883.

Tourkin, S., Parmer, R., Cox, S., & Zukerberg, A. (2005). (Inter) net gain? Experiments to increase response. Paper presented at the 60th Annual Conference of the American Association for Public Opinion Research, Miami Beach, FL, May.

Trouteaud, A. R. (2004). How you ask counts: A test of Internet-related components of response rates to a Web-based survey. *Social Science Computer Review, 22,* 385–392.

Tuten, T. L., Bosnjak, M., & Bandilla, W. (2000). Banner-advertised Web surveys. *Marketing Research, 11,* 17–21.

Tuten, T. L., Galešic, M., & Bosnjak, M. (2004). Effects of immediate versus delayed notification of prize draw results on response behavior in Web surveys: An experiment. *Social Science Computer Review, 22,* 377–384.

Vehovar, V., Lozar Manfreda, K., & Batagelj, Z. (1999). Design issues in WWW surveys. Paper presented at the 54th Annual Conference of the American Association for Public Opinion Research, Portland, OR, May.

Vonk, T., van Ossenbruggen, R., & Willems, P. (2006). The effects of panel recruitment and management on research results: A study across 19 panels. *Proceedings of ESOMAR World Research Conference, Panel Research 2006,* Barcelona, Spain, pp. 79–99 [CD].

Ware, C.. (2004). *Information visualization: Perception for design* (2nd ed.). Burlington MA: Morgan Kaufmann.

Werner, P. (2005). *On the cost-efficiency of probability sampling based mail surveys with a Web response option.* Department of Mathematics, Linköping University, Sweden: Ph.D. dissertation.

White, J. V. (1990). *Color for the electronic age.* New York: Watson-Guptill.

Wolfe, E. W., Converse, P. D., Airen, O., & Bodenhorn, N. (2009). Unit and item nonresponses and ancillary information in Web- and paper-based questionnaires administered to school counselors. *Measurement and Evaluation in Counseling and Development, 42,* 92–103.

Wroblewski, L. (2008). *Web form design: Filling in the blanks.* Brooklyn, NY: Rosenfeld Media.

Yan, T. (2005). *Gricean effects in self-administered surveys.* College Park, MD: University of Maryland, unpublished doctoral dissertation.

Yan, T., Conrad, F. G., Tourangeau, R., & Couper, M. P. (2011). Should I stay or should I go: The effects of progress feedback, promised task duration, and length of questionnaire on completing Web surveys. *International Journal of Public Opinion Research, 23,* 131–147.

Ye, C., Fulton, J., & Tourangeau, R. (2011). More positive or more extreme? A meta-analysis of mode differences in response choice. *Public Opinion Quarterly, 75,* 349–365.

Yeager, D. S., Krosnick, J. A., Chang, L., Javitz, H. S., Levendusky, M. S., Simpser, A., & Wang, R. (2011), "Comparing the accuracy of RDD telephone surveys and Internet surveys conducted with probability and non-probability samples. *Public Opinion Quarterly, 75,* 709–747.

Yoshimura, O. (2004). Adjusting responses in a non-probability Web panel survey by the propensity score weighting. In *Proceedings of the Survey Research Methods Section* (pp. 4660–4665). Alexandria, VA: American Statistical Association.

AUTHOR INDEX

SUBJECT INDEX